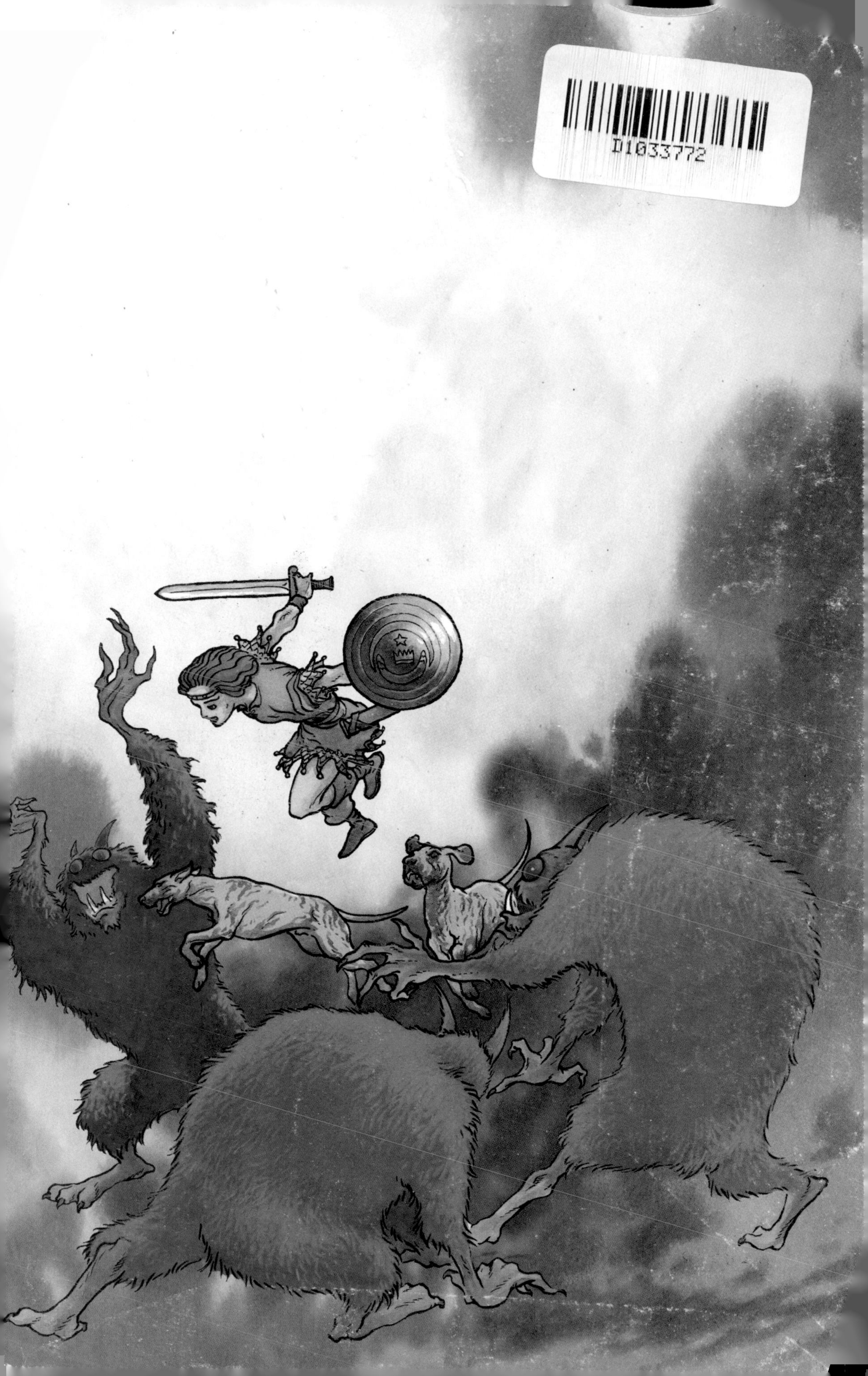

OTHER BOOKS BY JEFF SMITH

OUT FROM BONEVILLE

THE GREAT COW RACE

EYES OF THE STORM

THE DRAGONSLAYER

ROCKJAW, MASTER OF THE EASTERN BORDER

OLD MAN'S CAVE

GHOST CIRCLES

(WITH TOM SNIEGOSKI AND STAN SAKAI)
STUPID STUPID RAT-TAILS: THE ADVENTURES OF BIG JOHNSON BONE, FRONTIER HERO

OTHER BOOKS ILLUSTRATED BY CHARLES VESS

BEDROOM ASTRONOMY

STARDUST

BALLADS

SANDMAN: THE DREAM COUNTRY

THE C. VESS SKETCHBOOK

SPIDER-MAN: SPIRITS OF THE EARTH

THE DREAM MAKERS

LITTLE RED RIDINGHOOD

A MIDSUMMER NIGHTS DREAM

THE RAVEN BANNER

THE HORNS OF ELFLAND

THIS BOOK IS DEDICATED TO

KAREN
&
VIJAYA

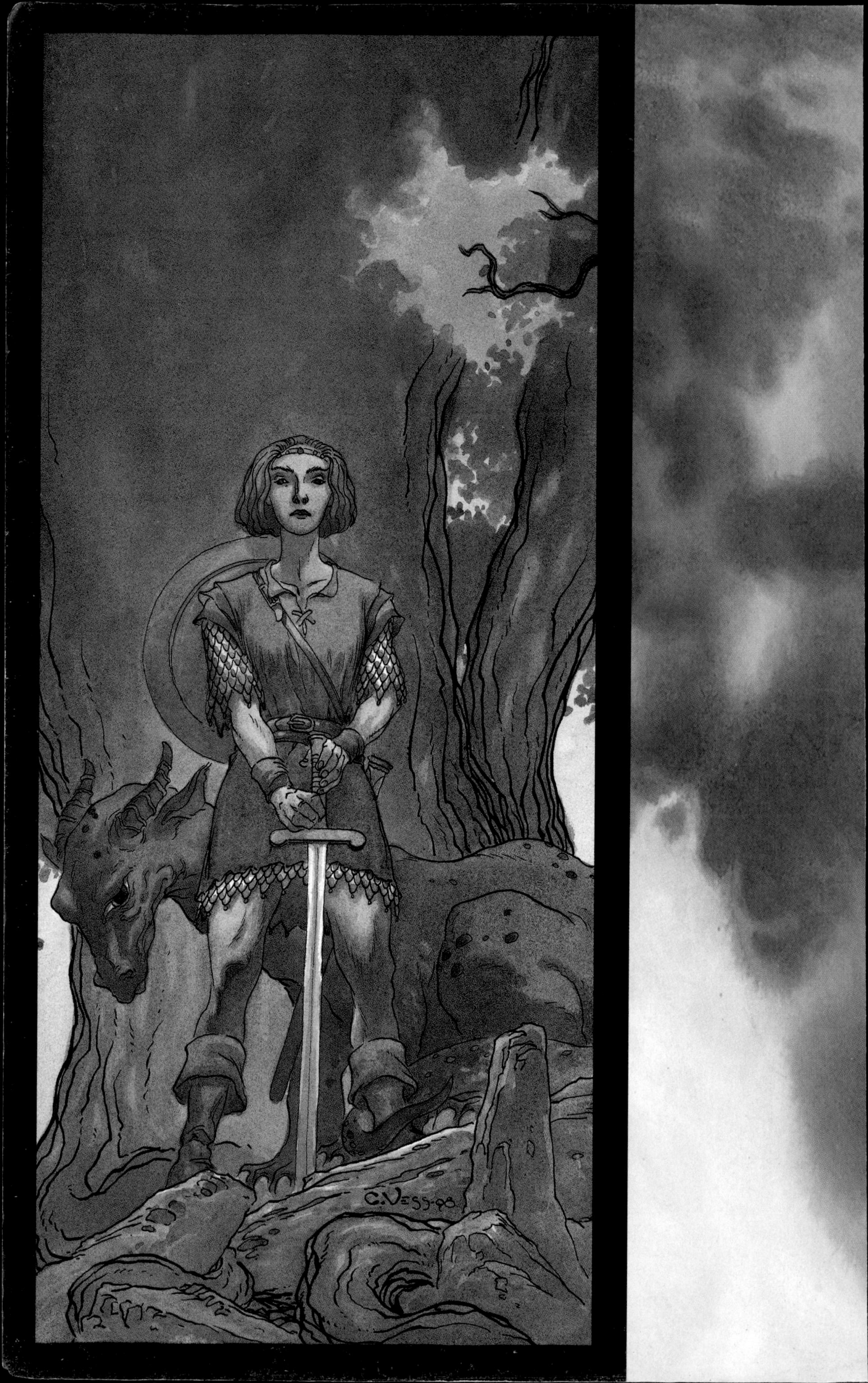
C.Vess-98

BY JEFF SMITH & CHARLES VESS

CARTOON BOOKS
COLUMBUS, OHIO

LETTERED
BY
STEVE HAMAKER

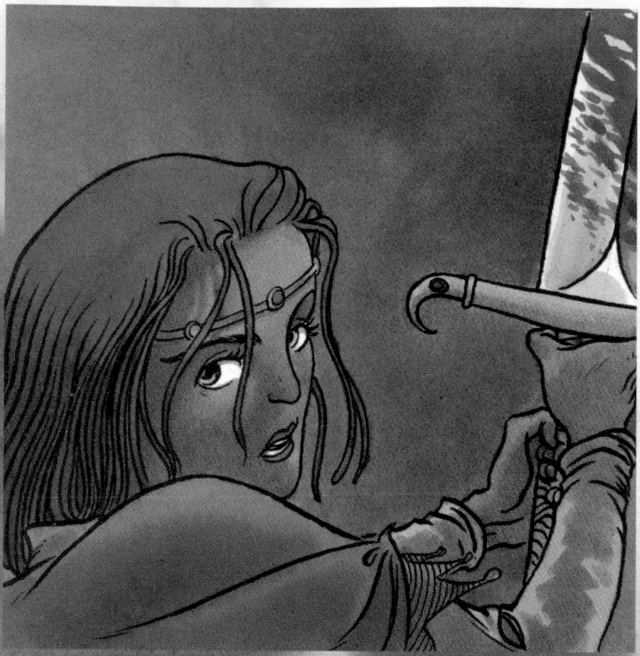

ILLUSTRATION AND
FONT DESIGN
BY
CHARLES VESS

Printed in Canada

Hardcover ISBN: 1-888963-10-7
Softcover ISBN: 1-888963-11-5

Library of Congress Catalog Card Number: 95-68403

10 9 8 7 6 5 4 3 2

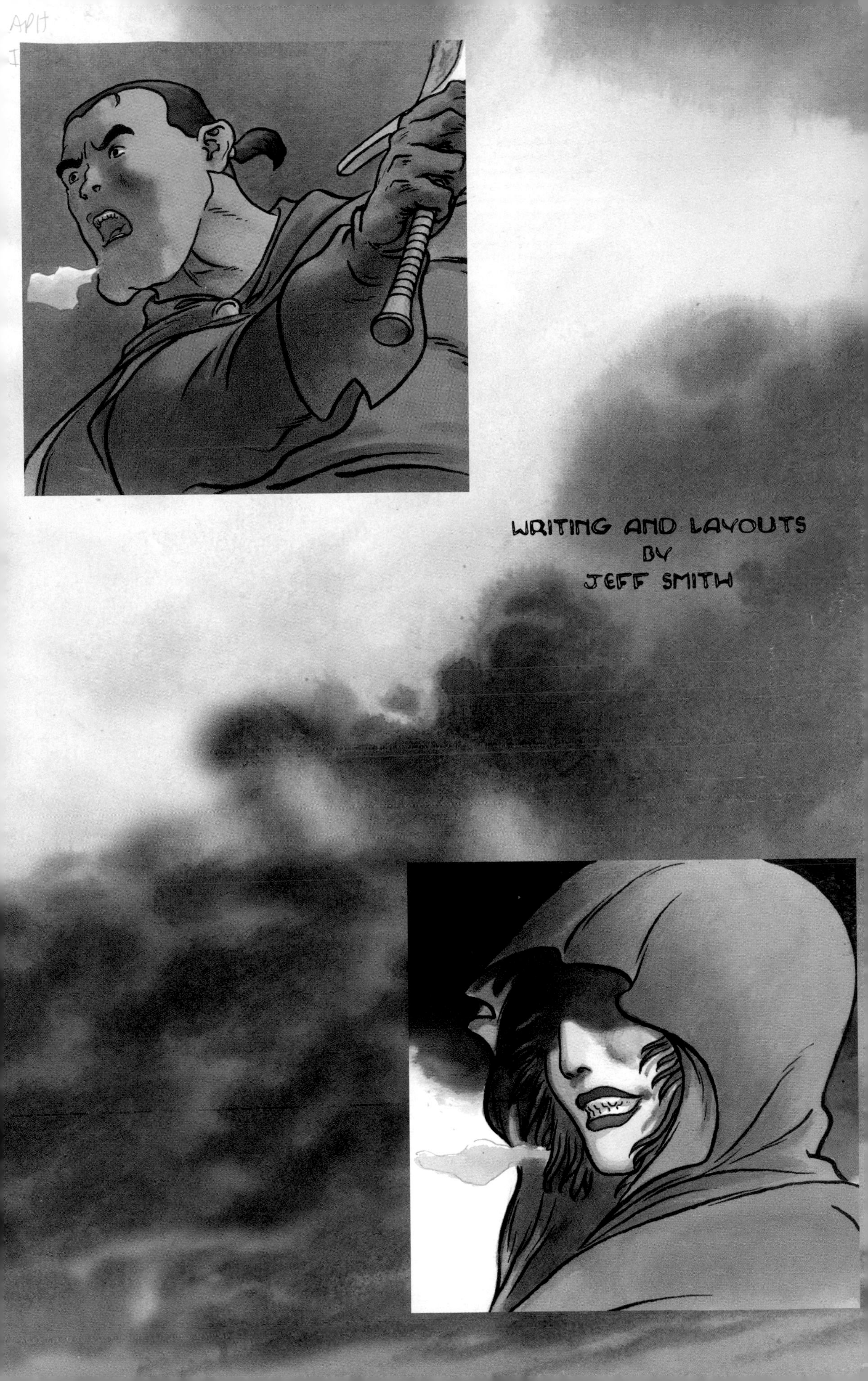
WRITING AND LAYOUTS
BY
JEFF SMITH

CAST OF CHARACTERS

ROSE HARVESTAR	A YOUNG PRINCESS
BRIAR HARVESTAR	HER OLDER SISTER
LUCIUS DOWN	CAPTAIN OF THE PALACE GUARD
THE HEADMASTER	SPIRITUAL LEADER OF THE DISCIPLES OF VENU
EUCLID & CLEO	ROSE'S DOGS
TOBY THE GIANT	A SOLDIER OF FORTUNE FROM THE LAND OF PAWA
BILL OAKS	A VILLAGER
BALSAAD	A RIVER DRAGON
MIM	QUEEN OF THE DRAGONS
THE GREAT RED DRAGON	SON OF MIM

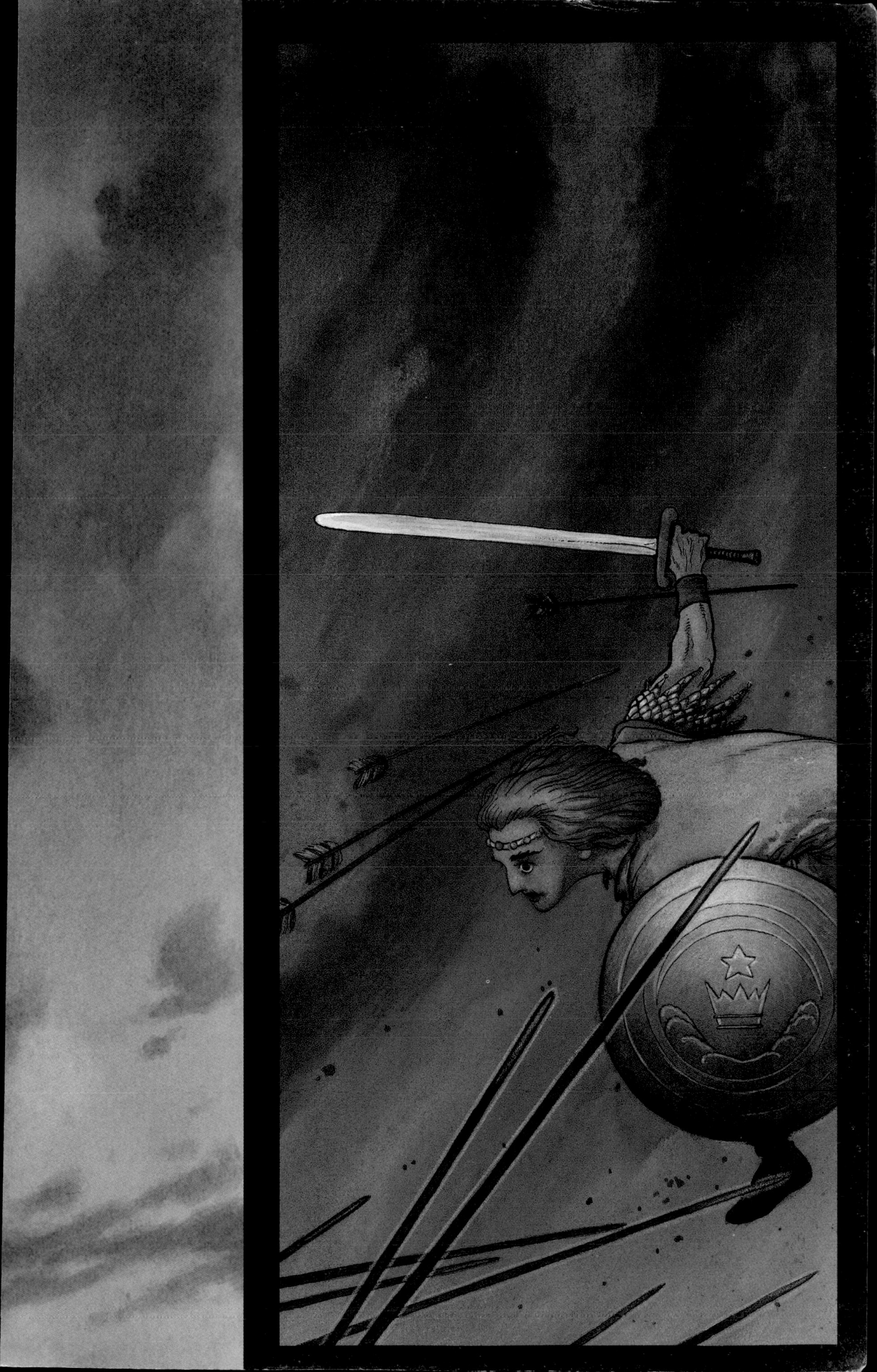

BRIAR
&
ROSE

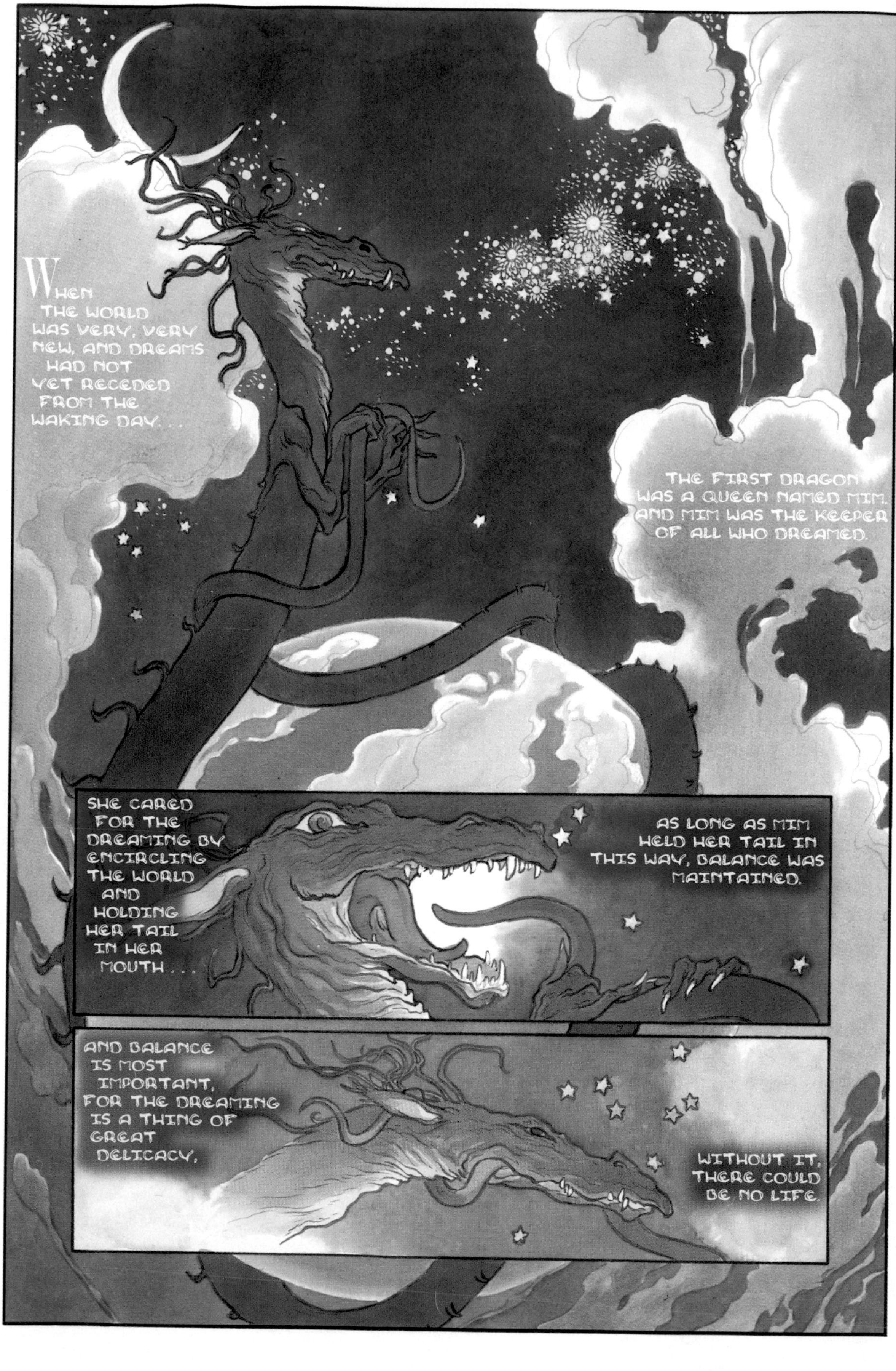
WHEN THE WORLD WAS VERY, VERY NEW, AND DREAMS HAD NOT YET RECEDED FROM THE WAKING DAY...
THE FIRST DRAGON WAS A QUEEN NAMED MIM. AND MIM WAS THE KEEPER OF ALL WHO DREAMED.
SHE CARED FOR THE DREAMING BY ENCIRCLING THE WORLD AND HOLDING HER TAIL IN HER MOUTH...
AS LONG AS MIM HELD HER TAIL IN THIS WAY, BALANCE WAS MAINTAINED.
AND BALANCE IS MOST IMPORTANT, FOR THE DREAMING IS A THING OF GREAT DELICACY,
WITHOUT IT, THERE COULD BE NO LIFE.

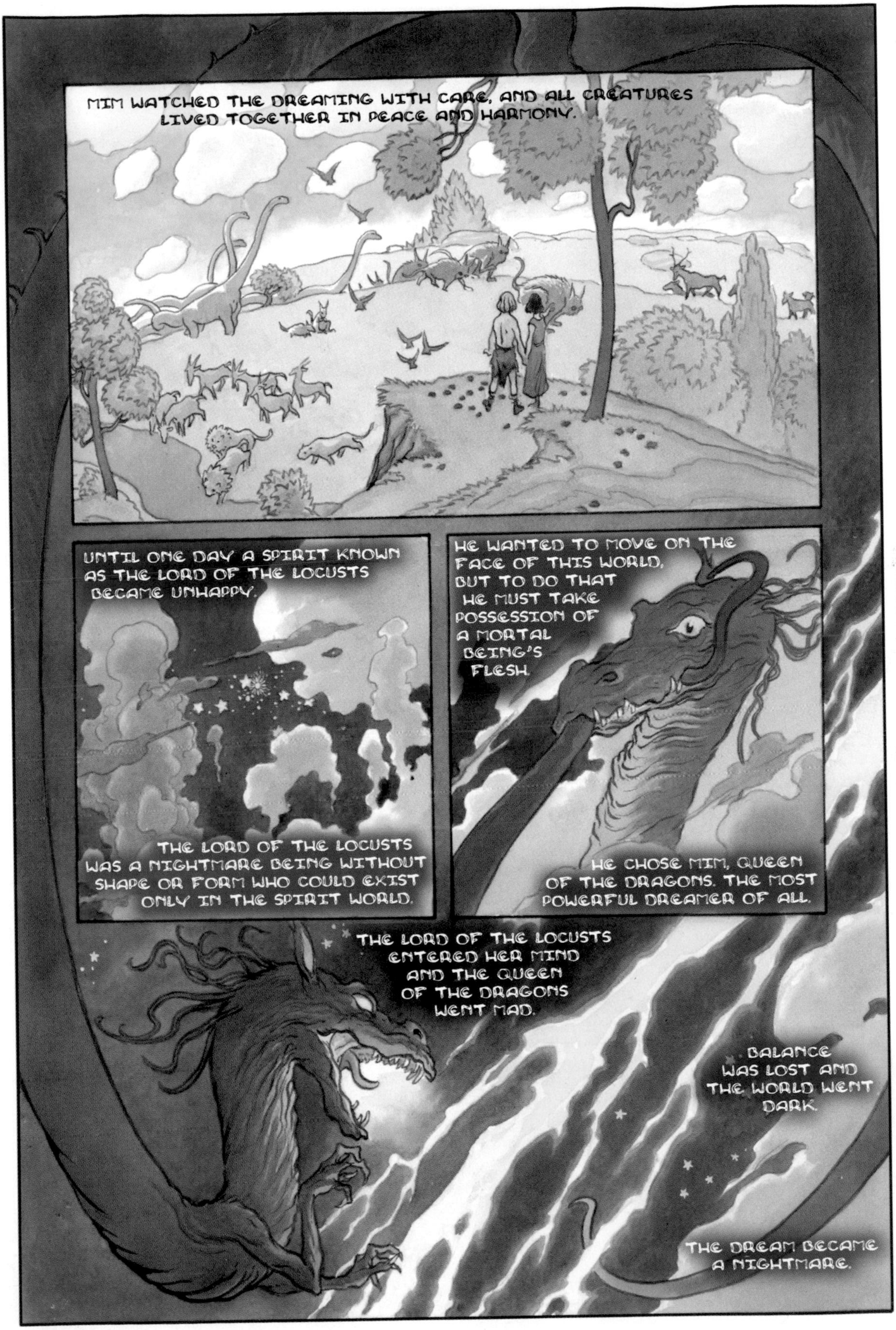
MIM WATCHED THE DREAMING WITH CARE, AND ALL CREATURES LIVED TOGETHER IN PEACE AND HARMONY.
UNTIL ONE DAY A SPIRIT KNOWN AS THE LORD OF THE LOCUSTS BECAME UNHAPPY.
THE LORD OF THE LOCUSTS WAS A NIGHTMARE BEING WITHOUT SHAPE OR FORM WHO COULD EXIST ONLY IN THE SPIRIT WORLD.
HE WANTED TO MOVE ON THE FACE OF THIS WORLD, BUT TO DO THAT HE MUST TAKE POSSESSION OF A MORTAL BEING'S FLESH.
HE CHOSE MIM, QUEEN OF THE DRAGONS, THE MOST POWERFUL DREAMER OF ALL.
THE LORD OF THE LOCUSTS ENTERED HER MIND AND THE QUEEN OF THE DRAGONS WENT MAD.
BALANCE WAS LOST AND THE WORLD WENT DARK.
THE DREAM BECAME A NIGHTMARE.

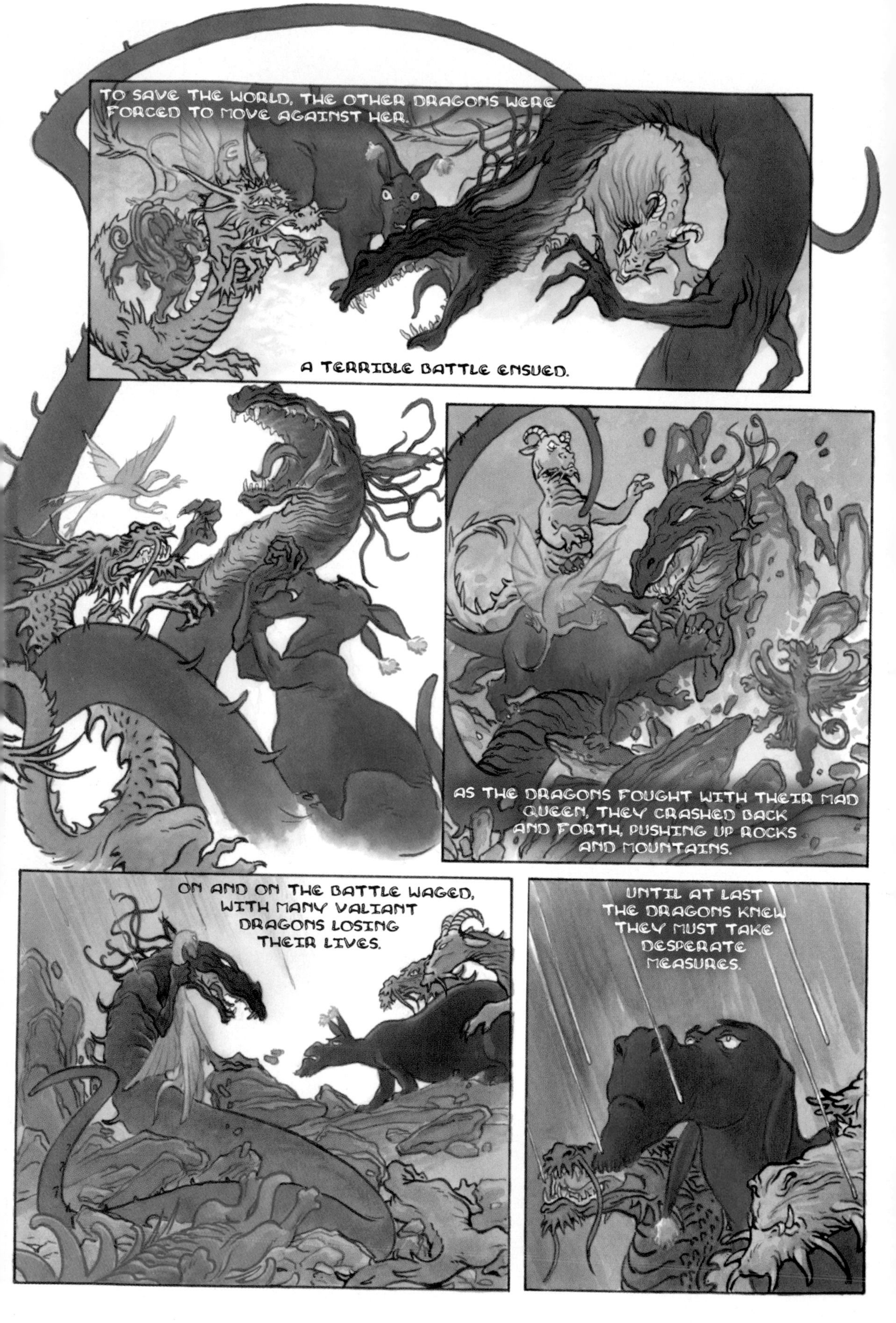
TO SAVE THE WORLD, THE OTHER DRAGONS WERE FORCED TO MOVE AGAINST HER.
A TERRIBLE BATTLE ENSUED.
AS THE DRAGONS FOUGHT WITH THEIR MAD QUEEN, THEY CRASHED BACK AND FORTH, PUSHING UP ROCKS AND MOUNTAINS.
ON AND ON THE BATTLE WAGED, WITH MANY VALIANT DRAGONS LOSING THEIR LIVES.
UNTIL AT LAST THE DRAGONS KNEW THEY MUST TAKE DESPERATE MEASURES.

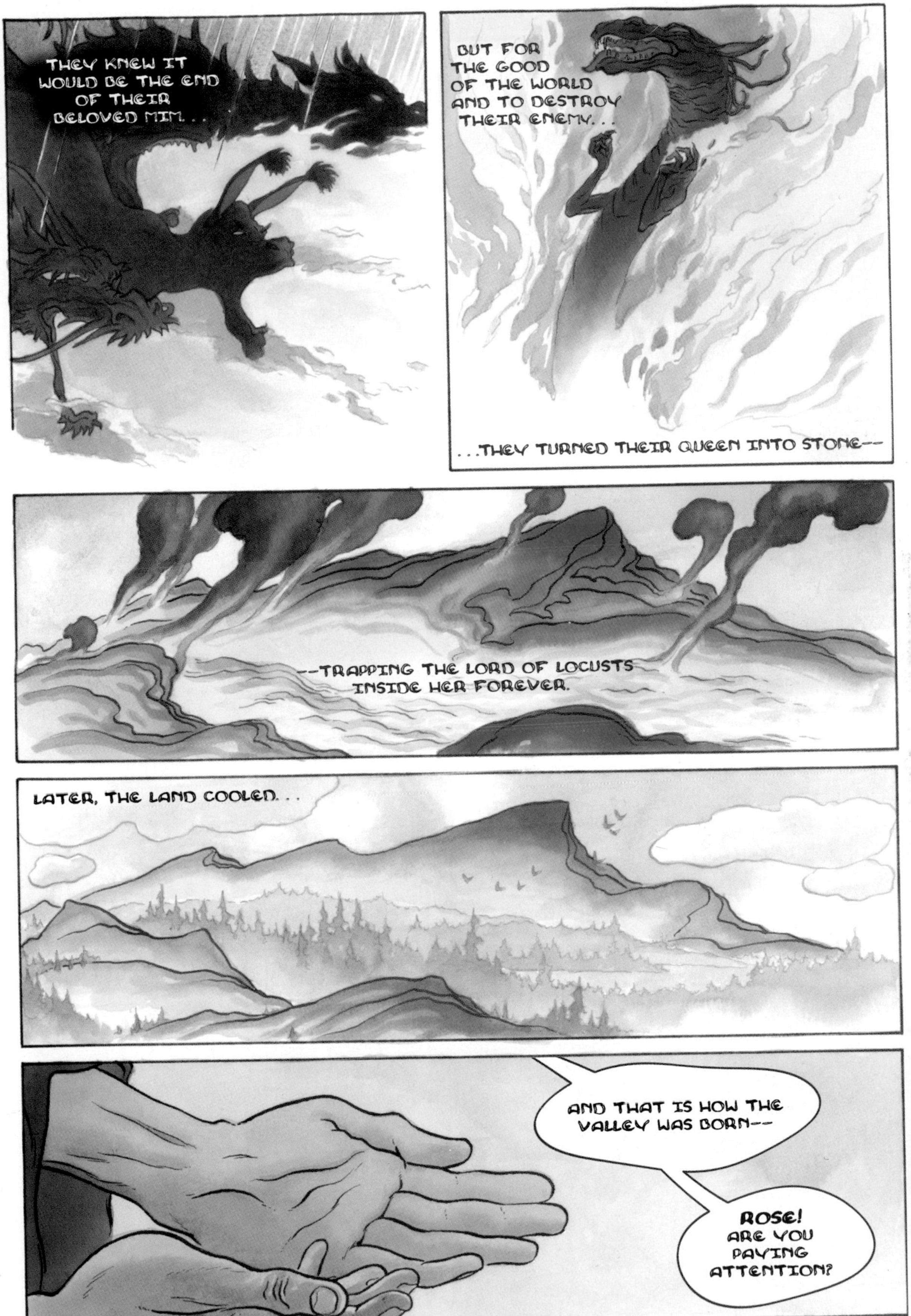
THEY KNEW IT WOULD BE THE END OF THEIR BELOVED MIM. . .
BUT FOR THE GOOD OF THE WORLD AND TO DESTROY THEIR ENEMY. . .
. . .THEY TURNED THEIR QUEEN INTO STONE--
--TRAPPING THE LORD OF LOCUSTS INSIDE HER FOREVER.
LATER, THE LAND COOLED. . .
AND THAT IS HOW THE VALLEY WAS BORN--
ROSE! ARE YOU PAYING ATTENTION?

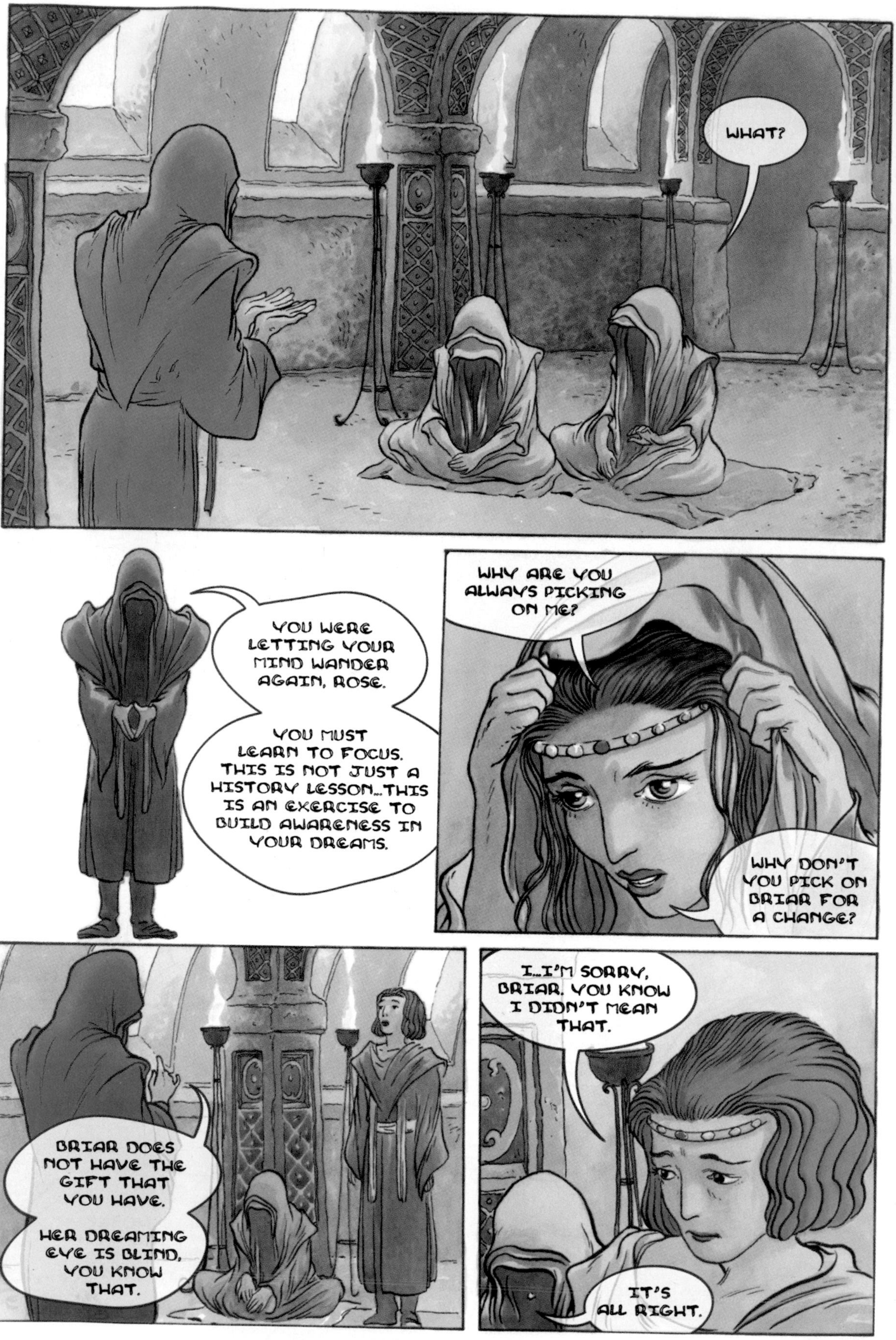
WHAT?
YOU WERE LETTING YOUR MIND WANDER AGAIN, ROSE.
YOU MUST LEARN TO FOCUS. THIS IS NOT JUST A HISTORY LESSON...THIS IS AN EXERCISE TO BUILD AWARENESS IN YOUR DREAMS.
WHY ARE YOU ALWAYS PICKING ON ME?
WHY DON'T YOU PICK ON BRIAR FOR A CHANGE?
BRIAR DOES NOT HAVE THE GIFT THAT YOU HAVE.
HER DREAMING EYE IS BLIND, YOU KNOW THAT.
I...I'M SORRY, BRIAR. YOU KNOW I DIDN'T MEAN THAT.
IT'S ALL RIGHT.

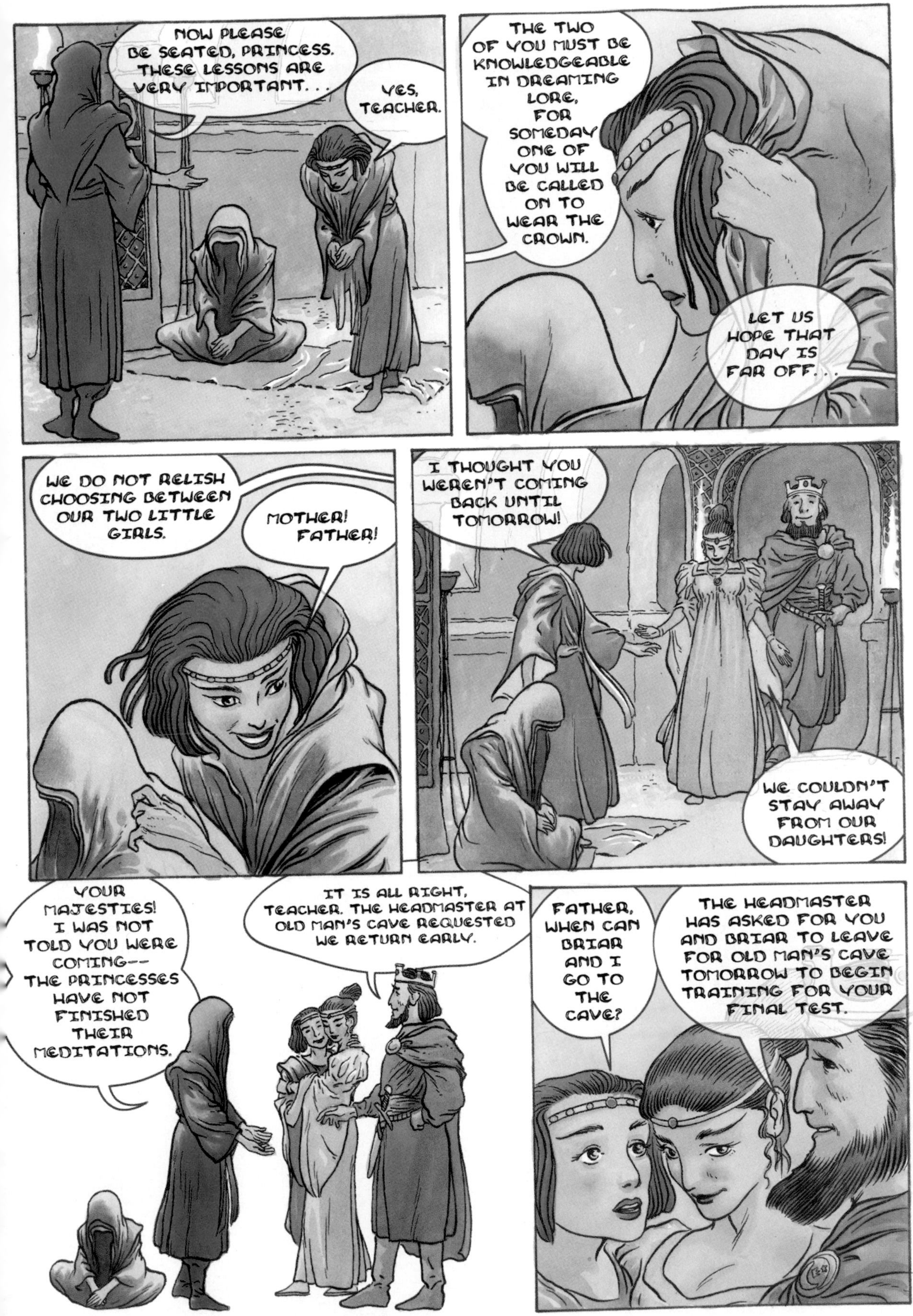
NOW PLEASE BE SEATED, PRINCESS. THESE LESSONS ARE VERY IMPORTANT...
YES, TEACHER.
THE TWO OF YOU MUST BE KNOWLEDGEABLE IN DREAMING LORE, FOR SOMEDAY ONE OF YOU WILL BE CALLED ON TO WEAR THE CROWN.
LET US HOPE THAT DAY IS FAR OFF...
WE DO NOT RELISH CHOOSING BETWEEN OUR TWO LITTLE GIRLS.
MOTHER! FATHER!
I THOUGHT YOU WEREN'T COMING BACK UNTIL TOMORROW!
WE COULDN'T STAY AWAY FROM OUR DAUGHTERS!
YOUR MAJESTIES! I WAS NOT TOLD YOU WERE COMING-- THE PRINCESSES HAVE NOT FINISHED THEIR MEDITATIONS.
IT IS ALL RIGHT, TEACHER. THE HEADMASTER AT OLD MAN'S CAVE REQUESTED WE RETURN EARLY.
FATHER, WHEN CAN BRIAR AND I GO TO THE CAVE?
THE HEADMASTER HAS ASKED FOR YOU AND BRIAR TO LEAVE FOR OLD MAN'S CAVE TOMORROW TO BEGIN TRAINING FOR YOUR FINAL TEST.

REALLY?! WE'RE GOING TO OLD MAN'S CAVE TOMORROW? BRIAR—— DID YOU HEAR THAT?

AREN'T YOU EXCITED? WE ARE GOING TO TAKE A JOURNEY TO THE NORTHERN END OF THE VALLEY! IT'S SO BEAUTIFUL THIS TIME OF YEAR.

WHY ARE WE GOING?

WE AREN'T SUPPOSED TO TAKE OUR FINAL TEST UNTIL WE ARE OLDER.

THE HEADMASTER FEELS YOU TWO ARE READY. THE CAPTAIN OF THE GUARD WILL ACCOMPANY YOU AT DAWN.

WILL YOU NOT RESPECT OUR WISHES, BRIAR? WE BELIEVE THERE IS STILL HOPE FOR YOU.

THERE IS NO HOPE. TAKING THE TEST IS A WASTE OF TIME.

BRIAR, HOW CAN YOU SAY SUCH A THING? I'M SURE YOUR DREAMING EYE WILL OPEN———

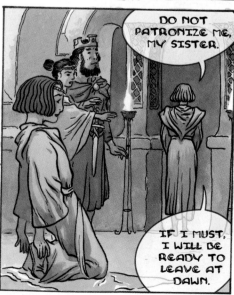

DO NOT PATRONIZE ME, MY SISTER.

IF I MUST, I WILL BE READY TO LEAVE AT DAWN.

OUR
BRIGHTEST
HOPE

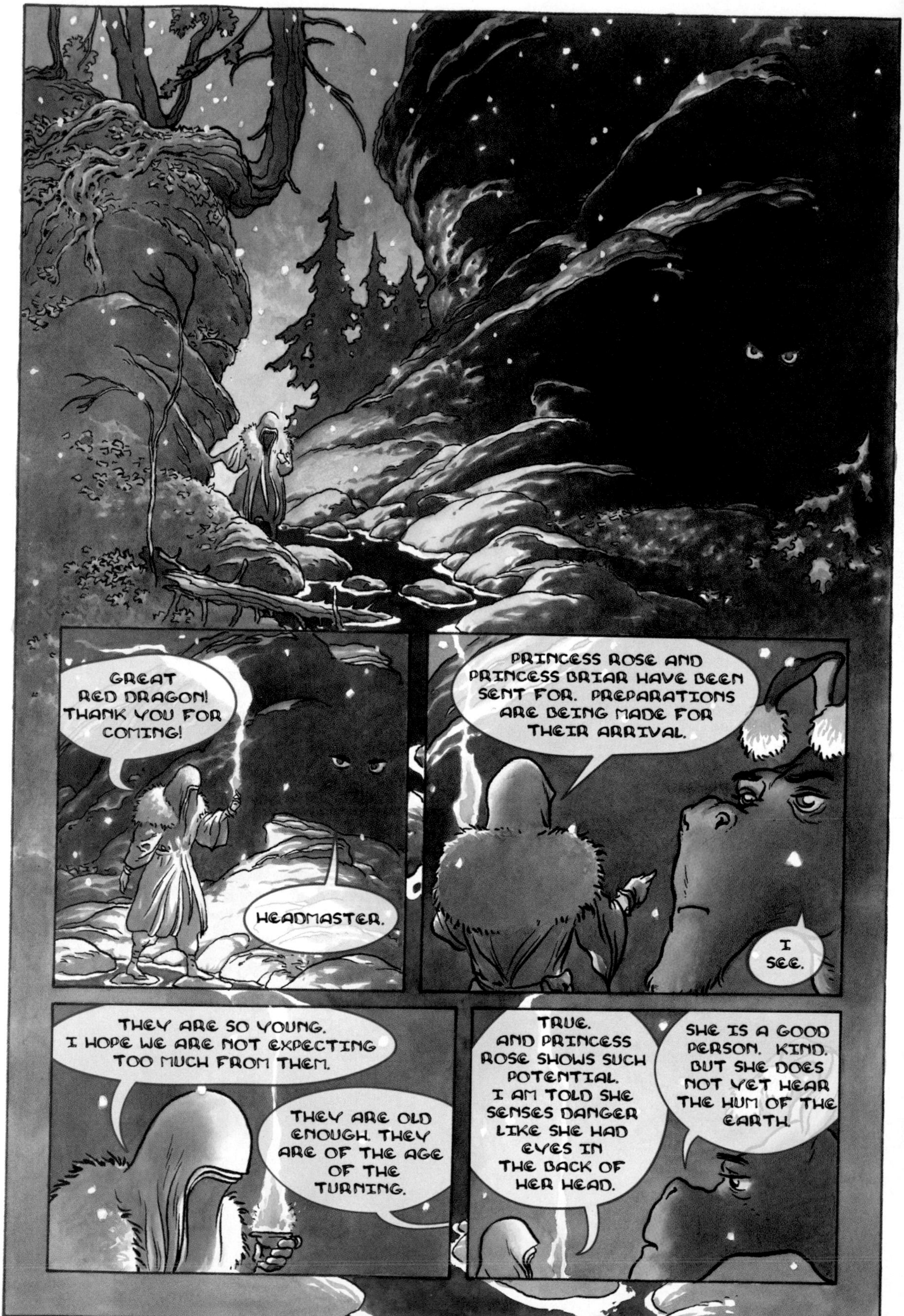
GREAT RED DRAGON! THANK YOU FOR COMING!
HEADMASTER.
PRINCESS ROSE AND PRINCESS BRIAR HAVE BEEN SENT FOR. PREPARATIONS ARE BEING MADE FOR THEIR ARRIVAL.
I SEE.
THEY ARE SO YOUNG. I HOPE WE ARE NOT EXPECTING TOO MUCH FROM THEM.
THEY ARE OLD ENOUGH. THEY ARE OF THE AGE OF THE TURNING.
TRUE. AND PRINCESS ROSE SHOWS SUCH POTENTIAL. I AM TOLD SHE SENSES DANGER LIKE SHE HAD EYES IN THE BACK OF HER HEAD.
SHE IS A GOOD PERSON. KIND. BUT SHE DOES NOT YET HEAR THE HUM OF THE EARTH.

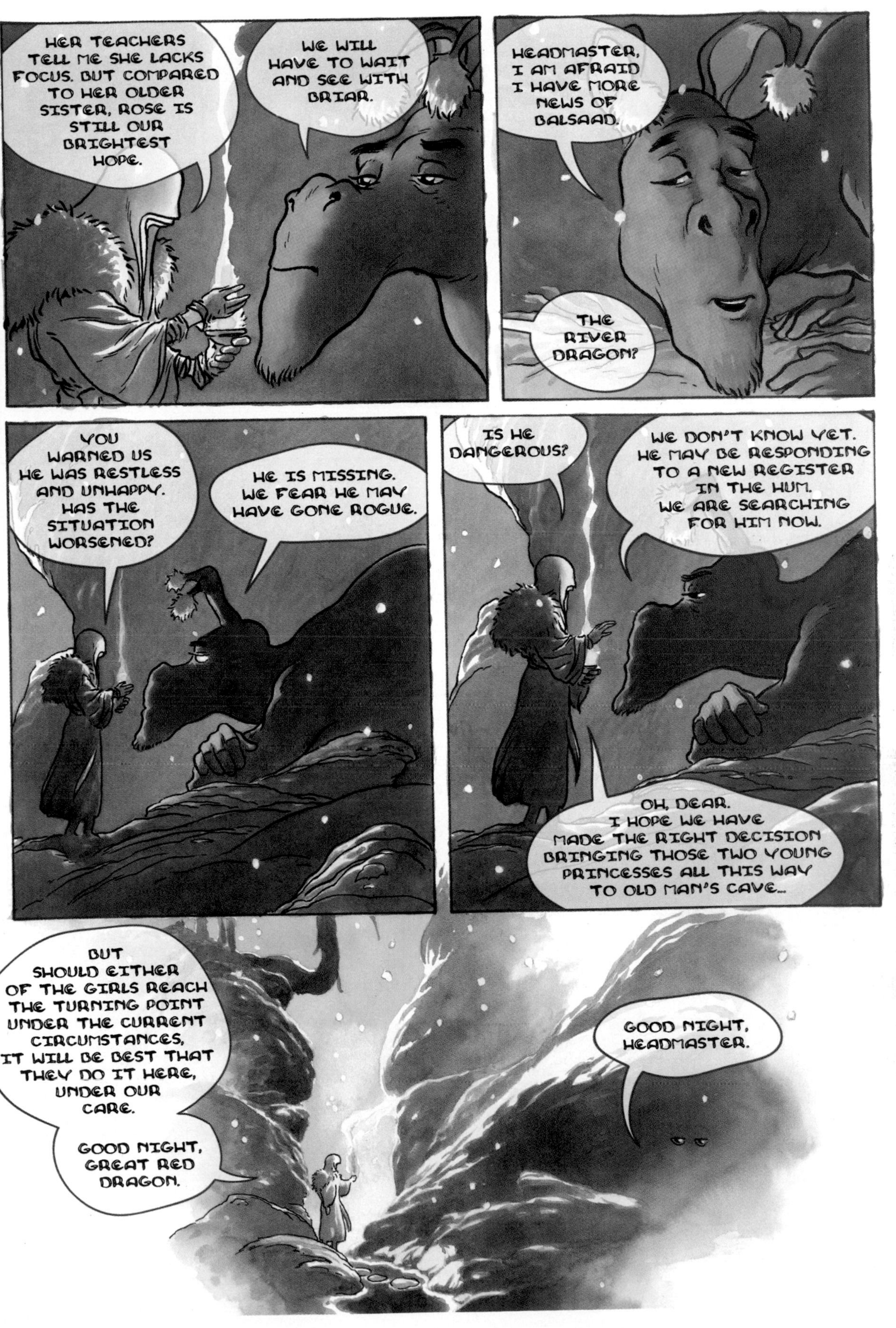
HER TEACHERS TELL ME SHE LACKS FOCUS. BUT COMPARED TO HER OLDER SISTER, ROSE IS STILL OUR BRIGHTEST HOPE.
WE WILL HAVE TO WAIT AND SEE WITH BRIAR.
HEADMASTER, I AM AFRAID I HAVE MORE NEWS OF BALSAAD.
THE RIVER DRAGON?
YOU WARNED US HE WAS RESTLESS AND UNHAPPY. HAS THE SITUATION WORSENED?
HE IS MISSING. WE FEAR HE MAY HAVE GONE ROGUE.
IS HE DANGEROUS?
WE DON'T KNOW YET. HE MAY BE RESPONDING TO A NEW REGISTER IN THE HUM. WE ARE SEARCHING FOR HIM NOW.
OH, DEAR. I HOPE WE HAVE MADE THE RIGHT DECISION BRINGING THOSE TWO YOUNG PRINCESSES ALL THIS WAY TO OLD MAN'S CAVE...
BUT SHOULD EITHER OF THE GIRLS REACH THE TURNING POINT UNDER THE CURRENT CIRCUMSTANCES, IT WILL BE BEST THAT THEY DO IT HERE, UNDER OUR CARE.
GOOD NIGHT, GREAT RED DRAGON.
GOOD NIGHT, HEADMASTER.

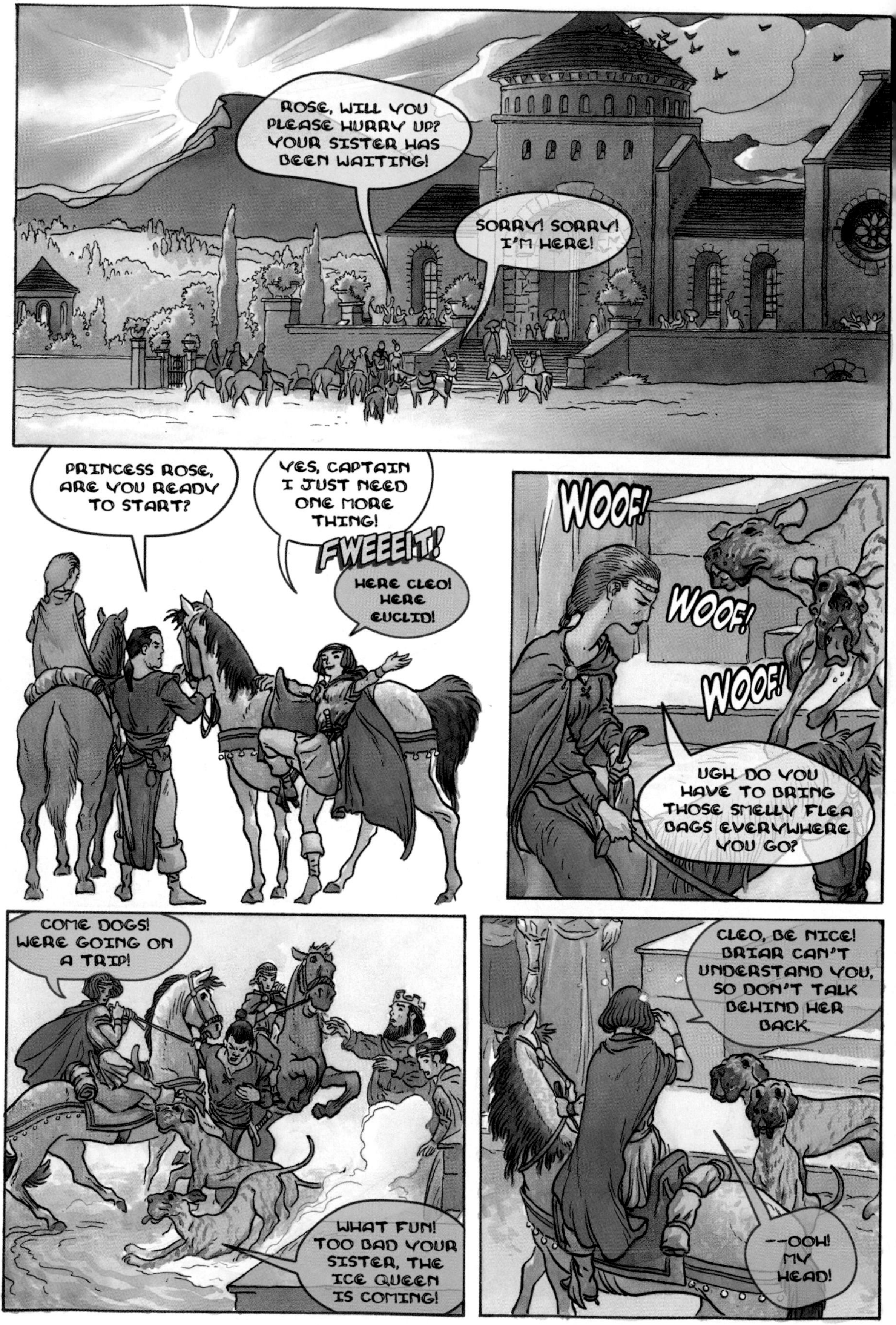
ROSE, WILL YOU PLEASE HURRY UP? YOUR SISTER HAS BEEN WAITING!
SORRY! SORRY! I'M HERE!
PRINCESS ROSE, ARE YOU READY TO START?
YES, CAPTAIN I JUST NEED ONE MORE THING!
FWEEEIT!
HERE CLEO! HERE EUCLID!
WOOF!
WOOF!
WOOF!
UGH. DO YOU HAVE TO BRING THOSE SMELLY FLEA BAGS EVERYWHERE YOU GO?
COME DOGS! WERE GOING ON A TRIP!
WHAT FUN! TOO BAD YOUR SISTER, THE ICE QUEEN IS COMING!
CLEO, BE NICE! BRIAR CAN'T UNDERSTAND YOU, SO DON'T TALK BEHIND HER BACK.
--OOH! MY HEAD!

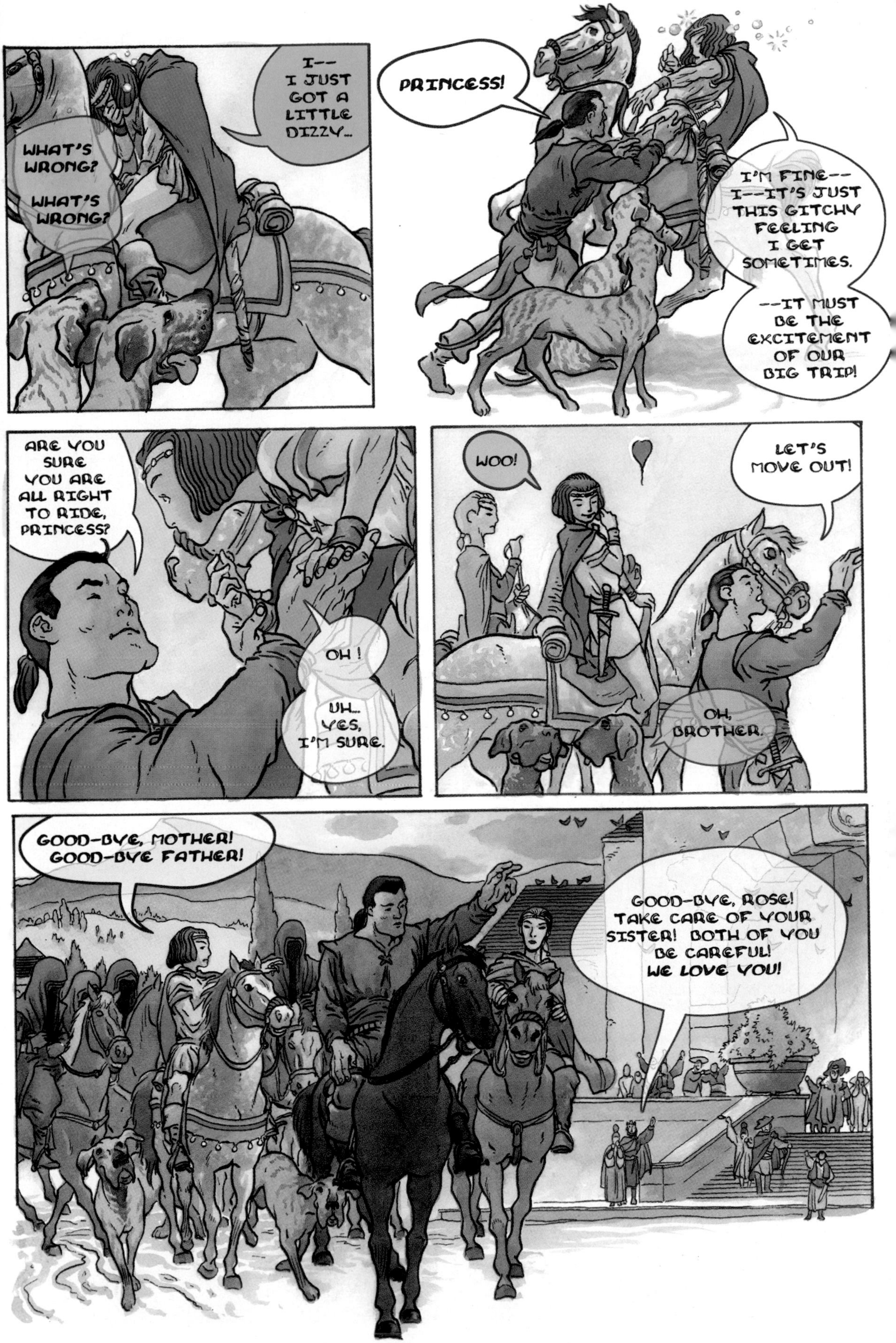
I-- I JUST GOT A LITTLE DIZZY...
WHAT'S WRONG? WHAT'S WRONG?
PRINCESS!
I'M FINE-- I--IT'S JUST THIS GITCHY FEELING I GET SOMETIMES.
--IT MUST BE THE EXCITEMENT OF OUR BIG TRIP!
ARE YOU SURE YOU ARE ALL RIGHT TO RIDE, PRINCESS?
OH !
UH... YES, I'M SURE.
WOO!
LET'S MOVE OUT!
OH, BROTHER.
GOOD-BYE, MOTHER! GOOD-BYE FATHER!
GOOD-BYE, ROSE! TAKE CARE OF YOUR SISTER! BOTH OF YOU BE CAREFUL! WE LOVE YOU!

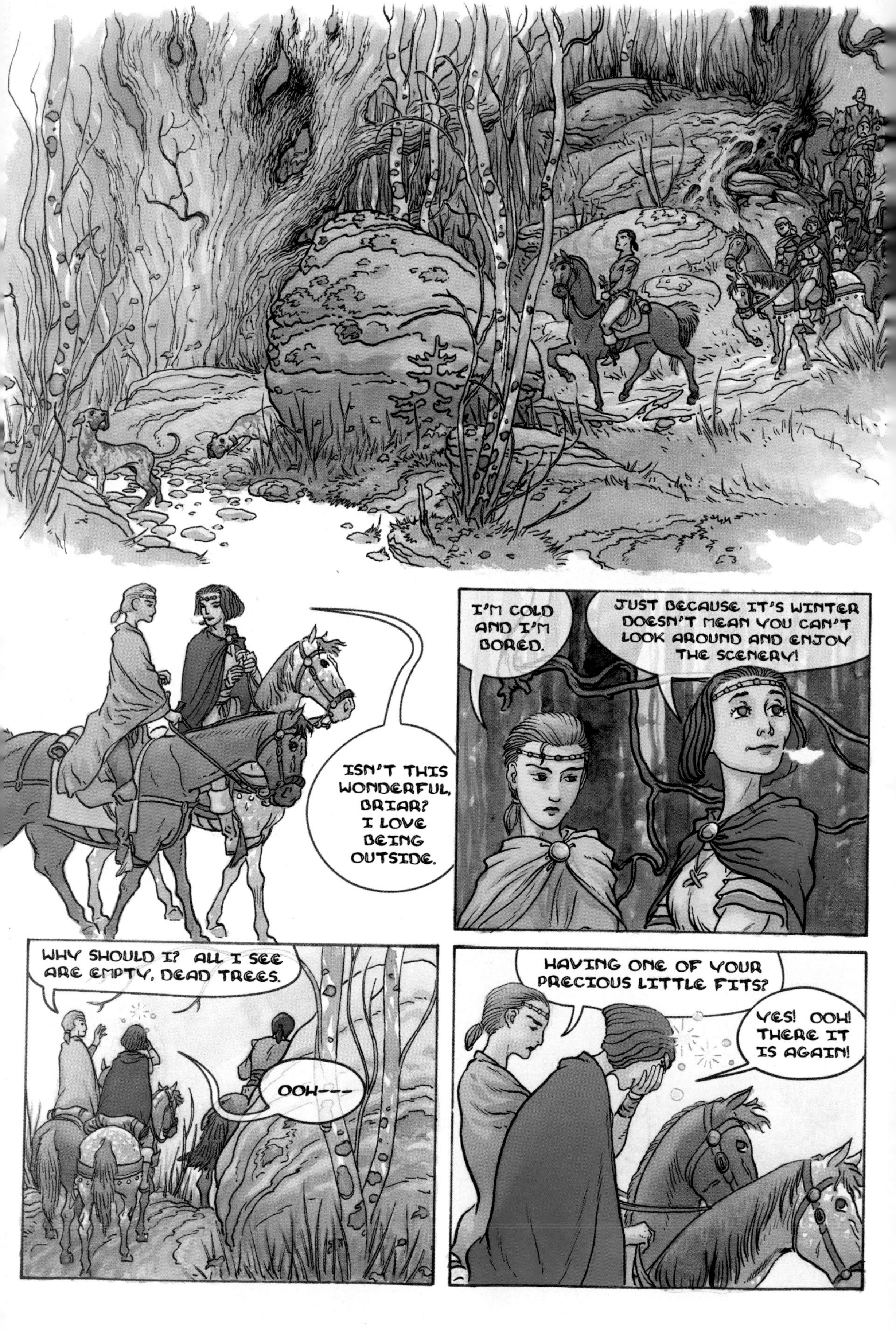

ISN'T THIS WONDERFUL, BRIAR? I LOVE BEING OUTSIDE.
I'M COLD AND I'M BORED.
JUST BECAUSE IT'S WINTER DOESN'T MEAN YOU CAN'T LOOK AROUND AND ENJOY THE SCENERY!
WHY SHOULD I? ALL I SEE ARE EMPTY, DEAD TREES.
OOH---
HAVING ONE OF YOUR PRECIOUS LITTLE FITS?
YES! OOH! THERE IT IS AGAIN!

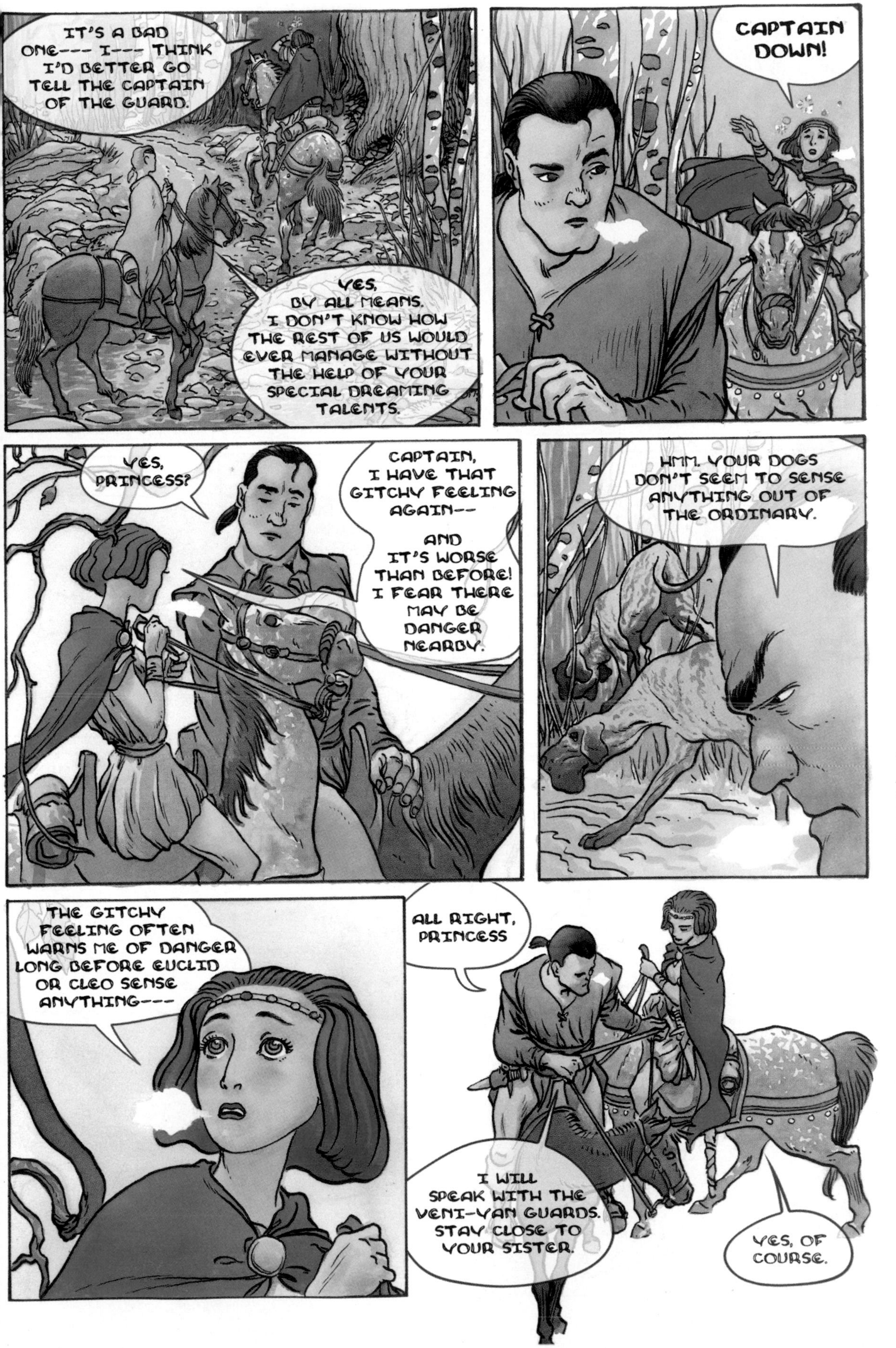
IT'S A BAD ONE--- I--- THINK I'D BETTER GO TELL THE CAPTAIN OF THE GUARD.
YES, BY ALL MEANS. I DON'T KNOW HOW THE REST OF US WOULD EVER MANAGE WITHOUT THE HELP OF YOUR SPECIAL DREAMING TALENTS.
CAPTAIN DOWN!
YES, PRINCESS?
CAPTAIN, I HAVE THAT GITCHY FEELING AGAIN--
AND IT'S WORSE THAN BEFORE! I FEAR THERE MAY BE DANGER NEARBY.
HMM. YOUR DOGS DON'T SEEM TO SENSE ANYTHING OUT OF THE ORDINARY.
THE GITCHY FEELING OFTEN WARNS ME OF DANGER LONG BEFORE EUCLID OR CLEO SENSE ANYTHING---
ALL RIGHT, PRINCESS
I WILL SPEAK WITH THE VENI-YAN GUARDS. STAY CLOSE TO YOUR SISTER.
YES, OF COURSE.

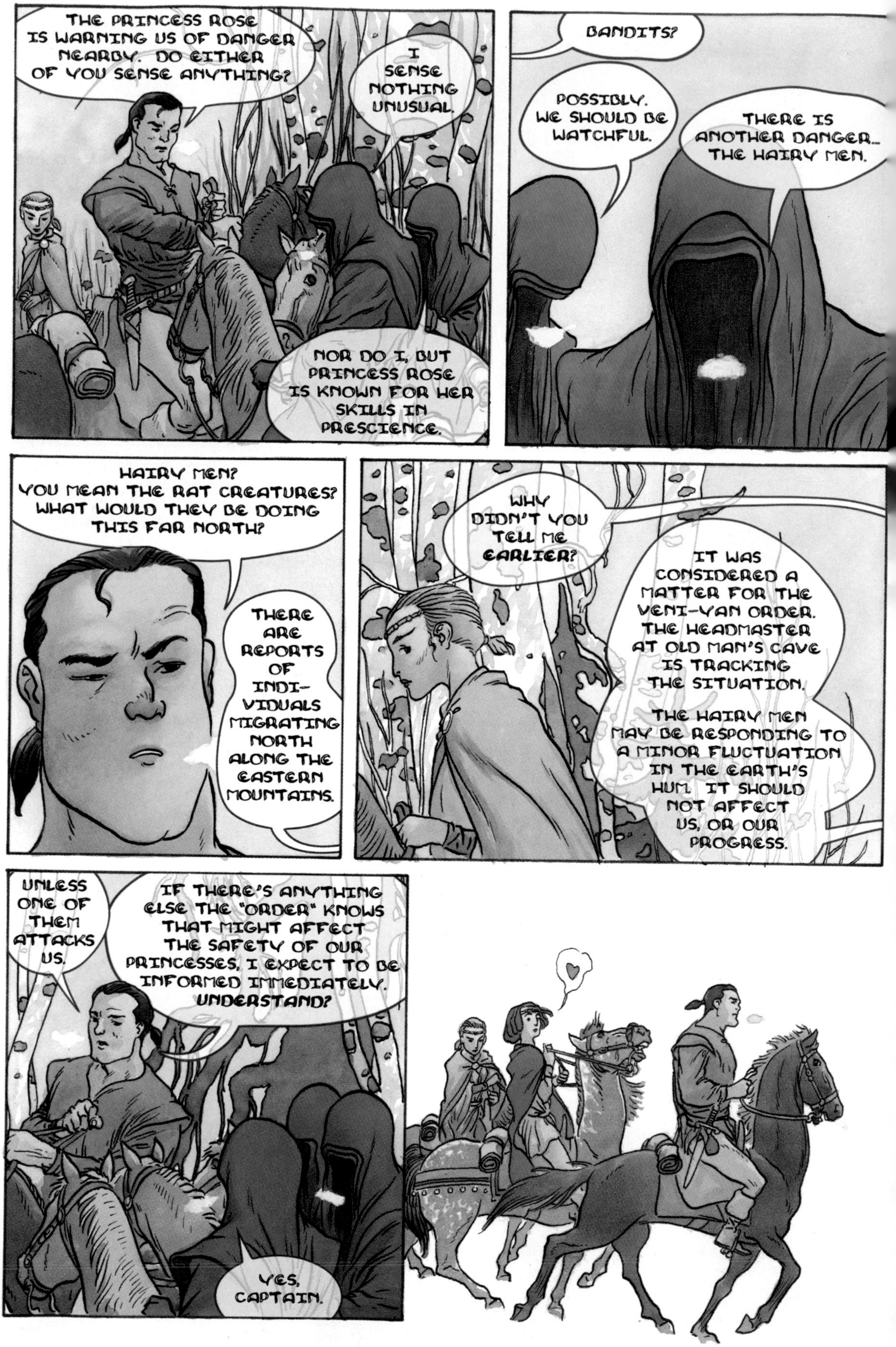

THE PRINCESS ROSE IS WARNING US OF DANGER NEARBY. DO EITHER OF YOU SENSE ANYTHING?
I SENSE NOTHING UNUSUAL.
NOR DO I, BUT PRINCESS ROSE IS KNOWN FOR HER SKILLS IN PRESCIENCE.
BANDITS?
POSSIBLY. WE SHOULD BE WATCHFUL.
THERE IS ANOTHER DANGER... THE HAIRY MEN.
HAIRY MEN? YOU MEAN THE RAT CREATURES? WHAT WOULD THEY BE DOING THIS FAR NORTH?
THERE ARE REPORTS OF INDIVIDUALS MIGRATING NORTH ALONG THE EASTERN MOUNTAINS.
WHY DIDN'T YOU TELL ME **EARLIER**?
IT WAS CONSIDERED A MATTER FOR THE VENI-YAN ORDER. THE HEADMASTER AT OLD MAN'S CAVE IS TRACKING THE SITUATION.
THE HAIRY MEN MAY BE RESPONDING TO A MINOR FLUCTUATION IN THE EARTH'S HUM. IT SHOULD NOT AFFECT US, OR OUR PROGRESS.
UNLESS ONE OF THEM ATTACKS US.
IF THERE'S ANYTHING ELSE THE "ORDER" KNOWS THAT MIGHT AFFECT THE SAFETY OF OUR PRINCESSES, I EXPECT TO BE INFORMED IMMEDIATELY. **UNDERSTAND?**
YES, CAPTAIN.

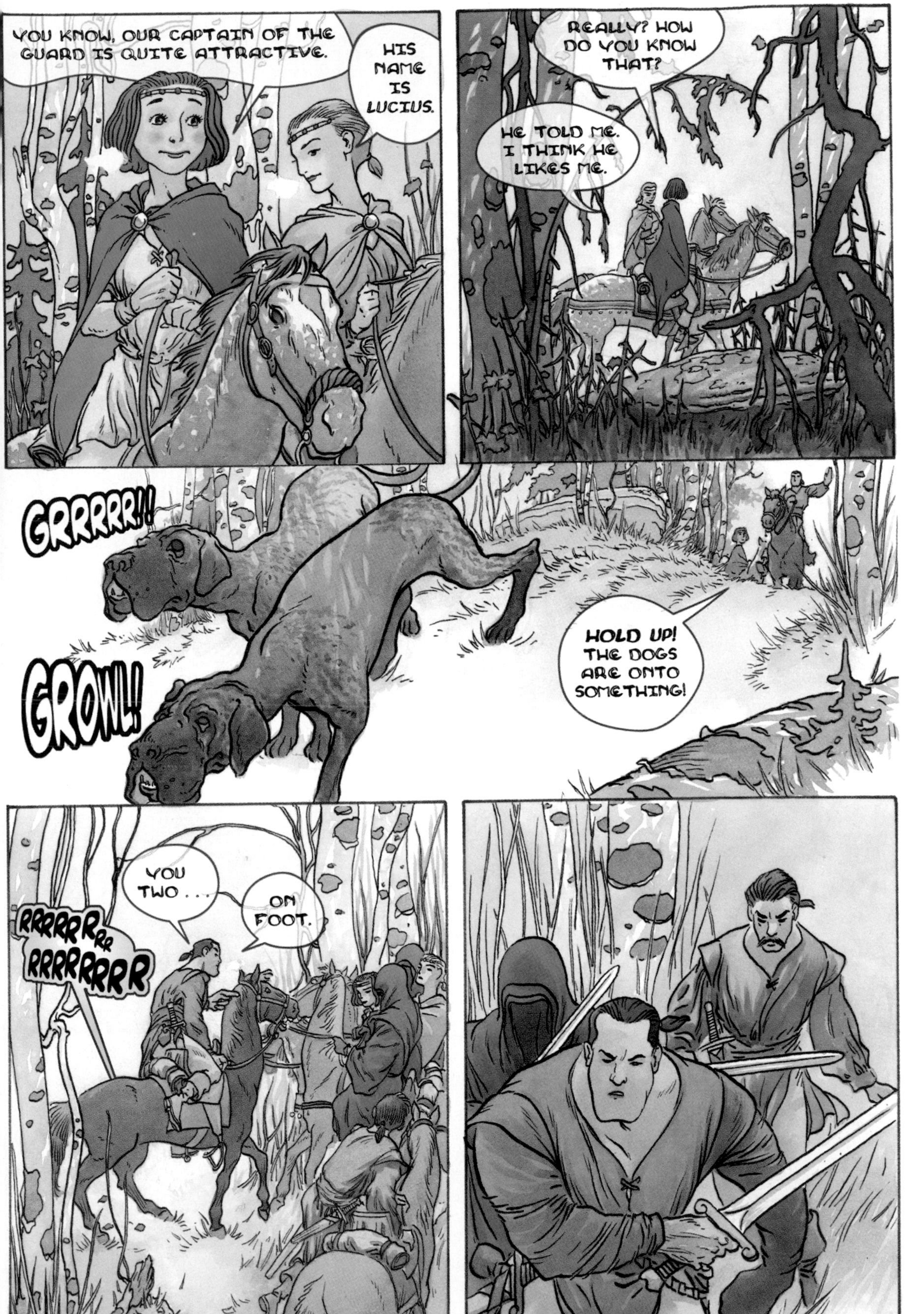
YOU KNOW, OUR CAPTAIN OF THE GUARD IS QUITE ATTRACTIVE.
HIS NAME IS LUCIUS.
REALLY? HOW DO YOU KNOW THAT?
HE TOLD ME. I THINK HE LIKES ME.
GRRRRR!!
GROWL!
HOLD UP! THE DOGS ARE ONTO SOMETHING!
RRRRRRRR RRRRRRRR
YOU TWO . . .
ON FOOT.

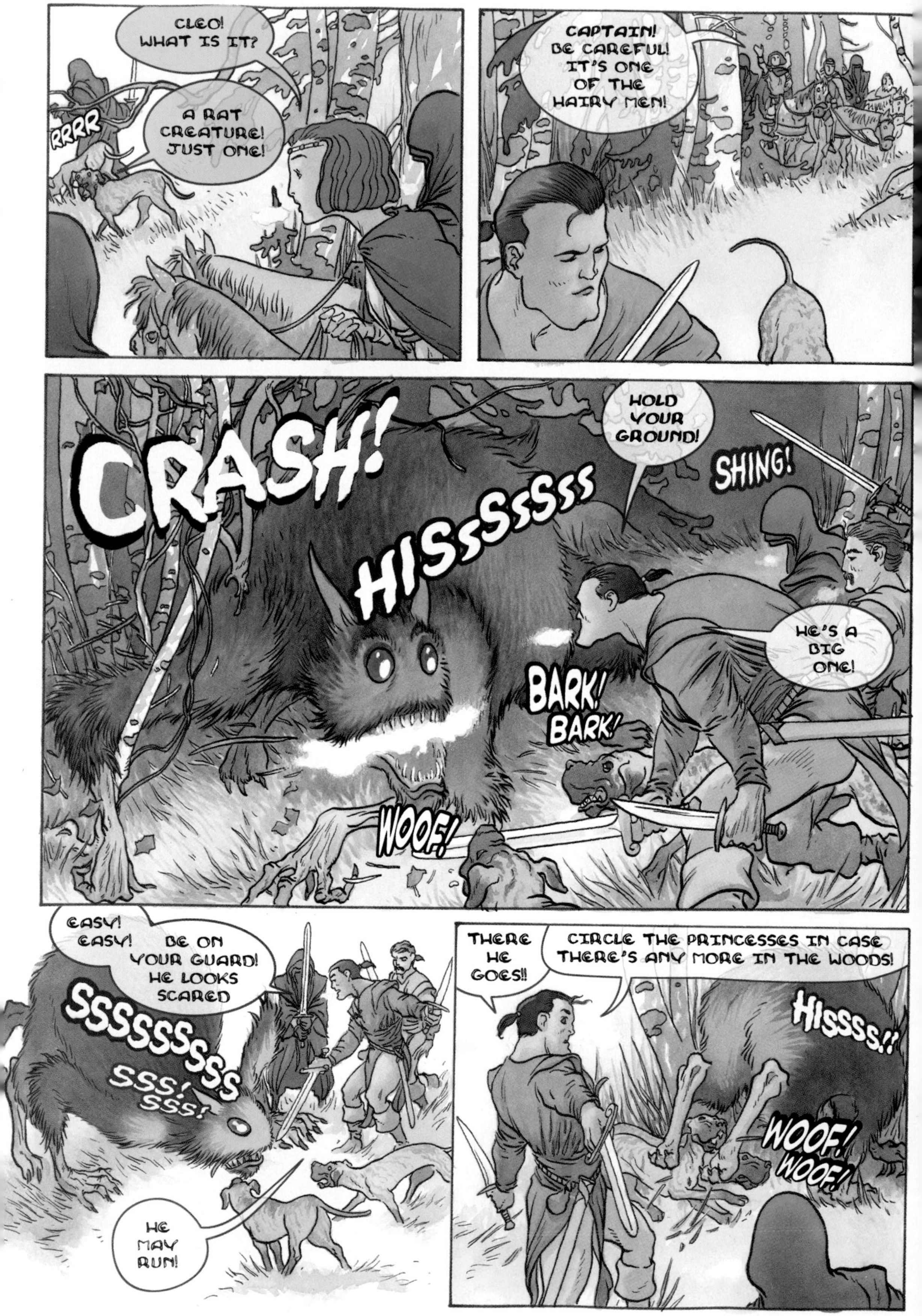
CLEO! WHAT IS IT?
RRRR
A RAT CREATURE! JUST ONE!
CAPTAIN! BE CAREFUL! IT'S ONE OF THE HAIRY MEN!
CRASH!
HISsSsSss
HOLD YOUR GROUND!
SHING!
HE'S A BIG ONE!
BARK! BARK!
WOOF!
EASY! EASY! BE ON YOUR GUARD! HE LOOKS SCARED
SSSSSSSSS
SSS! SSS!
HE MAY RUN!
THERE HE GOES!!
CIRCLE THE PRINCESSES IN CASE THERE'S ANY MORE IN THE WOODS!
HISSSS.!!
WOOF! WOOF!

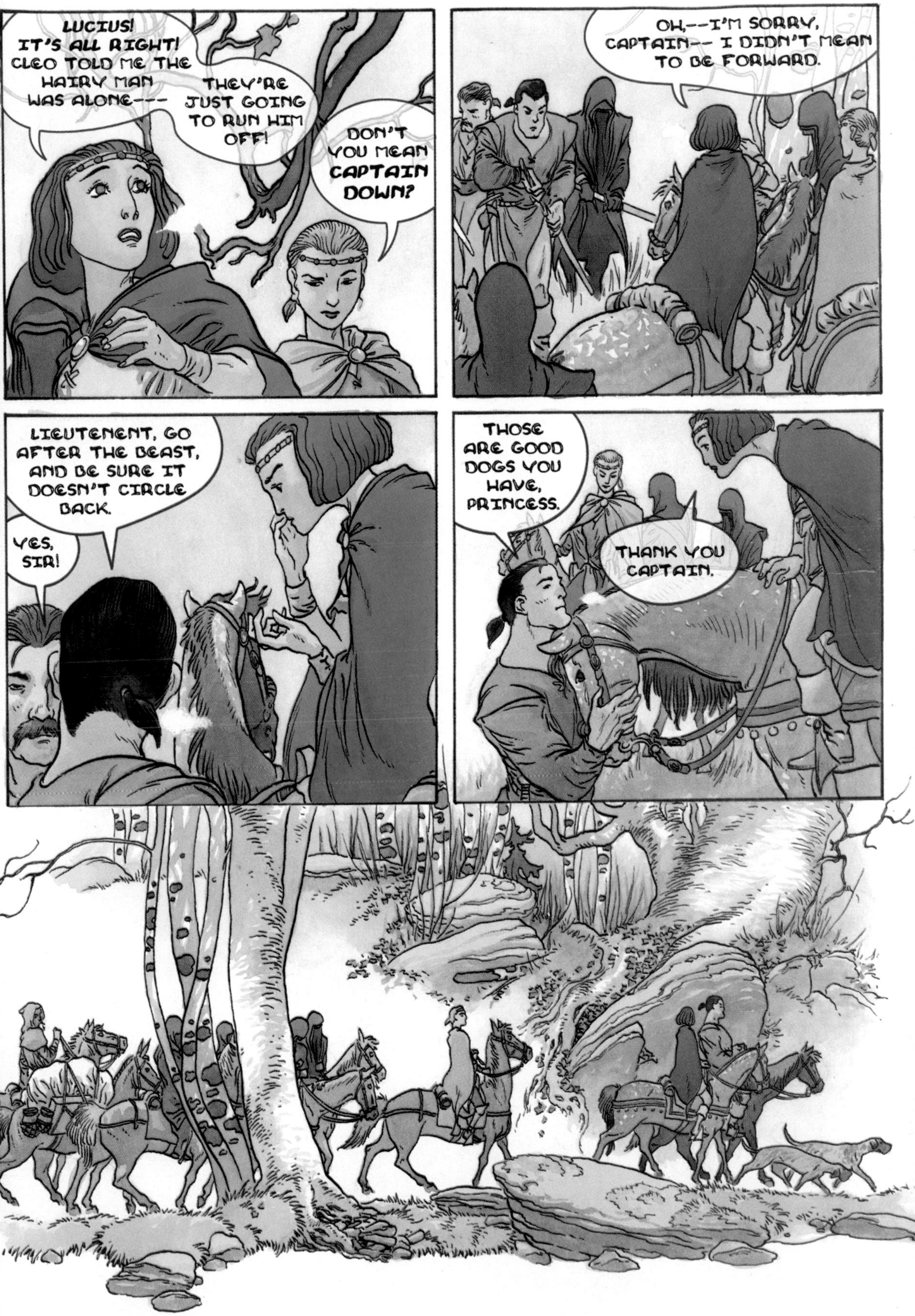
LUCIUS! IT'S ALL RIGHT! CLEO TOLD ME THE HAIRY MAN WAS ALONE---
THEY'RE JUST GOING TO RUN HIM OFF!
DON'T YOU MEAN CAPTAIN DOWN?
OH,--I'M SORRY, CAPTAIN-- I DIDN'T MEAN TO BE FORWARD.
LIEUTENENT, GO AFTER THE BEAST, AND BE SURE IT DOESN'T CIRCLE BACK.
YES, SIR!
THOSE ARE GOOD DOGS YOU HAVE, PRINCESS.
THANK YOU CAPTAIN.

THE
ICE
QUEEN

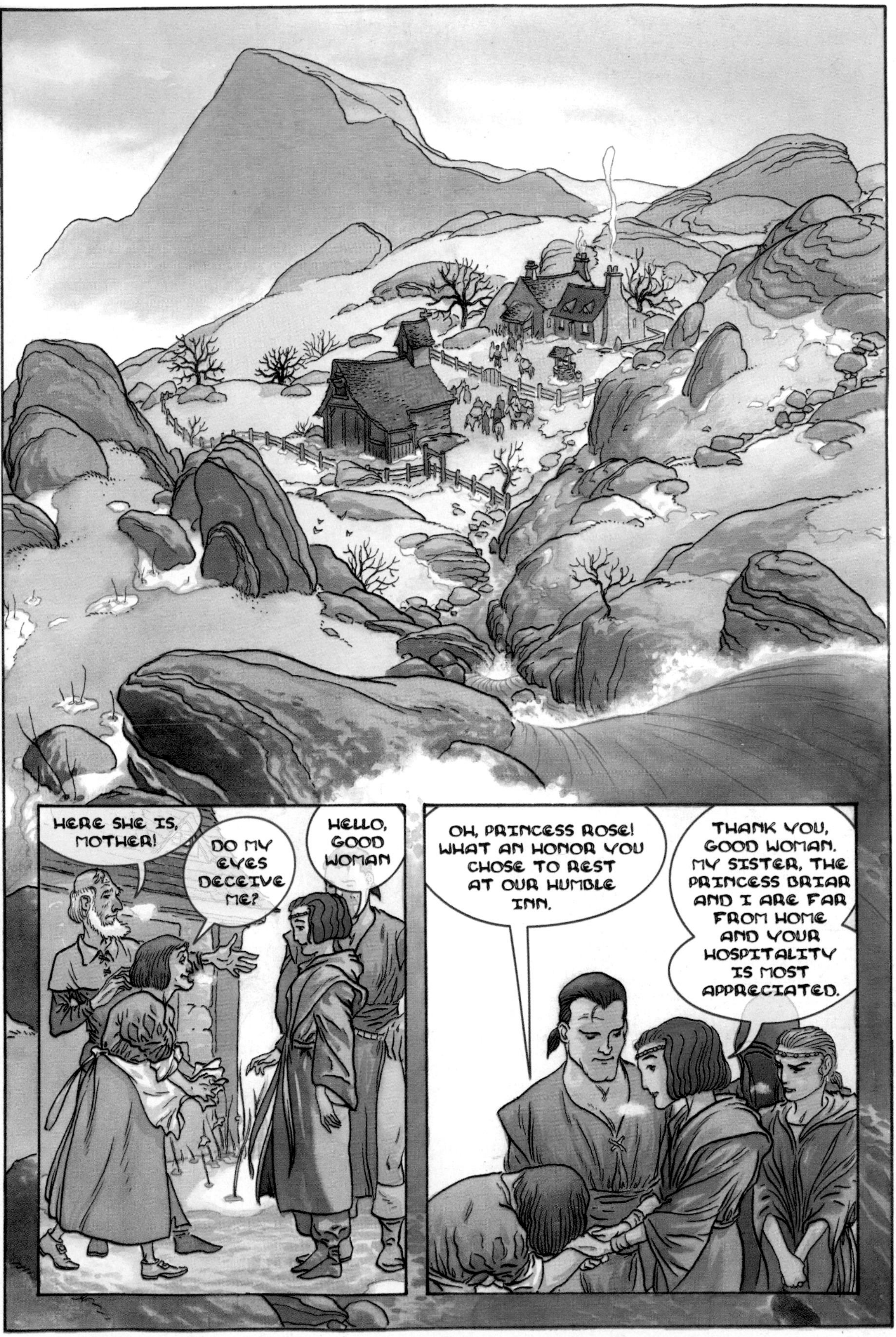
HERE SHE IS, MOTHER!
DO MY EYES DECEIVE ME?
HELLO, GOOD WOMAN
OH, PRINCESS ROSE! WHAT AN HONOR YOU CHOSE TO REST AT OUR HUMBLE INN.
THANK YOU, GOOD WOMAN. MY SISTER, THE PRINCESS BRIAR AND I ARE FAR FROM HOME AND YOUR HOSPITALITY IS MOST APPRECIATED.

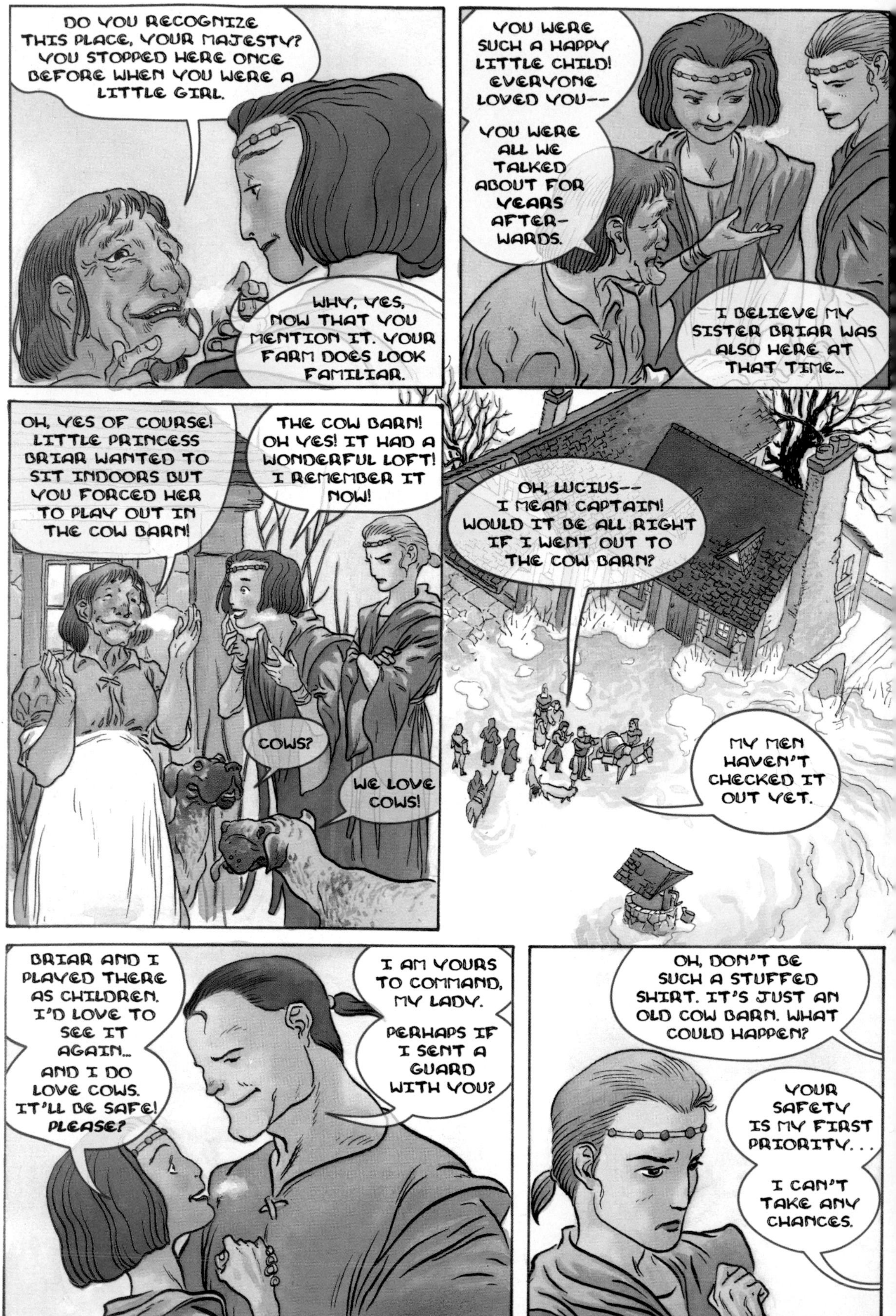
DO YOU RECOGNIZE THIS PLACE, YOUR MAJESTY? YOU STOPPED HERE ONCE BEFORE WHEN YOU WERE A LITTLE GIRL.
WHY, YES, NOW THAT YOU MENTION IT. YOUR FARM DOES LOOK FAMILIAR.
YOU WERE SUCH A HAPPY LITTLE CHILD! EVERYONE LOVED YOU--
YOU WERE ALL WE TALKED ABOUT FOR YEARS AFTER-WARDS.
I BELIEVE MY SISTER BRIAR WAS ALSO HERE AT THAT TIME...
OH, YES OF COURSE! LITTLE PRINCESS BRIAR WANTED TO SIT INDOORS BUT YOU FORCED HER TO PLAY OUT IN THE COW BARN!
THE COW BARN! OH YES! IT HAD A WONDERFUL LOFT! I REMEMBER IT NOW!
COWS?
WE LOVE COWS!
OH, LUCIUS-- I MEAN CAPTAIN! WOULD IT BE ALL RIGHT IF I WENT OUT TO THE COW BARN?
MY MEN HAVEN'T CHECKED IT OUT YET.
BRIAR AND I PLAYED THERE AS CHILDREN. I'D LOVE TO SEE IT AGAIN...
AND I DO LOVE COWS. IT'LL BE SAFE! PLEASE?
I AM YOURS TO COMMAND, MY LADY.
PERHAPS IF I SENT A GUARD WITH YOU?
OH, DON'T BE SUCH A STUFFED SHIRT. IT'S JUST AN OLD COW BARN. WHAT COULD HAPPEN?
YOUR SAFETY IS MY FIRST PRIORITY...
I CAN'T TAKE ANY CHANCES.

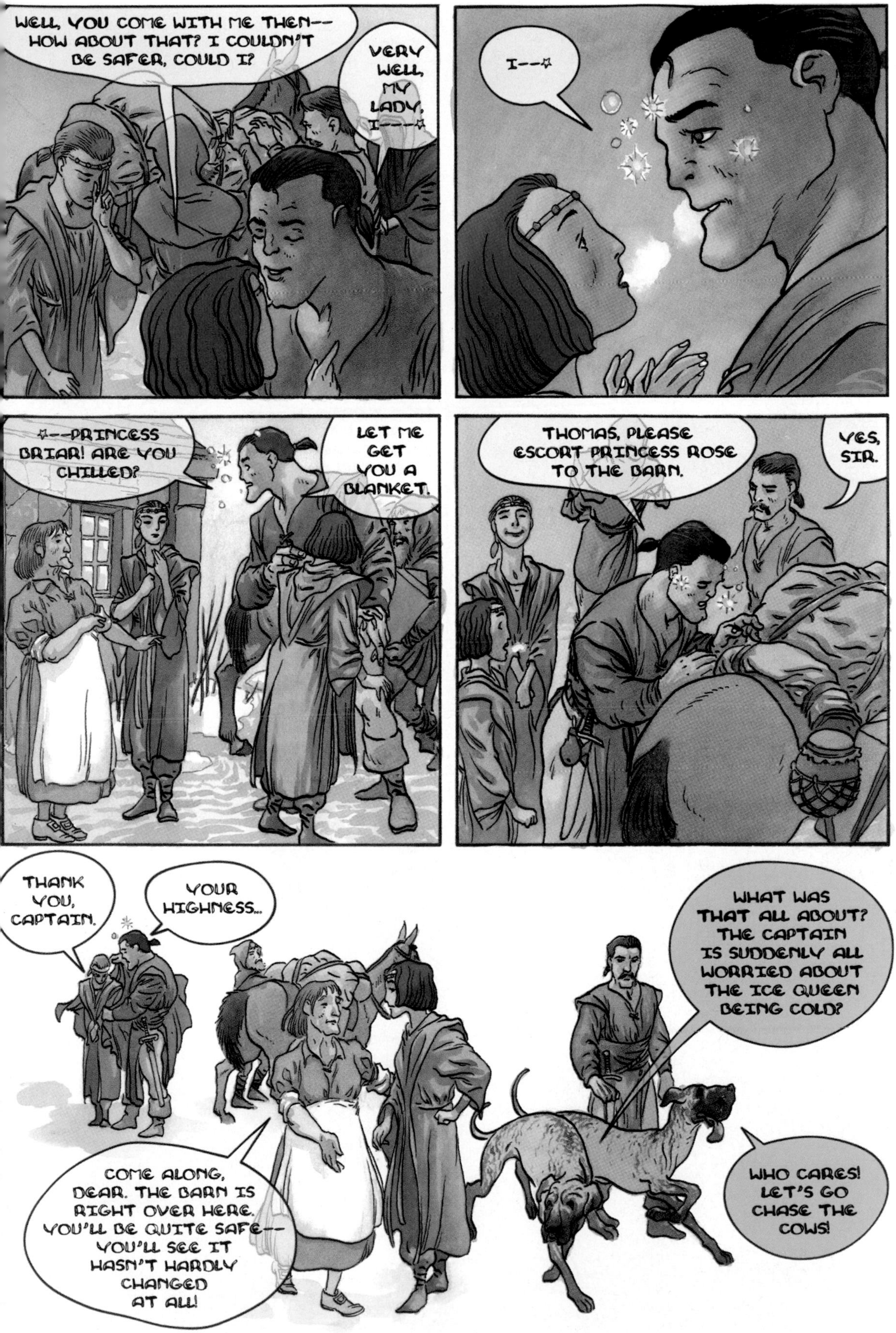
WELL, YOU COME WITH ME THEN-- HOW ABOUT THAT? I COULDN'T BE SAFER, COULD I?
VERY WELL, MY LADY, I---☆
I--☆
☆--PRINCESS BRIAR! ARE YOU CHILLED?
LET ME GET YOU A BLANKET.
THOMAS, PLEASE ESCORT PRINCESS ROSE TO THE BARN.
YES, SIR.
THANK YOU, CAPTAIN.
YOUR HIGHNESS...
WHAT WAS THAT ALL ABOUT? THE CAPTAIN IS SUDDENLY ALL WORRIED ABOUT THE ICE QUEEN BEING COLD?
COME ALONG, DEAR. THE BARN IS RIGHT OVER HERE. YOU'LL BE QUITE SAFE-- YOU'LL SEE IT HASN'T HARDLY CHANGED AT ALL!
WHO CARES! LET'S GO CHASE THE COWS!

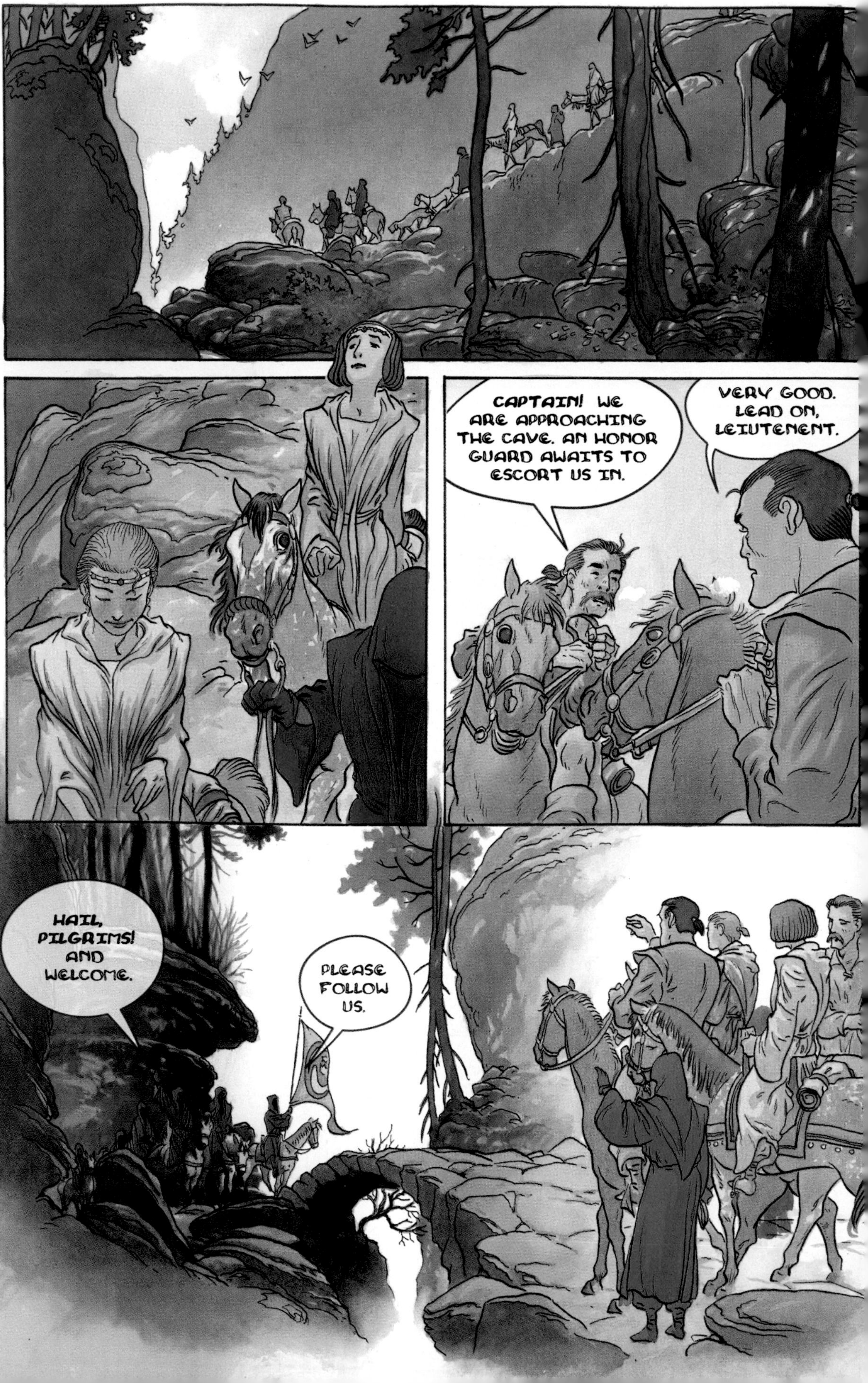
CAPTAIN! WE ARE APPROACHING THE CAVE. AN HONOR GUARD AWAITS TO ESCORT US IN.
VERY GOOD. LEAD ON, LEIUTENENT.
HAIL, PILGRIMS! AND WELCOME.
PLEASE FOLLOW US.

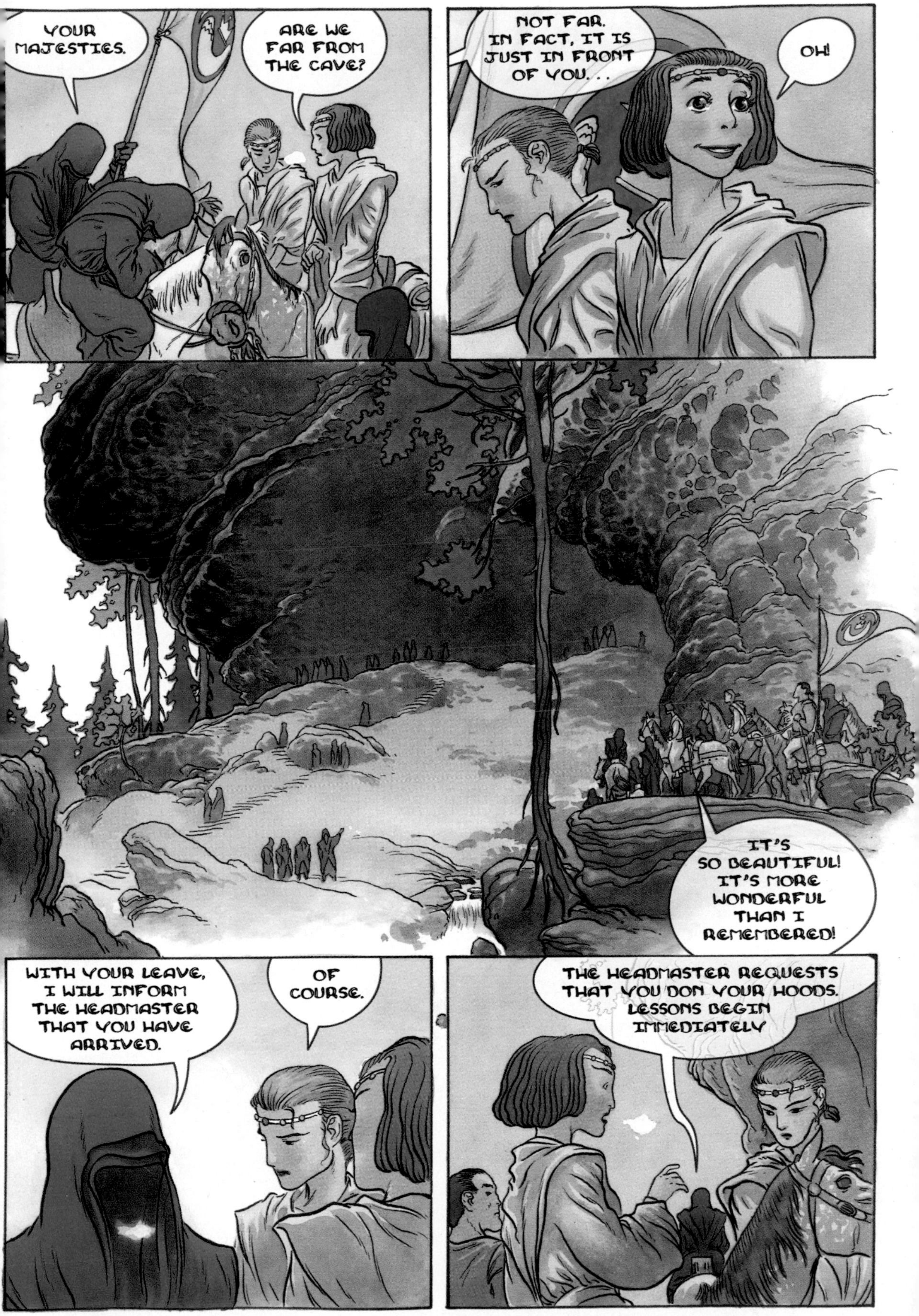
YOUR MAJESTIES.
ARE WE FAR FROM THE CAVE?
NOT FAR. IN FACT, IT IS JUST IN FRONT OF YOU. . .
OH!
IT'S SO BEAUTIFUL! IT'S MORE WONDERFUL THAN I REMEMBERED!
WITH YOUR LEAVE, I WILL INFORM THE HEADMASTER THAT YOU HAVE ARRIVED.
OF COURSE.
THE HEADMASTER REQUESTS THAT YOU DON YOUR HOODS. LESSONS BEGIN IMMEDIATELY

WE ASK,
TEACH

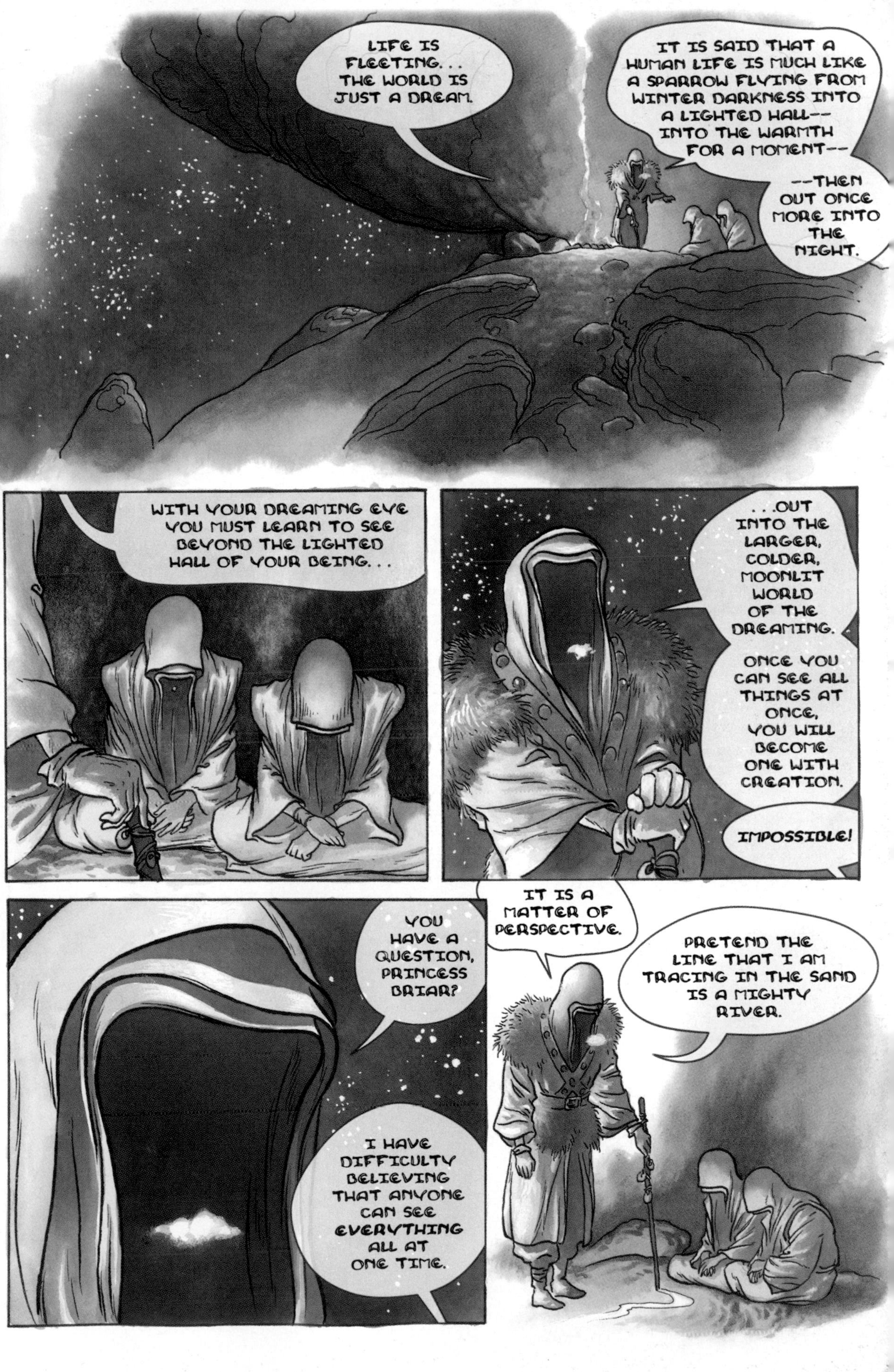
LIFE IS FLEETING. . . THE WORLD IS JUST A DREAM.
IT IS SAID THAT A HUMAN LIFE IS MUCH LIKE A SPARROW FLYING FROM WINTER DARKNESS INTO A LIGHTED HALL-- INTO THE WARMTH FOR A MOMENT--
--THEN OUT ONCE MORE INTO THE NIGHT.
WITH YOUR DREAMING EYE YOU MUST LEARN TO SEE BEYOND THE LIGHTED HALL OF YOUR BEING. . .
. . .OUT INTO THE LARGER, COLDER, MOONLIT WORLD OF THE DREAMING.
ONCE YOU CAN SEE ALL THINGS AT ONCE, YOU WILL BECOME ONE WITH CREATION.
IMPOSSIBLE!
YOU HAVE A QUESTION, PRINCESS BRIAR?
I HAVE DIFFICULTY BELIEVING THAT ANYONE CAN SEE EVERYTHING ALL AT ONE TIME.
IT IS A MATTER OF PERSPECTIVE.
PRETEND THE LINE THAT I AM TRACING IN THE SAND IS A MIGHTY RIVER.

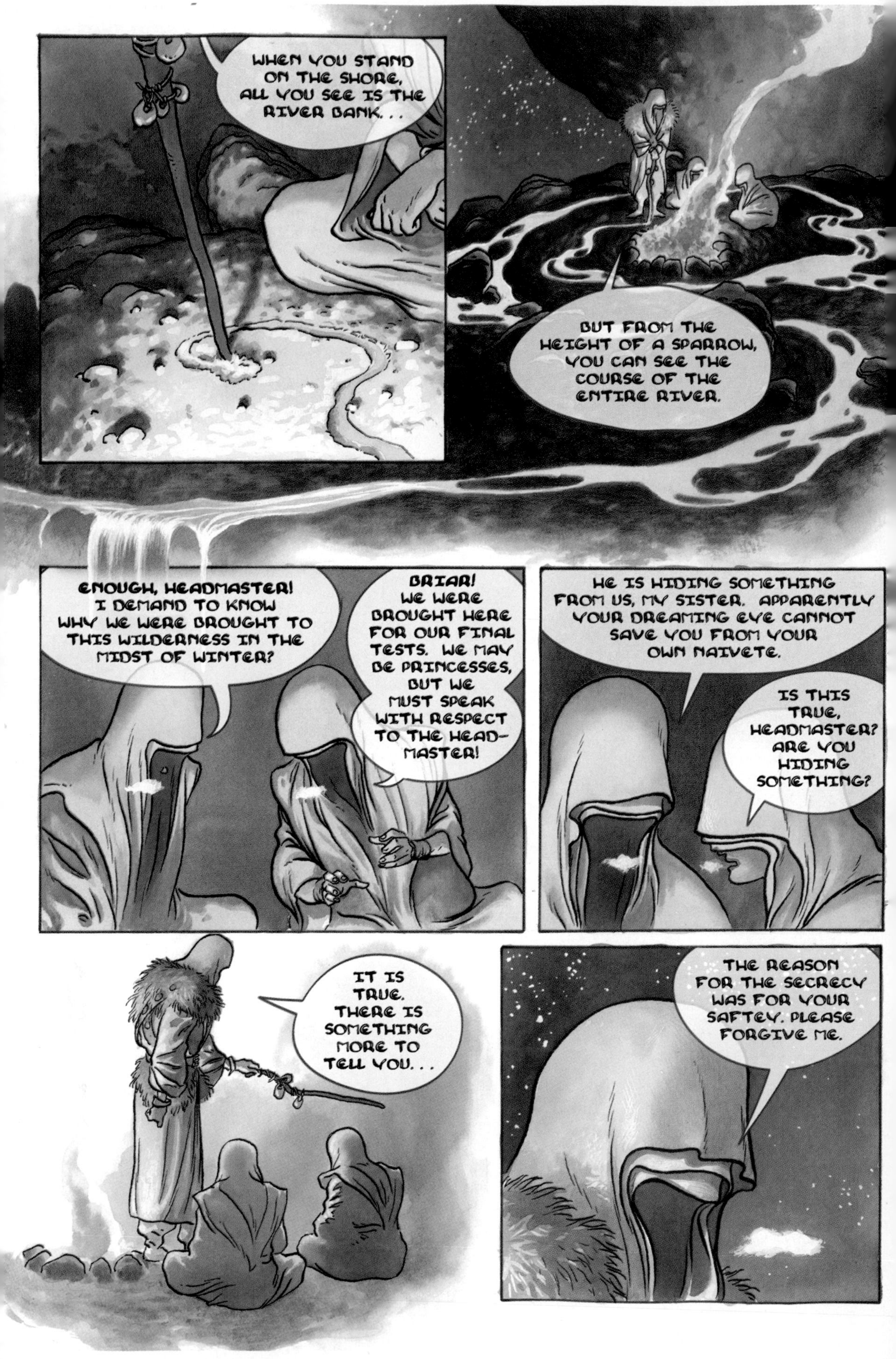
WHEN YOU STAND ON THE SHORE, ALL YOU SEE IS THE RIVER BANK. . .
BUT FROM THE HEIGHT OF A SPARROW, YOU CAN SEE THE COURSE OF THE ENTIRE RIVER.
ENOUGH, HEADMASTER! I DEMAND TO KNOW WHY WE WERE BROUGHT TO THIS WILDERNESS IN THE MIDST OF WINTER?
BRIAR! WE WERE BROUGHT HERE FOR OUR FINAL TESTS. WE MAY BE PRINCESSES, BUT WE MUST SPEAK WITH RESPECT TO THE HEAD-MASTER!
HE IS HIDING SOMETHING FROM US, MY SISTER. APPARENTLY YOUR DREAMING EYE CANNOT SAVE YOU FROM YOUR OWN NAIVETE.
IS THIS TRUE, HEADMASTER? ARE YOU HIDING SOMETHING?
IT IS TRUE. THERE IS SOMETHING MORE TO TELL YOU. . .
THE REASON FOR THE SECRECY WAS FOR YOUR SAFTEY. PLEASE FORGIVE ME.

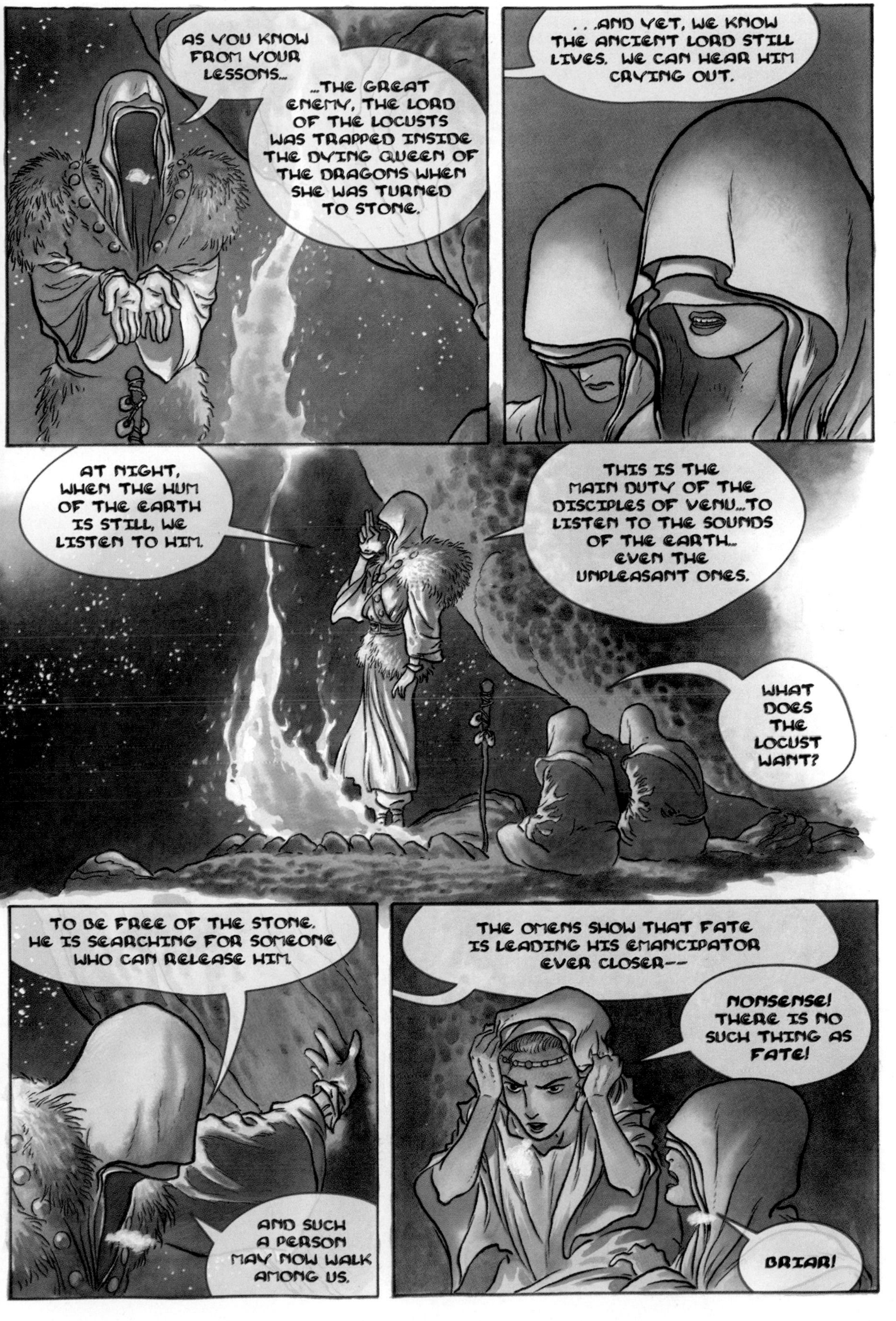
AS YOU KNOW FROM YOUR LESSONS...
...THE GREAT ENEMY, THE LORD OF THE LOCUSTS WAS TRAPPED INSIDE THE DYING QUEEN OF THE DRAGONS WHEN SHE WAS TURNED TO STONE.
. . .AND YET, WE KNOW THE ANCIENT LORD STILL LIVES. WE CAN HEAR HIM CRYING OUT.
AT NIGHT, WHEN THE HUM OF THE EARTH IS STILL, WE LISTEN TO HIM.
THIS IS THE MAIN DUTY OF THE DISCIPLES OF VENU...TO LISTEN TO THE SOUNDS OF THE EARTH... EVEN THE UNPLEASANT ONES.
WHAT DOES THE LOCUST WANT?
TO BE FREE OF THE STONE. HE IS SEARCHING FOR SOMEONE WHO CAN RELEASE HIM.
AND SUCH A PERSON MAY NOW WALK AMONG US.
THE OMENS SHOW THAT FATE IS LEADING HIS EMANCIPATOR EVER CLOSER---
NONSENSE! THERE IS NO SUCH THING AS FATE!
BRIAR!

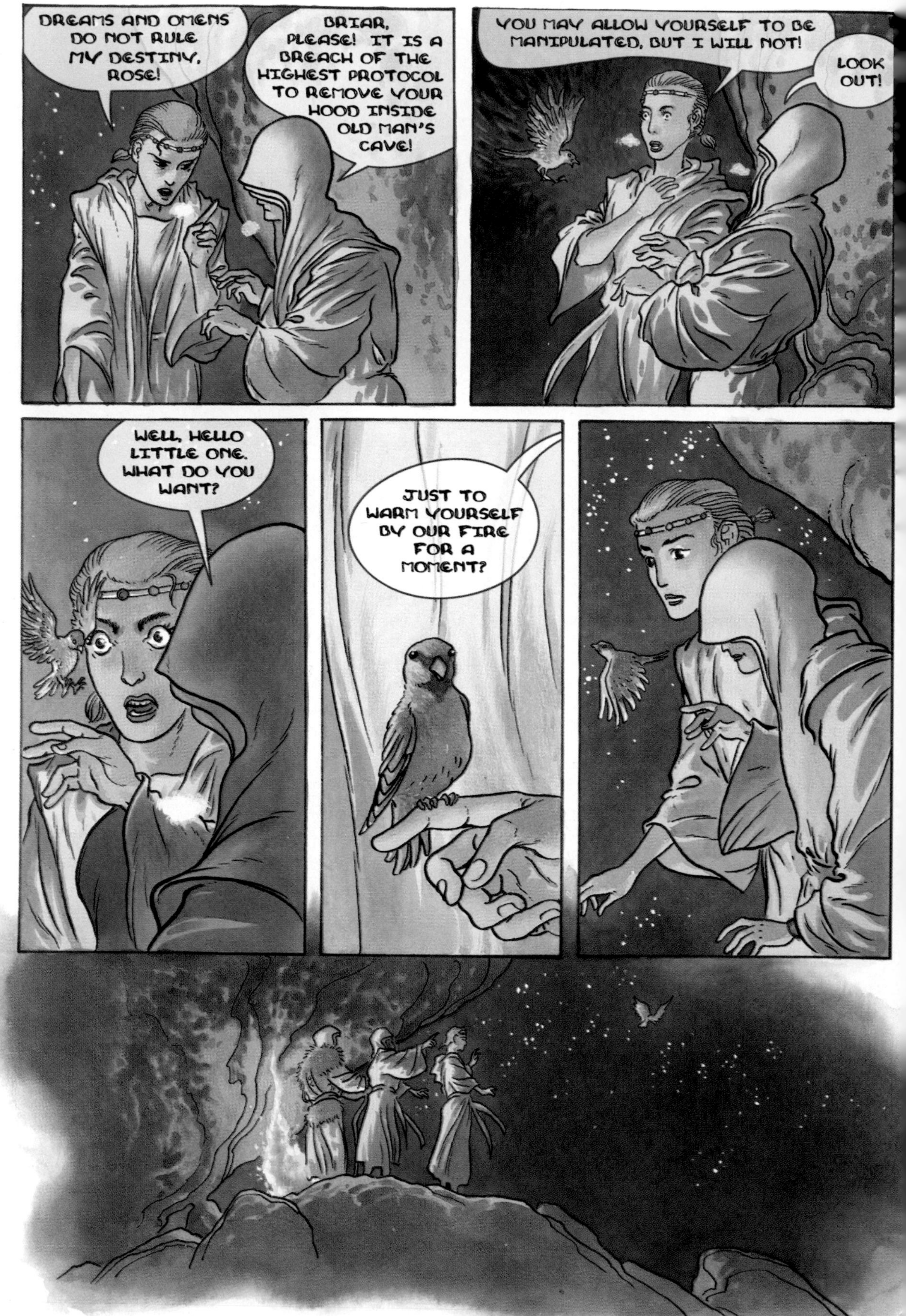
DREAMS AND OMENS DO NOT RULE MY DESTINY, ROSE!
BRIAR, PLEASE! IT IS A BREACH OF THE HIGHEST PROTOCOL TO REMOVE YOUR HOOD INSIDE OLD MAN'S CAVE!
YOU MAY ALLOW YOURSELF TO BE MANIPULATED, BUT I WILL NOT!
LOOK OUT!
WELL, HELLO LITTLE ONE. WHAT DO YOU WANT?
JUST TO WARM YOURSELF BY OUR FIRE FOR A MOMENT?

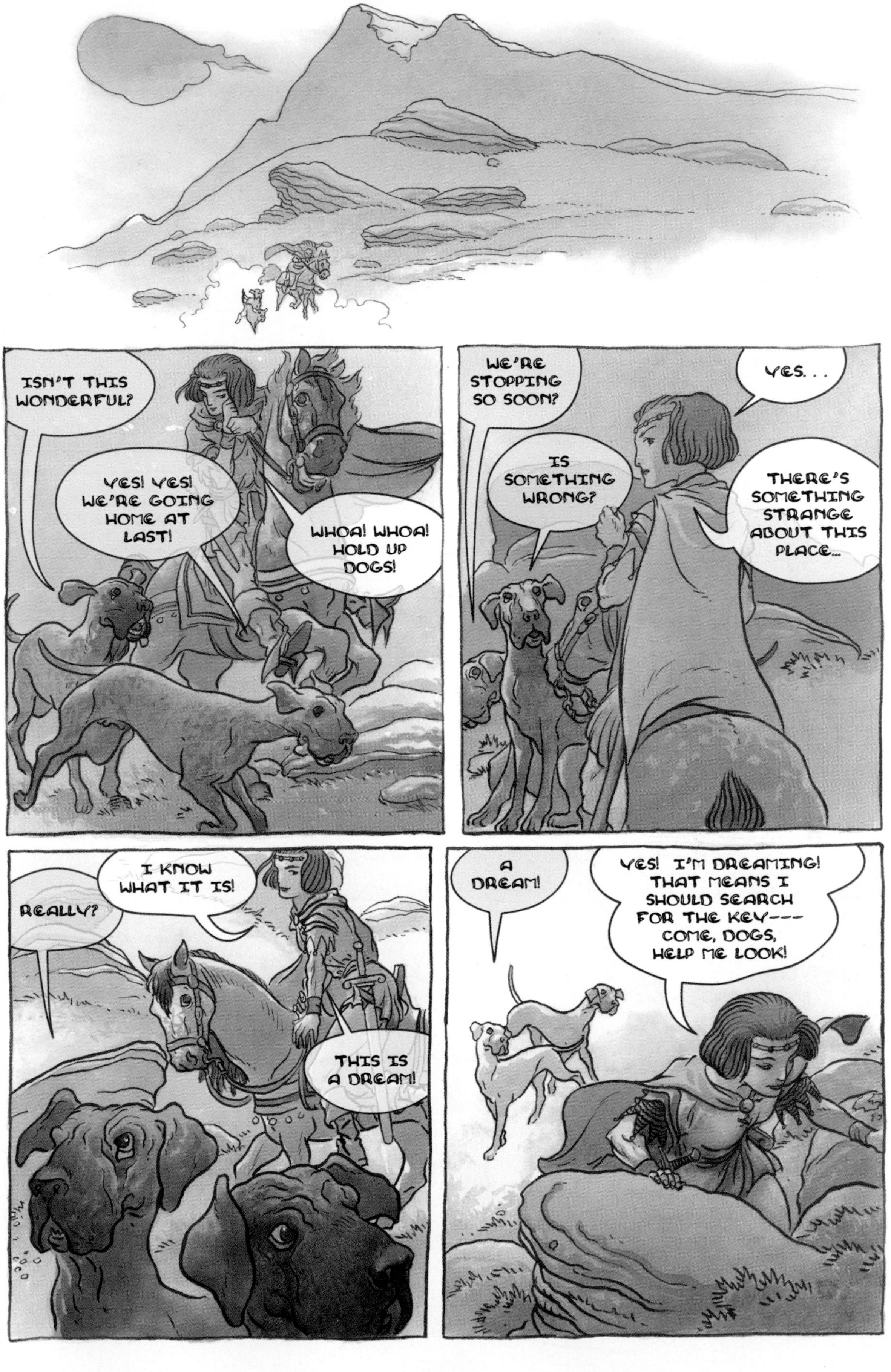
ISN'T THIS WONDERFUL?
YES! YES! WE'RE GOING HOME AT LAST!
WHOA! WHOA! HOLD UP DOGS!
WE'RE STOPPING SO SOON?
YES. . .
IS SOMETHING WRONG?
THERE'S SOMETHING STRANGE ABOUT THIS PLACE...
I KNOW WHAT IT IS!
REALLY?
THIS IS A DREAM!
A DREAM!
YES! I'M DREAMING! THAT MEANS I SHOULD SEARCH FOR THE KEY---
COME, DOGS, HELP ME LOOK!

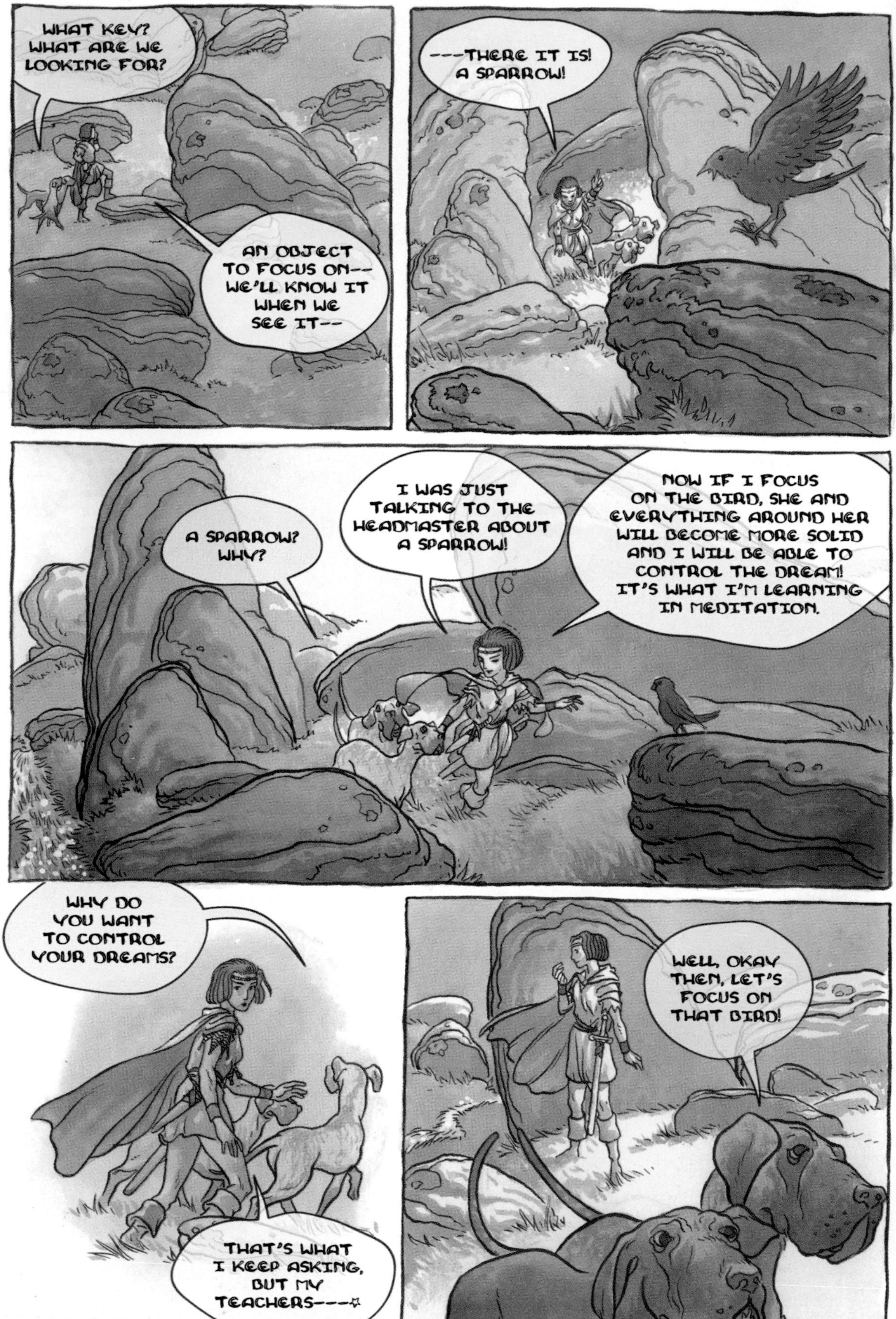
WHAT KEY? WHAT ARE WE LOOKING FOR?
AN OBJECT TO FOCUS ON-- WE'LL KNOW IT WHEN WE SEE IT--
---THERE IT IS! A SPARROW!
A SPARROW? WHY?
I WAS JUST TALKING TO THE HEADMASTER ABOUT A SPARROW!
NOW IF I FOCUS ON THE BIRD, SHE AND EVERYTHING AROUND HER WILL BECOME MORE SOLID AND I WILL BE ABLE TO CONTROL THE DREAM! IT'S WHAT I'M LEARNING IN MEDITATION.
WHY DO YOU WANT TO CONTROL YOUR DREAMS?
THAT'S WHAT I KEEP ASKING, BUT MY TEACHERS---☆
WELL, OKAY THEN, LET'S FOCUS ON THAT BIRD!

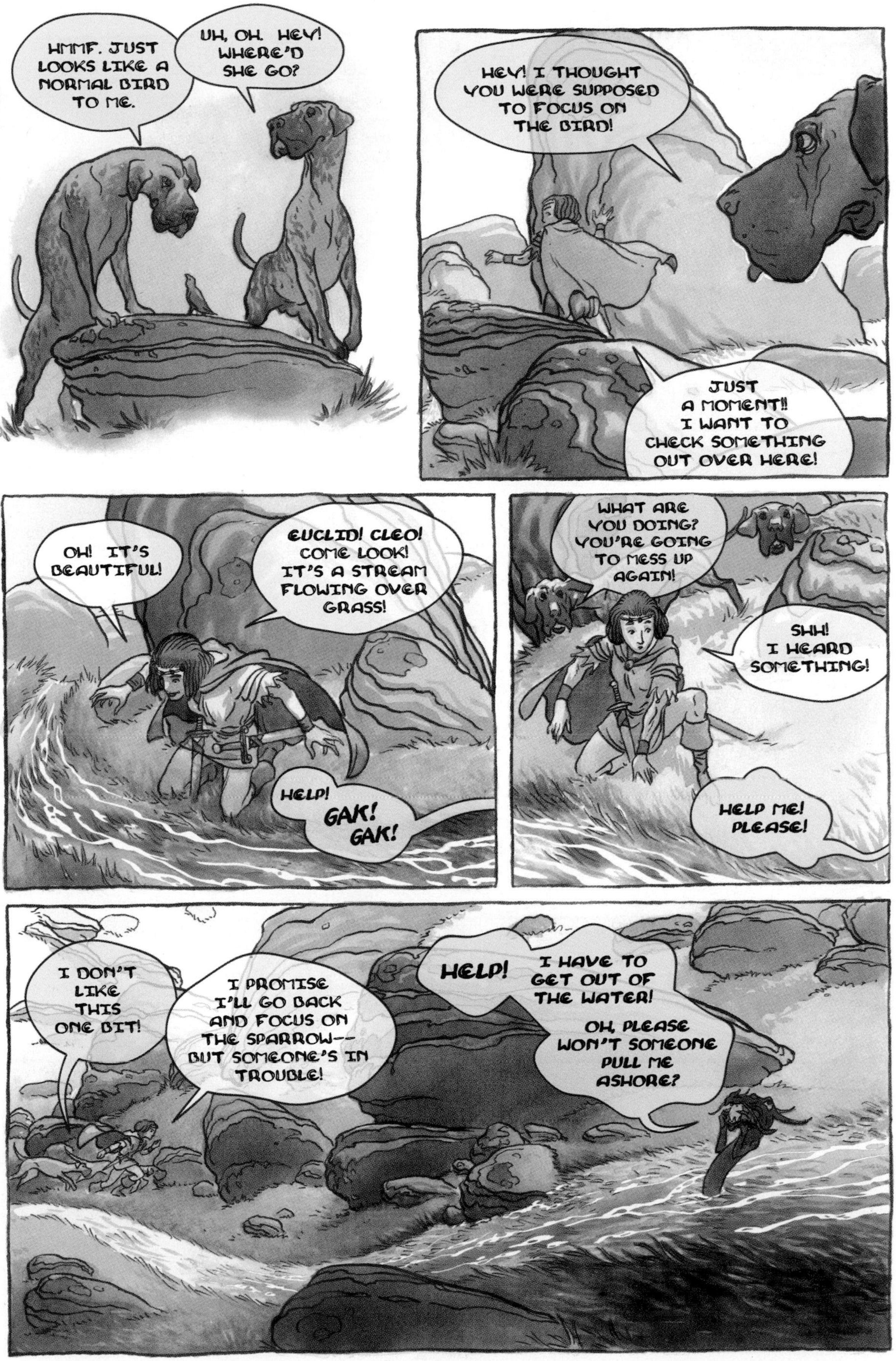
HMMF. JUST LOOKS LIKE A NORMAL BIRD TO ME.
UH, OH. HEY! WHERE'D SHE GO?
HEY! I THOUGHT YOU WERE SUPPOSED TO FOCUS ON THE BIRD!
JUST A MOMENT!! I WANT TO CHECK SOMETHING OUT OVER HERE!
OH! IT'S BEAUTIFUL!
EUCLID! CLEO! COME LOOK! IT'S A STREAM FLOWING OVER GRASS!
HELP! GAK! GAK!
WHAT ARE YOU DOING? YOU'RE GOING TO MESS UP AGAIN!
SHH! I HEARD SOMETHING!
HELP ME! PLEASE!
I DON'T LIKE THIS ONE BIT!
I PROMISE I'LL GO BACK AND FOCUS ON THE SPARROW-- BUT SOMEONE'S IN TROUBLE!
HELP!
I HAVE TO GET OUT OF THE WATER!
OH, PLEASE WON'T SOMEONE PULL ME ASHORE?

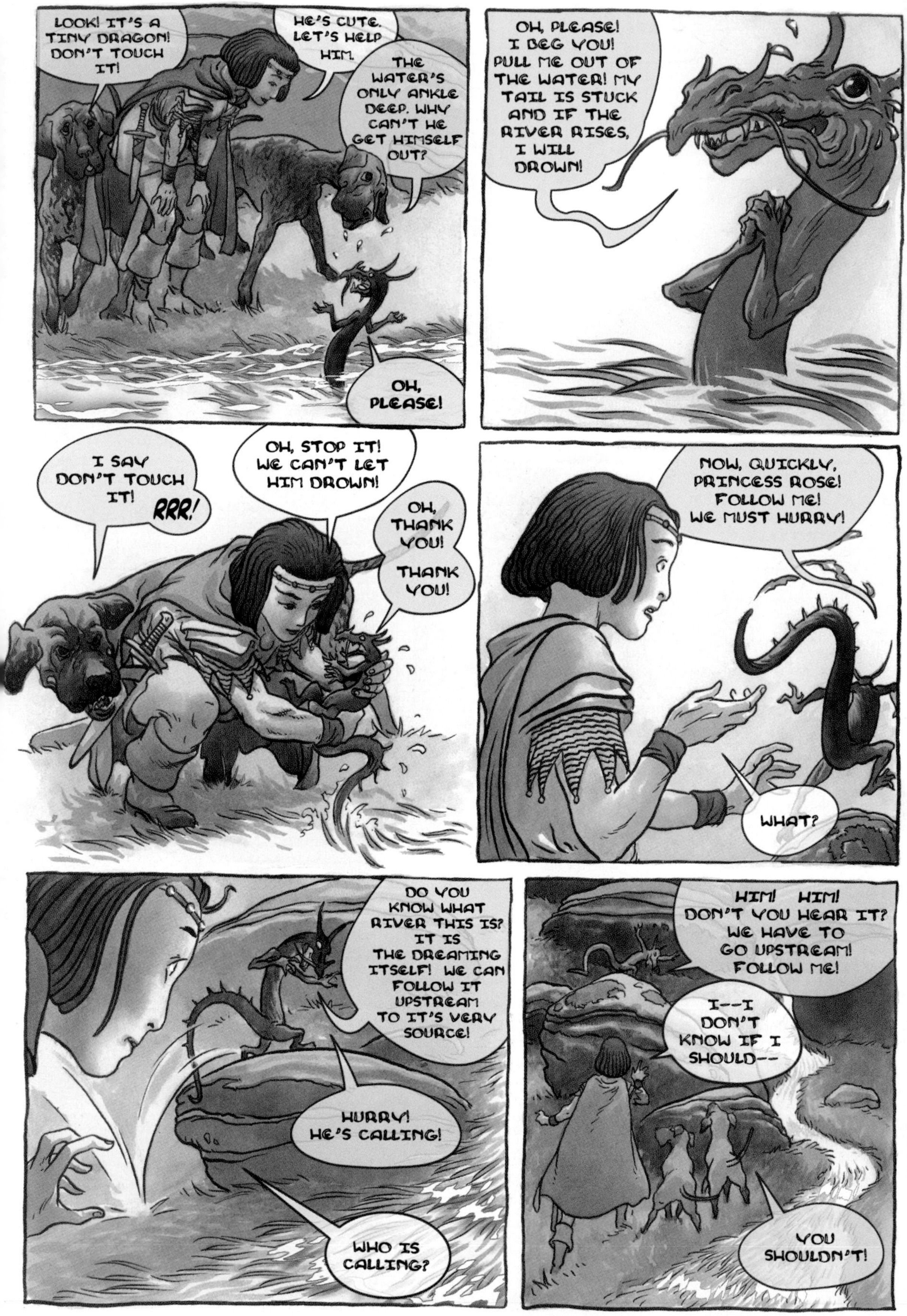
LOOK! IT'S A TINY DRAGON! DON'T TOUCH IT!
HE'S CUTE. LET'S HELP HIM.
THE WATER'S ONLY ANKLE DEEP. WHY CAN'T HE GET HIMSELF OUT?
OH, PLEASE!
OH, PLEASE! I BEG YOU! PULL ME OUT OF THE WATER! MY TAIL IS STUCK AND IF THE RIVER RISES, I WILL DROWN!
I SAY DON'T TOUCH IT!
RRR!
OH, STOP IT! WE CAN'T LET HIM DROWN!
OH, THANK YOU!
THANK YOU!
NOW, QUICKLY, PRINCESS ROSE! FOLLOW ME! WE MUST HURRY!
WHAT?
DO YOU KNOW WHAT RIVER THIS IS? IT IS THE DREAMING ITSELF! WE CAN FOLLOW IT UPSTREAM TO IT'S VERY SOURCE!
HURRY! HE'S CALLING!
WHO IS CALLING?
HIM! HIM! DON'T YOU HEAR IT? WE HAVE TO GO UPSTREAM! FOLLOW ME!
I--I DON'T KNOW IF I SHOULD--
YOU SHOULDN'T!

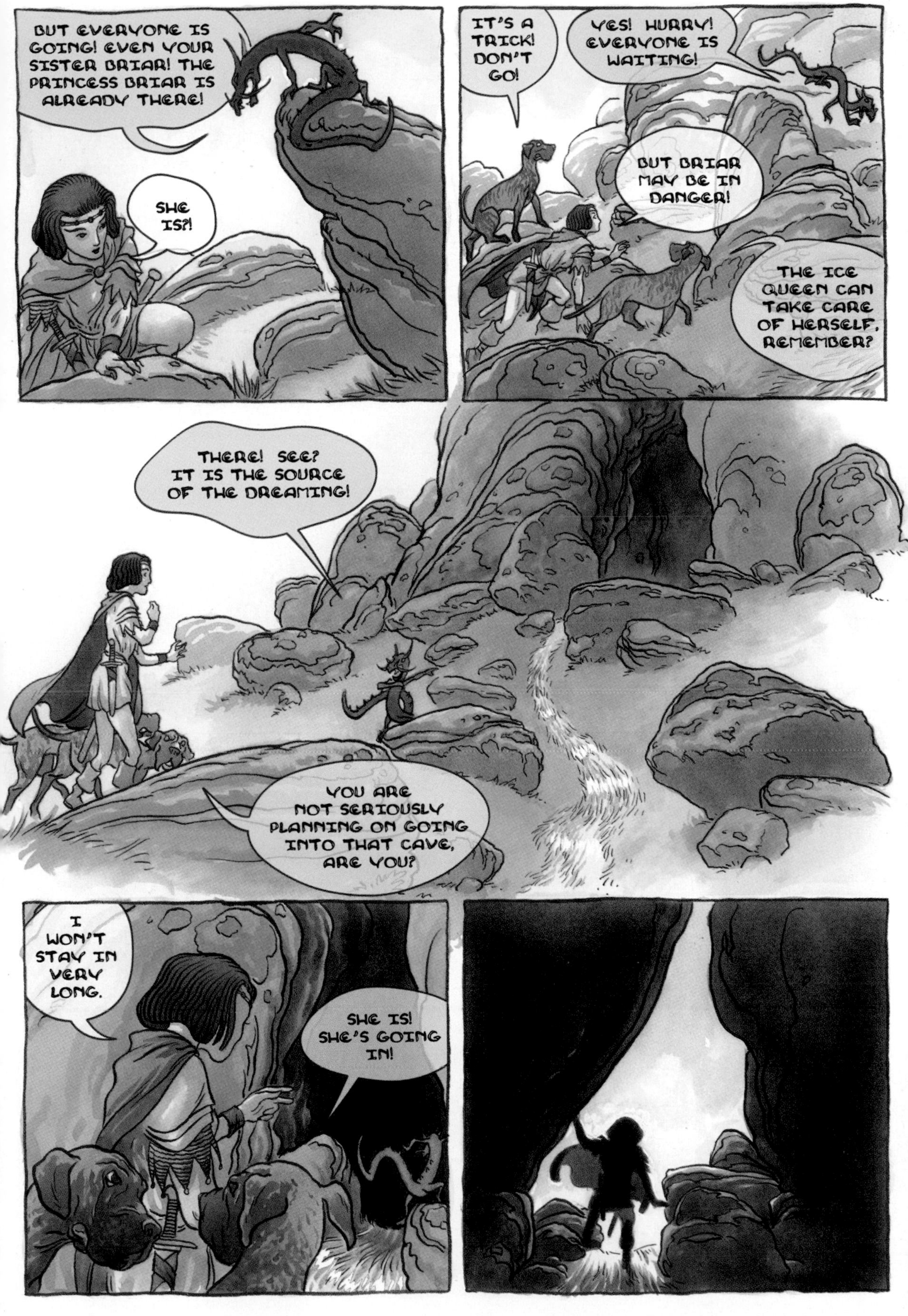
BUT EVERYONE IS GOING! EVEN YOUR SISTER BRIAR! THE PRINCESS BRIAR IS ALREADY THERE!
SHE IS?!
IT'S A TRICK! DON'T GO!
YES! HURRY! EVERYONE IS WAITING!
BUT BRIAR MAY BE IN DANGER!
THE ICE QUEEN CAN TAKE CARE OF HERSELF, REMEMBER?
THERE! SEE? IT IS THE SOURCE OF THE DREAMING!
YOU ARE NOT SERIOUSLY PLANNING ON GOING INTO THAT CAVE, ARE YOU?
I WON'T STAY IN VERY LONG.
SHE IS! SHE'S GOING IN!

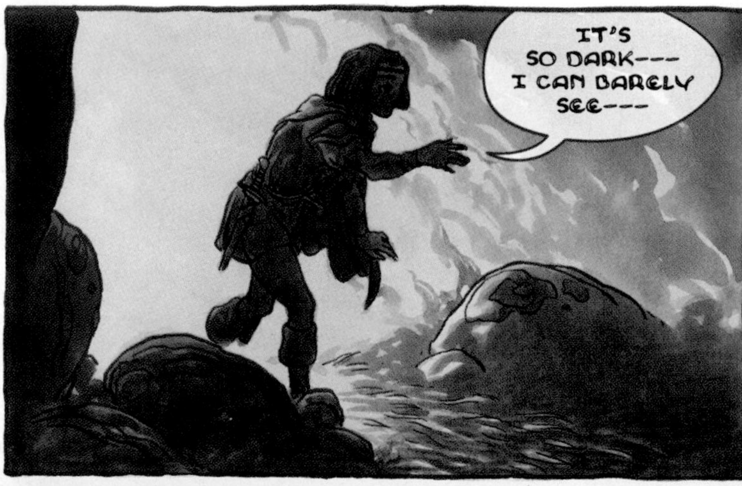
IT'S SO DARK--- I CAN BARELY SEE---

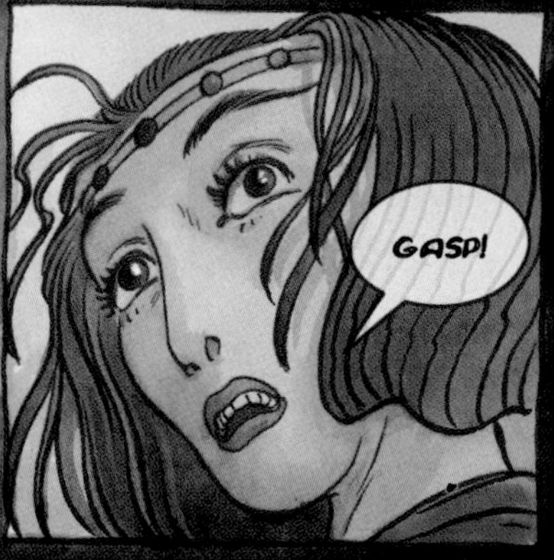
GASP!

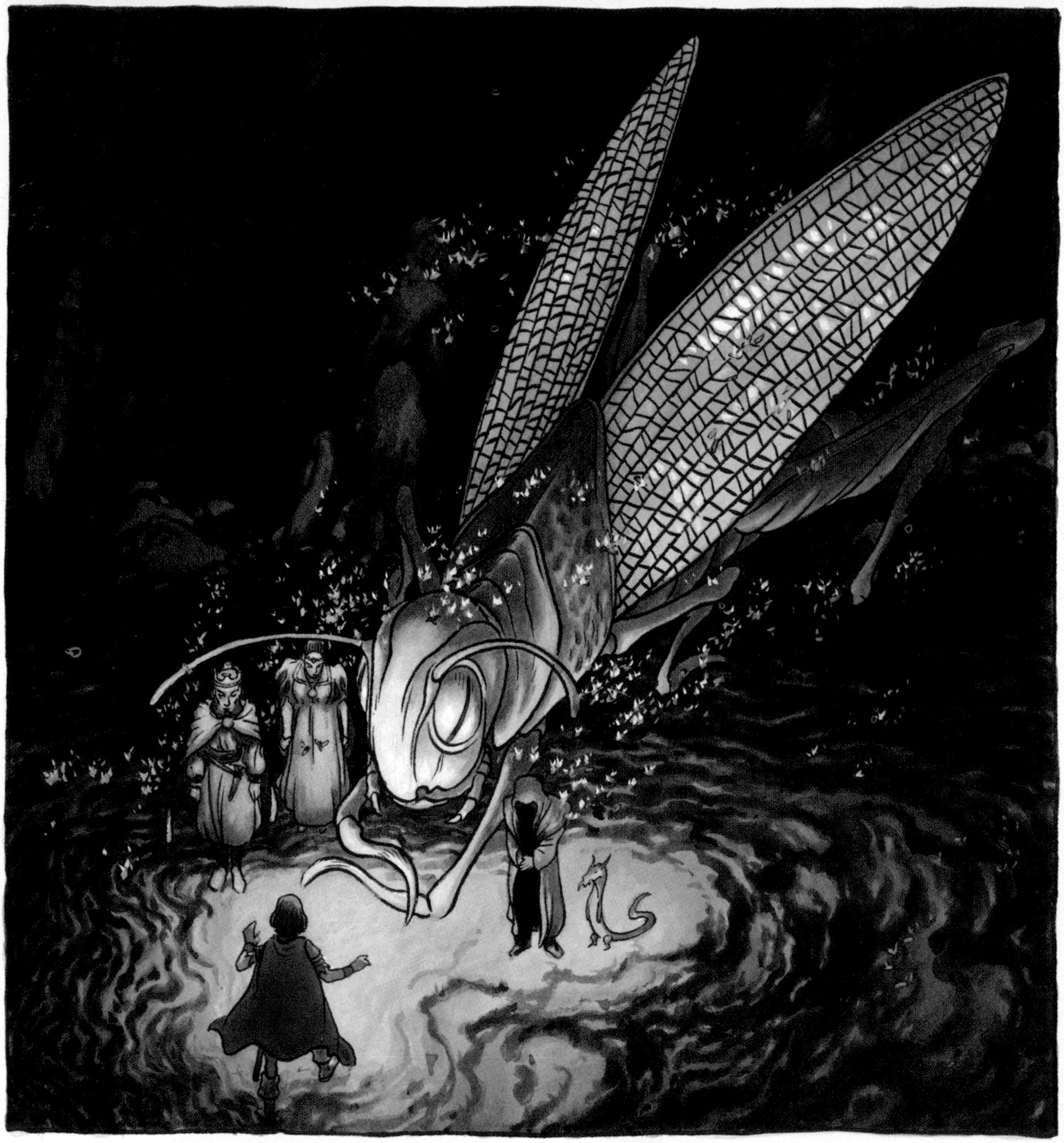

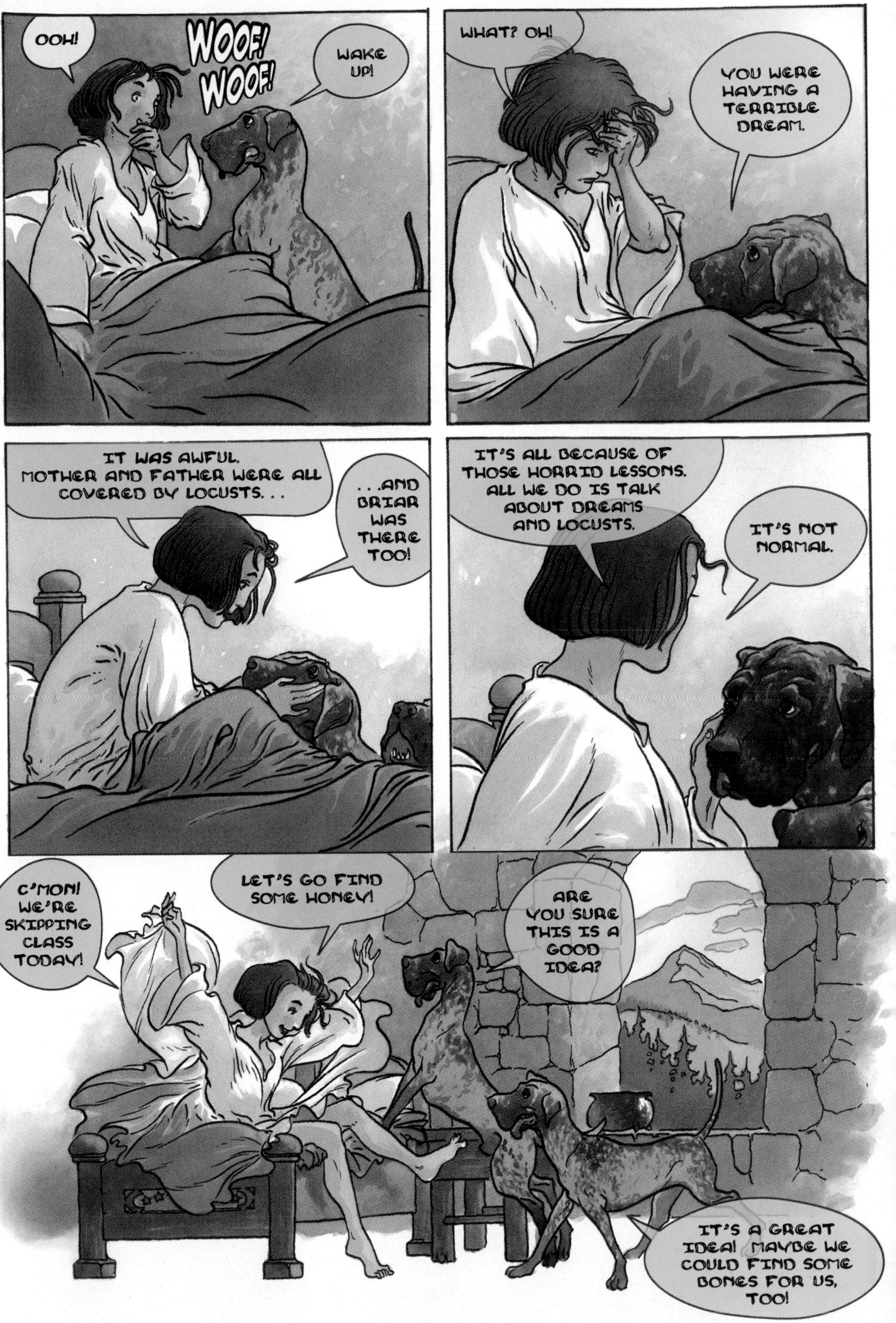
OOH!
WOOF! WOOF!
WAKE UP!
WHAT? OH!
YOU WERE HAVING A TERRIBLE DREAM.
IT WAS AWFUL. MOTHER AND FATHER WERE ALL COVERED BY LOCUSTS. . .
. . .AND BRIAR WAS THERE TOO!
IT'S ALL BECAUSE OF THOSE HORRID LESSONS. ALL WE DO IS TALK ABOUT DREAMS AND LOCUSTS.
IT'S NOT NORMAL.
C'MON! WE'RE SKIPPING CLASS TODAY!
LET'S GO FIND SOME HONEY!
ARE YOU SURE THIS IS A GOOD IDEA?
IT'S A GREAT IDEA! MAYBE WE COULD FIND SOME BONES FOR US, TOO!

TURN
BACK

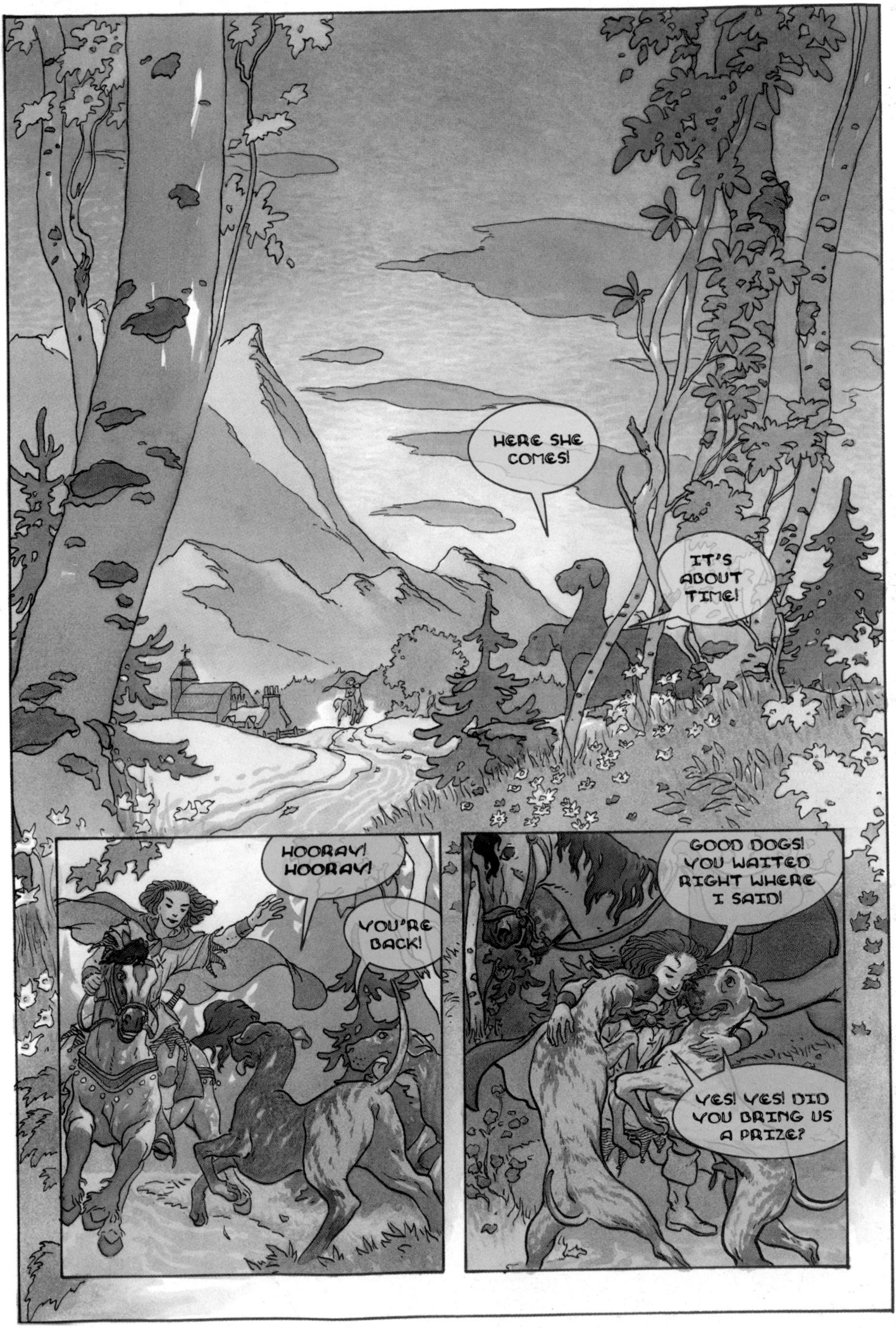
HERE SHE COMES!
IT'S ABOUT TIME!
HOORAY! HOORAY!
YOU'RE BACK!
GOOD DOGS! YOU WAITED RIGHT WHERE I SAID!
YES! YES! DID YOU BRING US A PRIZE?

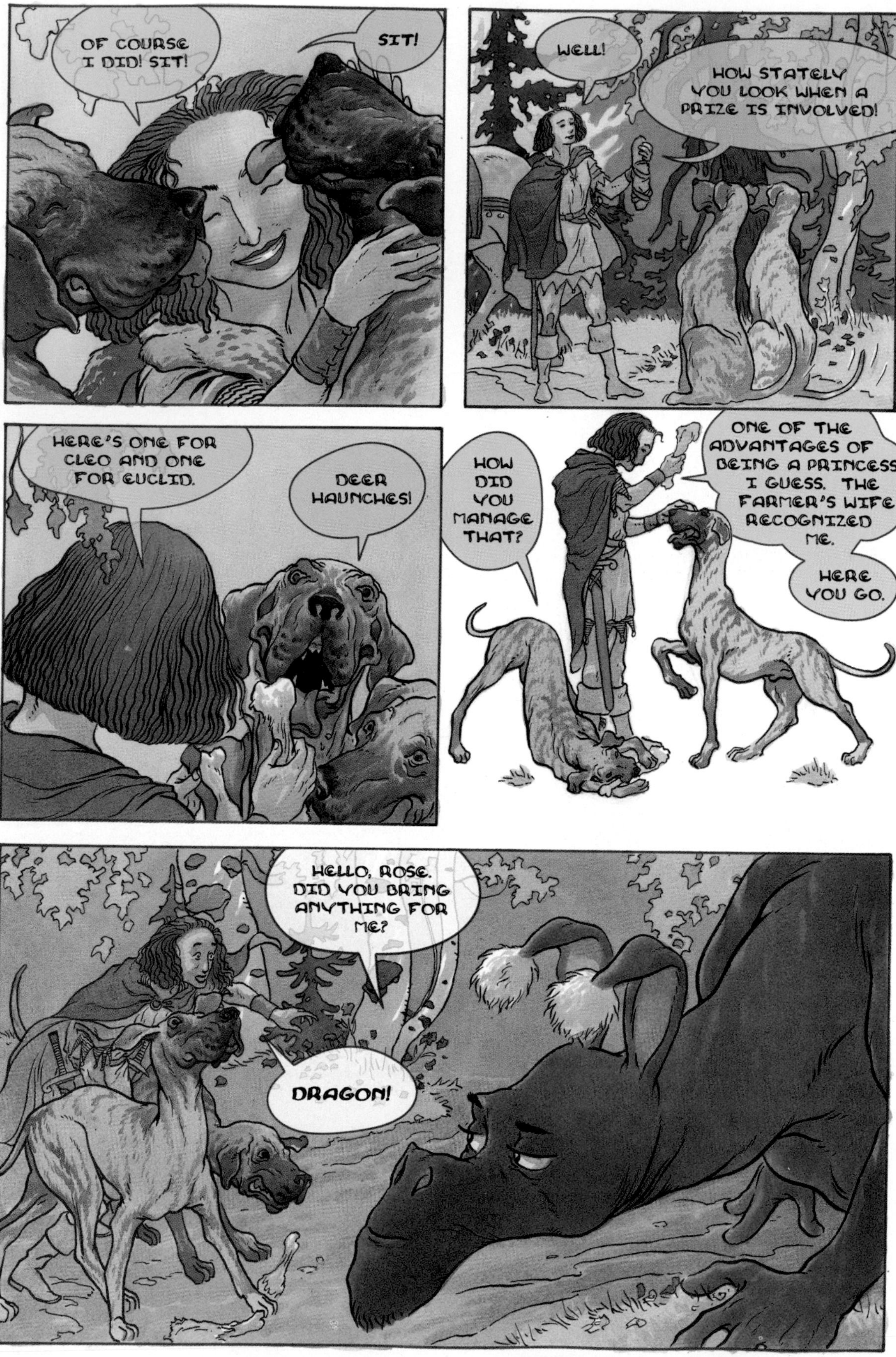
OF COURSE I DID! SIT!
SIT!
WELL!
HOW STATELY YOU LOOK WHEN A PRIZE IS INVOLVED!
HERE'S ONE FOR CLEO AND ONE FOR EUCLID.
DEER HAUNCHES!
HOW DID YOU MANAGE THAT?
ONE OF THE ADVANTAGES OF BEING A PRINCESS, I GUESS. THE FARMER'S WIFE RECOGNIZED ME.
HERE YOU GO.
HELLO, ROSE. DID YOU BRING ANYTHING FOR ME?
DRAGON!

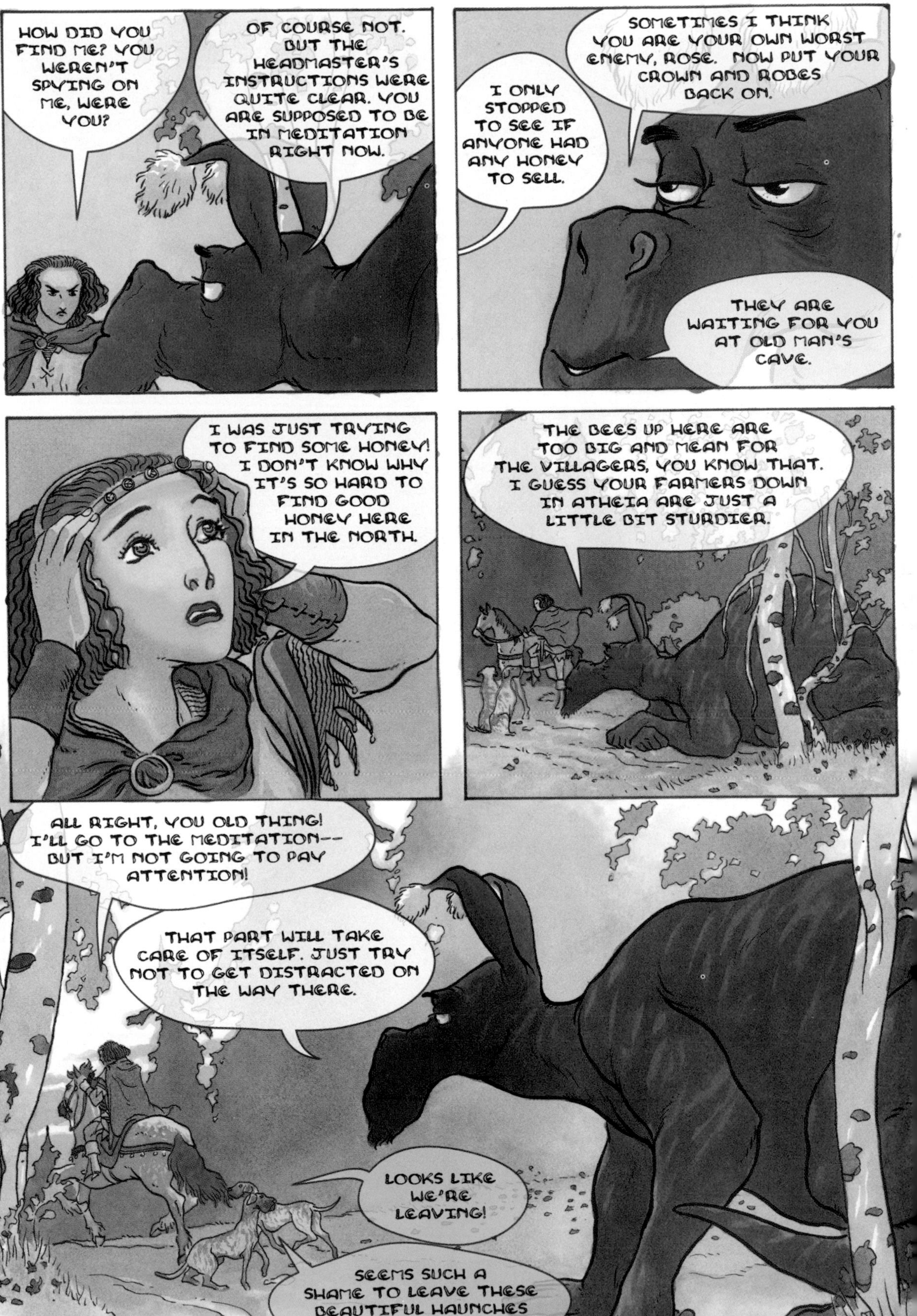
HOW DID YOU FIND ME? YOU WEREN'T SPYING ON ME, WERE YOU?
OF COURSE NOT. BUT THE HEADMASTER'S INSTRUCTIONS WERE QUITE CLEAR. YOU ARE SUPPOSED TO BE IN MEDITATION RIGHT NOW.
I ONLY STOPPED TO SEE IF ANYONE HAD ANY HONEY TO SELL.
SOMETIMES I THINK YOU ARE YOUR OWN WORST ENEMY, ROSE. NOW PUT YOUR CROWN AND ROBES BACK ON.
THEY ARE WAITING FOR YOU AT OLD MAN'S CAVE.
I WAS JUST TRYING TO FIND SOME HONEY! I DON'T KNOW WHY IT'S SO HARD TO FIND GOOD HONEY HERE IN THE NORTH.
THE BEES UP HERE ARE TOO BIG AND MEAN FOR THE VILLAGERS, YOU KNOW THAT. I GUESS YOUR FARMERS DOWN IN ATHEIA ARE JUST A LITTLE BIT STURDIER.
ALL RIGHT, YOU OLD THING! I'LL GO TO THE MEDITATION-- BUT I'M NOT GOING TO PAY ATTENTION!
THAT PART WILL TAKE CARE OF ITSELF. JUST TRY NOT TO GET DISTRACTED ON THE WAY THERE.
LOOKS LIKE WE'RE LEAVING!
SEEMS SUCH A SHAME TO LEAVE THESE BEAUTIFUL HAUNCHES BEHIND.

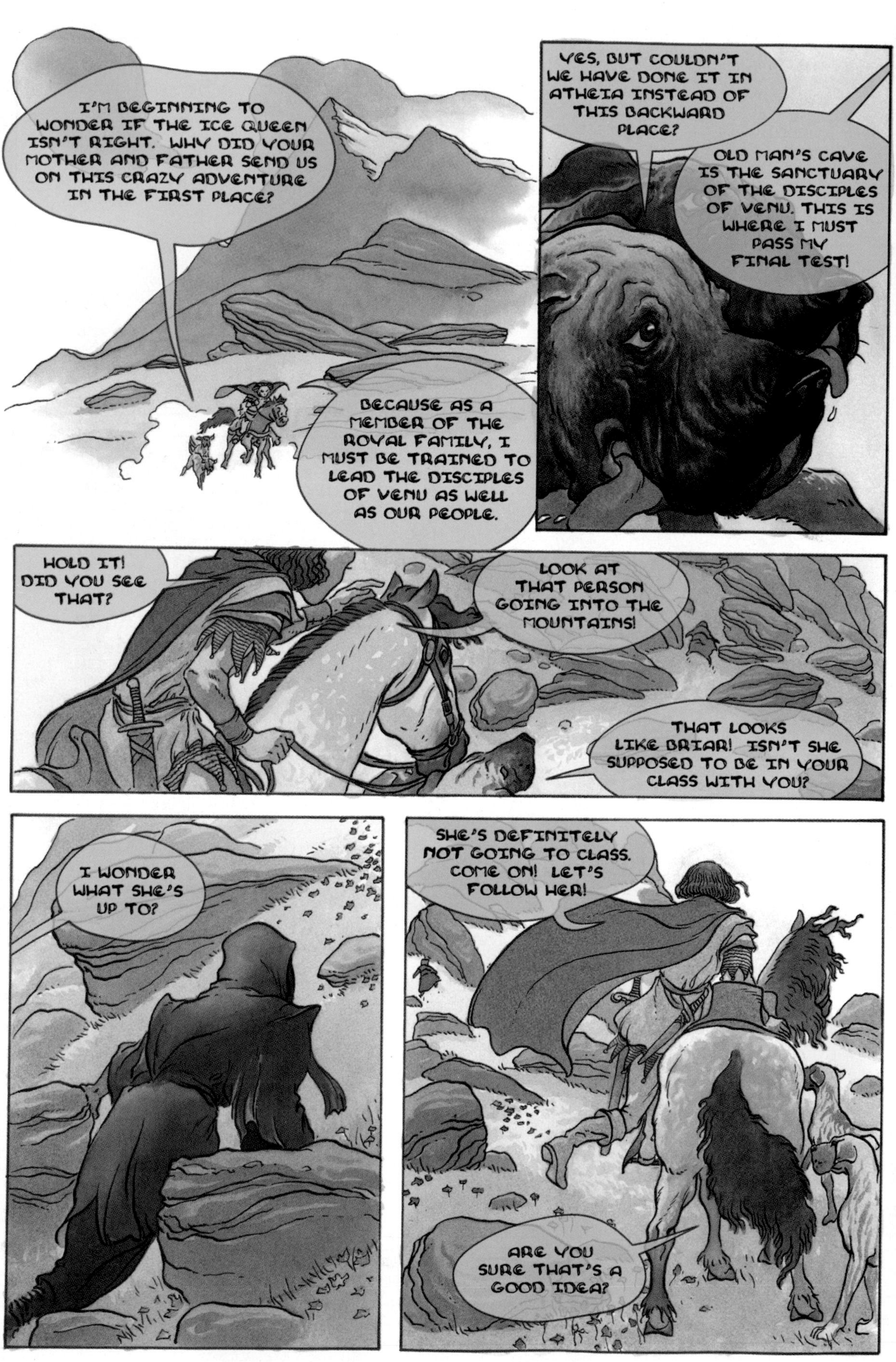
I'M BEGINNING TO WONDER IF THE ICE QUEEN ISN'T RIGHT. WHY DID YOUR MOTHER AND FATHER SEND US ON THIS CRAZY ADVENTURE IN THE FIRST PLACE?
BECAUSE AS A MEMBER OF THE ROYAL FAMILY, I MUST BE TRAINED TO LEAD THE DISCIPLES OF VENU AS WELL AS OUR PEOPLE.
YES, BUT COULDN'T WE HAVE DONE IT IN ATHEIA INSTEAD OF THIS BACKWARD PLACE?
OLD MAN'S CAVE IS THE SANCTUARY OF THE DISCIPLES OF VENU. THIS IS WHERE I MUST PASS MY FINAL TEST!
HOLD IT! DID YOU SEE THAT?
LOOK AT THAT PERSON GOING INTO THE MOUNTAINS!
THAT LOOKS LIKE BRIAR! ISN'T SHE SUPPOSED TO BE IN YOUR CLASS WITH YOU?
I WONDER WHAT SHE'S UP TO?
SHE'S DEFINITELY NOT GOING TO CLASS. COME ON! LET'S FOLLOW HER!
ARE YOU SURE THAT'S A GOOD IDEA?

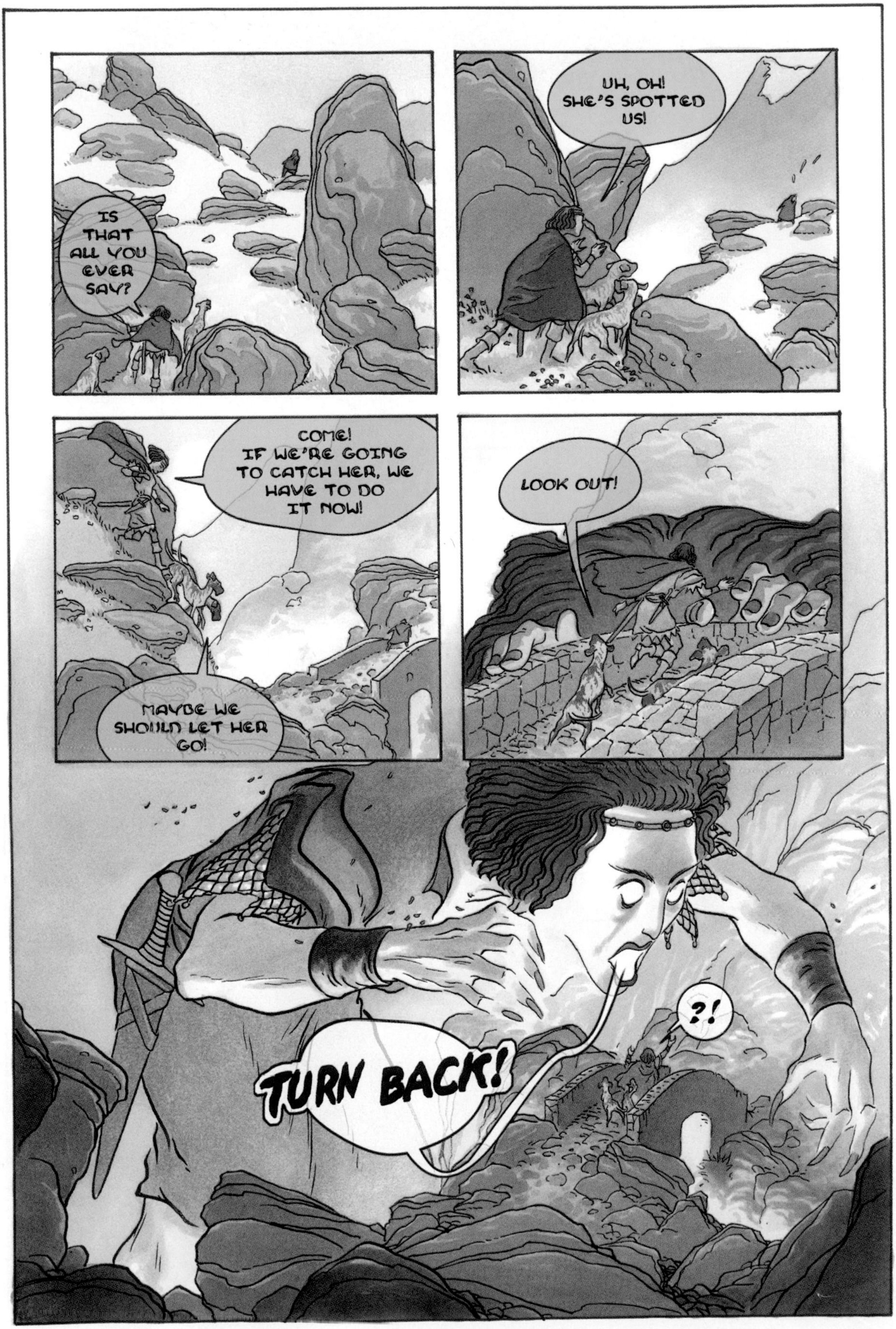
IS THAT ALL YOU EVER SAY?
UH, OH! SHE'S SPOTTED US!
COME! IF WE'RE GOING TO CATCH HER, WE HAVE TO DO IT NOW!
MAYBE WE SHOULD LET HER GO!
LOOK OUT!
TURN BACK!
?!

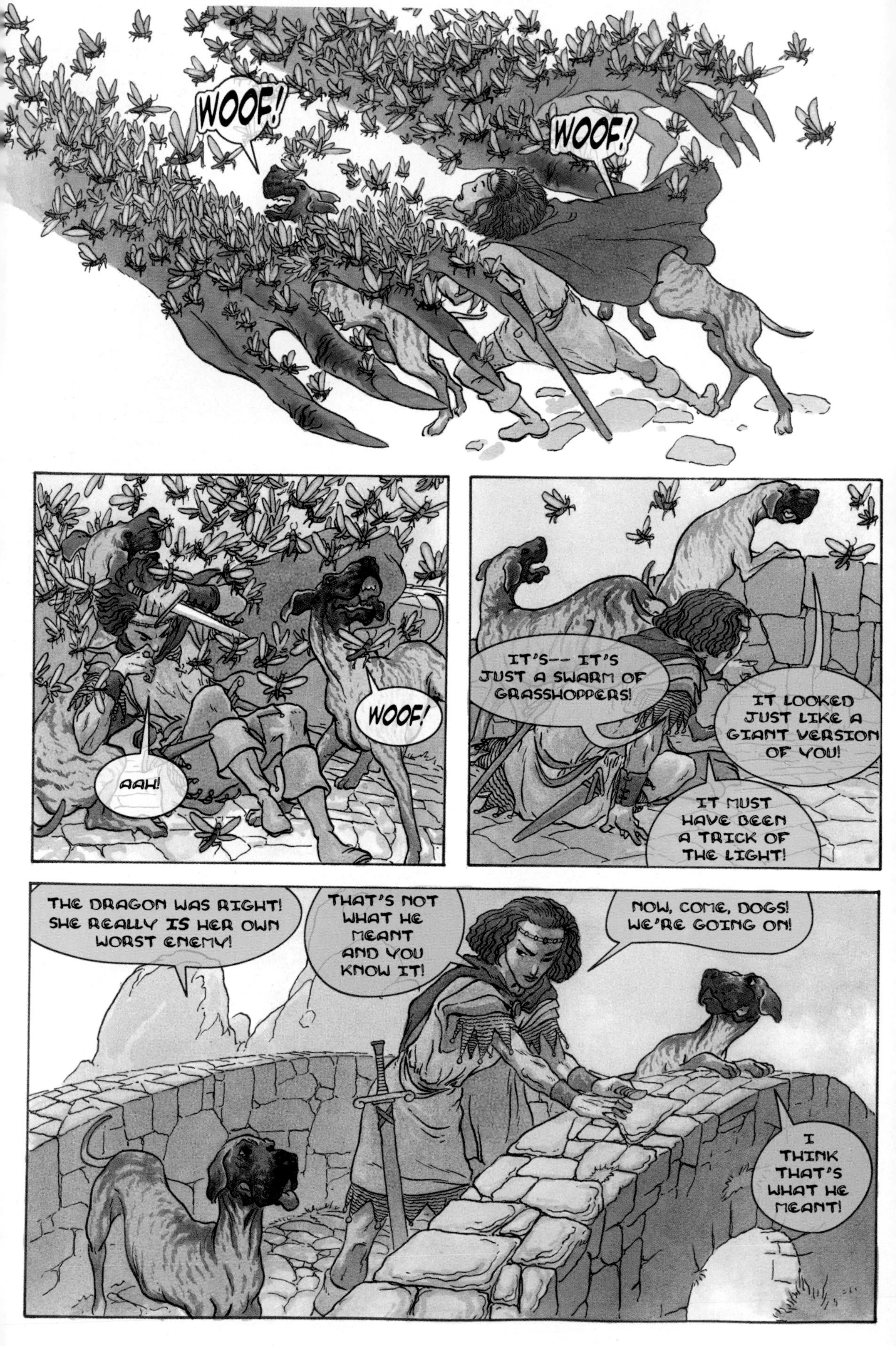
WOOF!
WOOF!
AAH!
WOOF!
IT'S-- IT'S JUST A SWARM OF GRASSHOPPERS!
IT LOOKED JUST LIKE A GIANT VERSION OF YOU!
IT MUST HAVE BEEN A TRICK OF THE LIGHT!
THE DRAGON WAS RIGHT! SHE REALLY IS HER OWN WORST ENEMY!
THAT'S NOT WHAT HE MEANT AND YOU KNOW IT!
NOW, COME, DOGS! WE'RE GOING ON!
I THINK THAT'S WHAT HE MEANT!

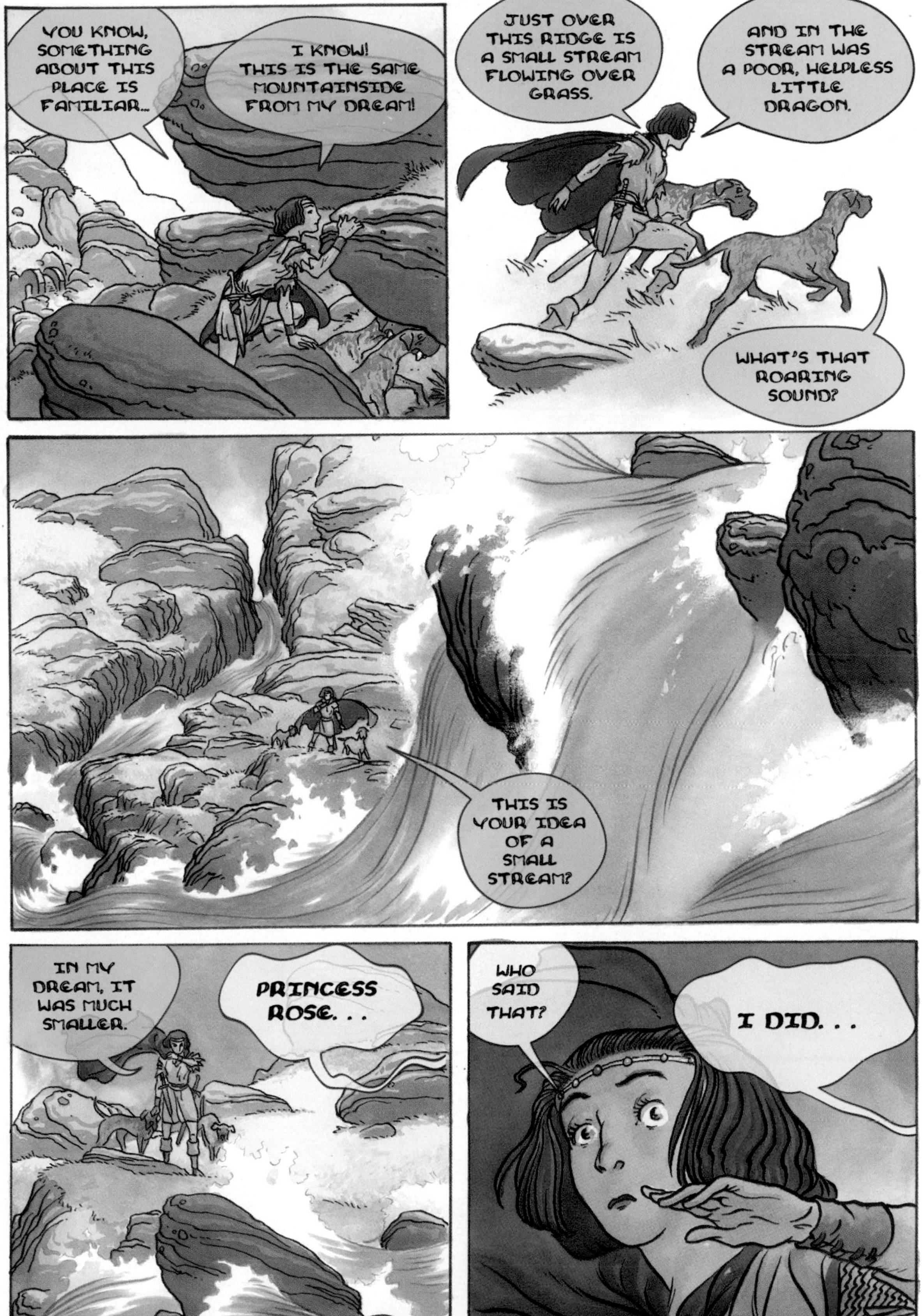
YOU KNOW, SOMETHING ABOUT THIS PLACE IS FAMILIAR...
I KNOW! THIS IS THE SAME MOUNTAINSIDE FROM MY DREAM!
JUST OVER THIS RIDGE IS A SMALL STREAM FLOWING OVER GRASS.
AND IN THE STREAM WAS A POOR, HELPLESS LITTLE DRAGON.
WHAT'S THAT ROARING SOUND?
THIS IS YOUR IDEA OF A SMALL STREAM?
IN MY DREAM, IT WAS MUCH SMALLER.
PRINCESS ROSE. . .
WHO SAID THAT?
I DID. . .

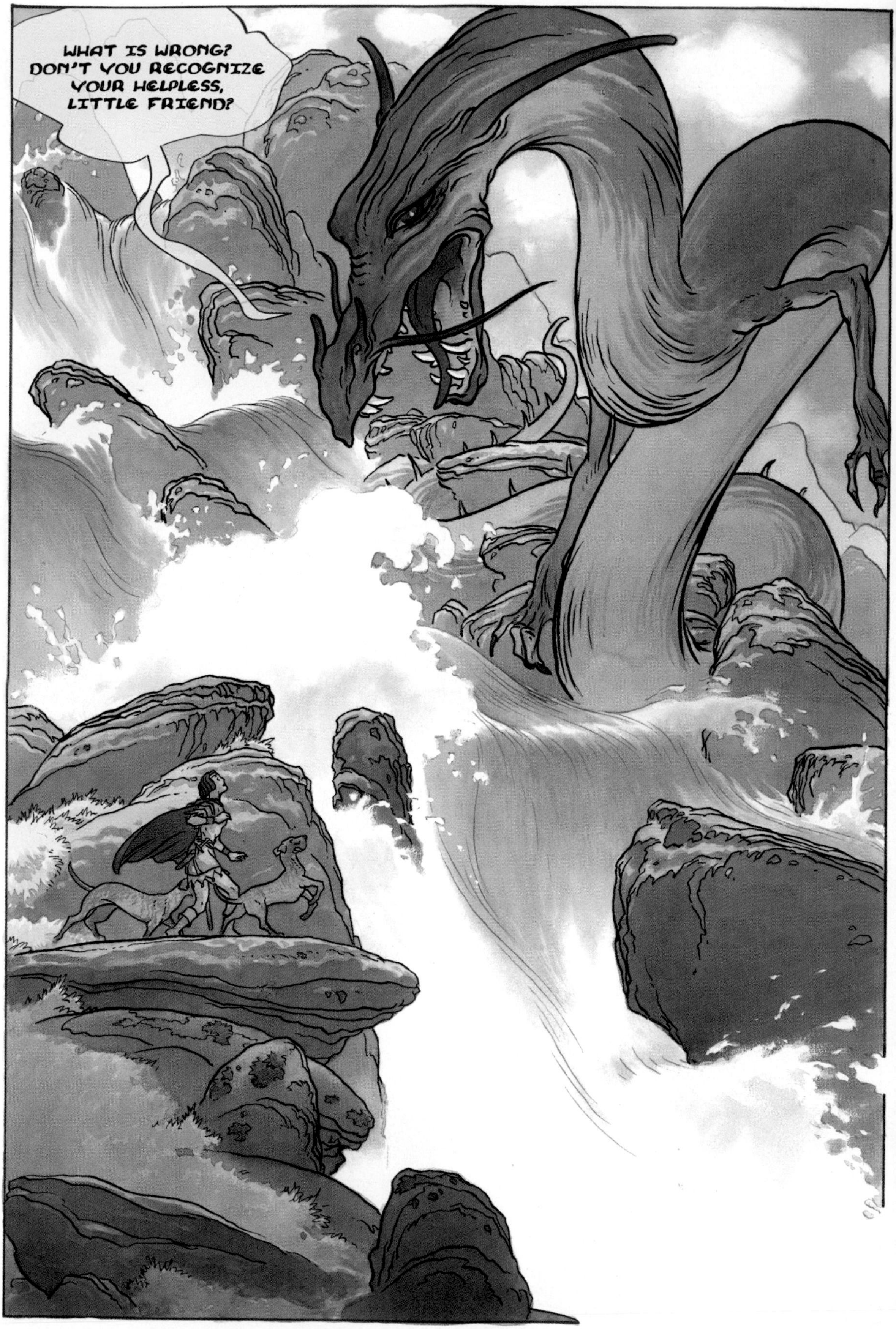
WHAT IS WRONG? DON'T YOU RECOGNIZE YOUR HELPLESS, LITTLE FRIEND?

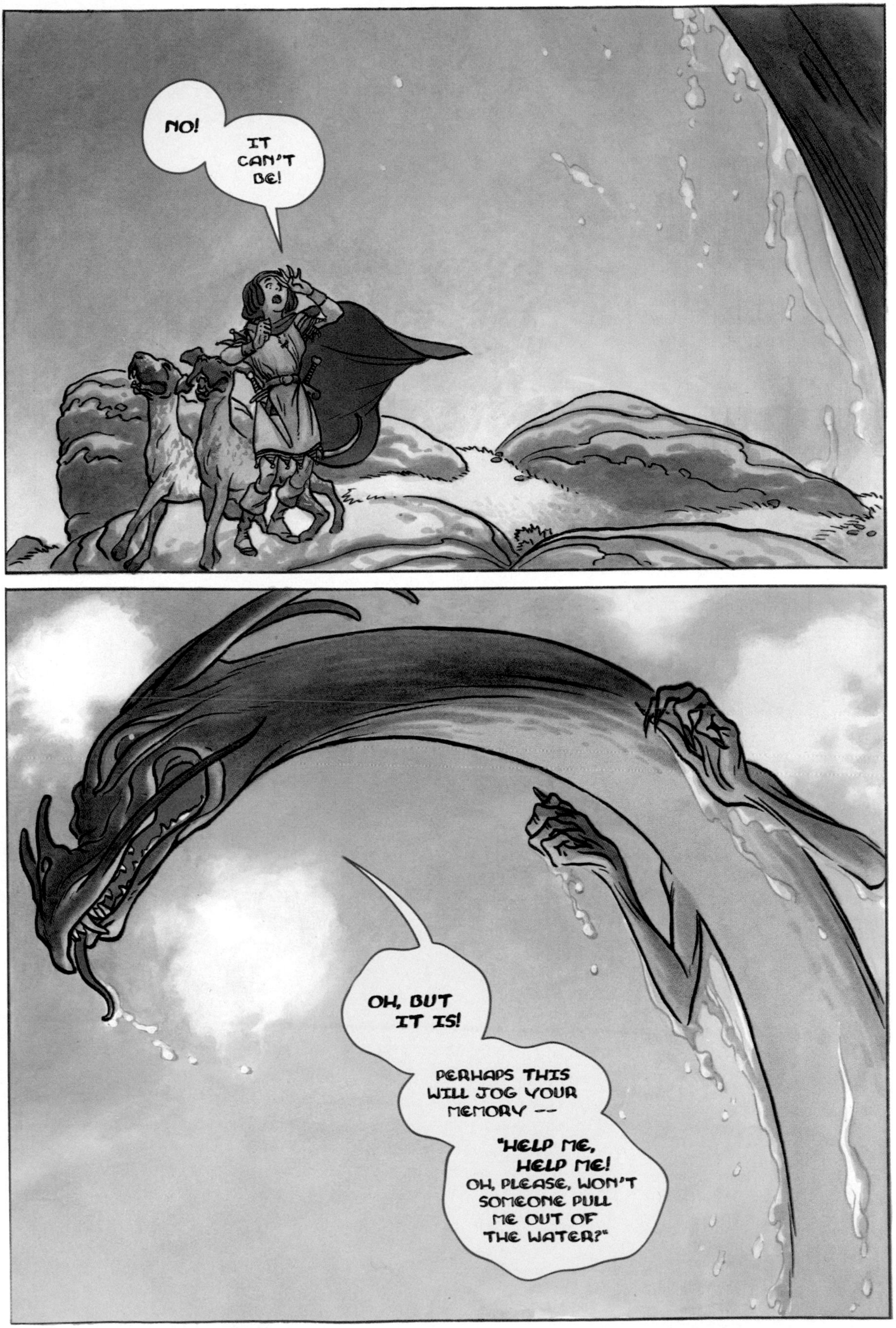
NO!
IT CAN'T BE!
OH, BUT IT IS!
PERHAPS THIS WILL JOG YOUR MEMORY --
"HELP ME, HELP ME! OH, PLEASE, WON'T SOMEONE PULL ME OUT OF THE WATER?"

BALSAAD

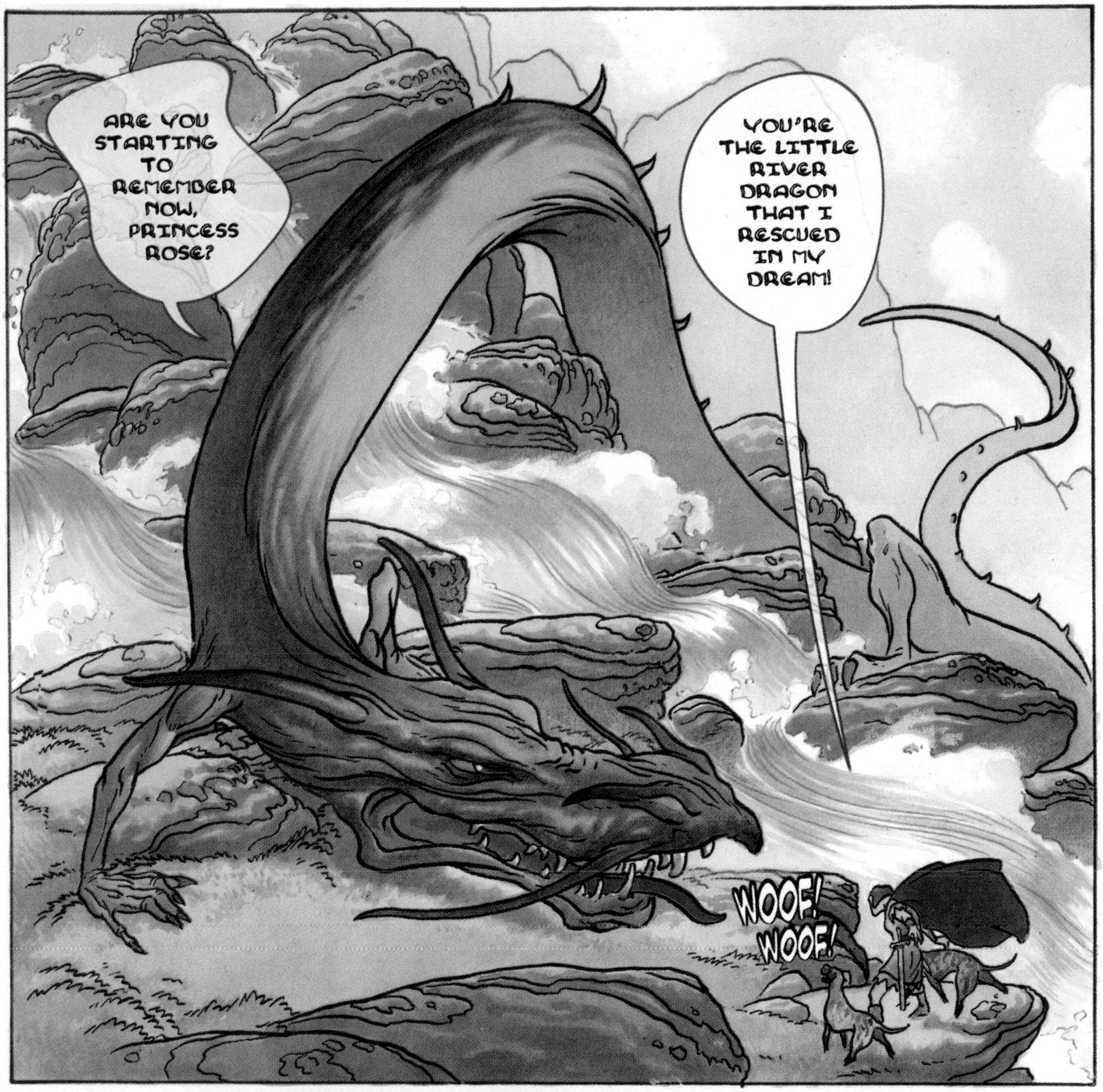
ARE YOU STARTING TO REMEMBER NOW, PRINCESS ROSE?
YOU'RE THE LITTLE RIVER DRAGON THAT I RESCUED IN MY DREAM!
WOOF! WOOF!
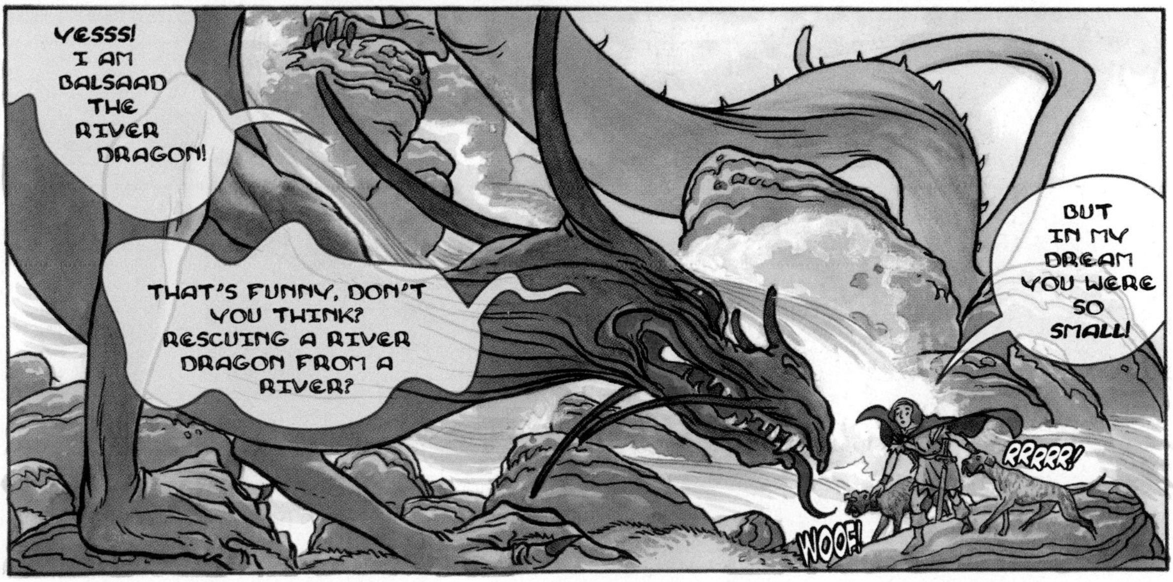
YESSS! I AM BALSAAD THE RIVER DRAGON!
BUT IN MY DREAM YOU WERE SO SMALL!
THAT'S FUNNY, DON'T YOU THINK? RESCUING A RIVER DRAGON FROM A RIVER?
RRRRR!
WOOF!

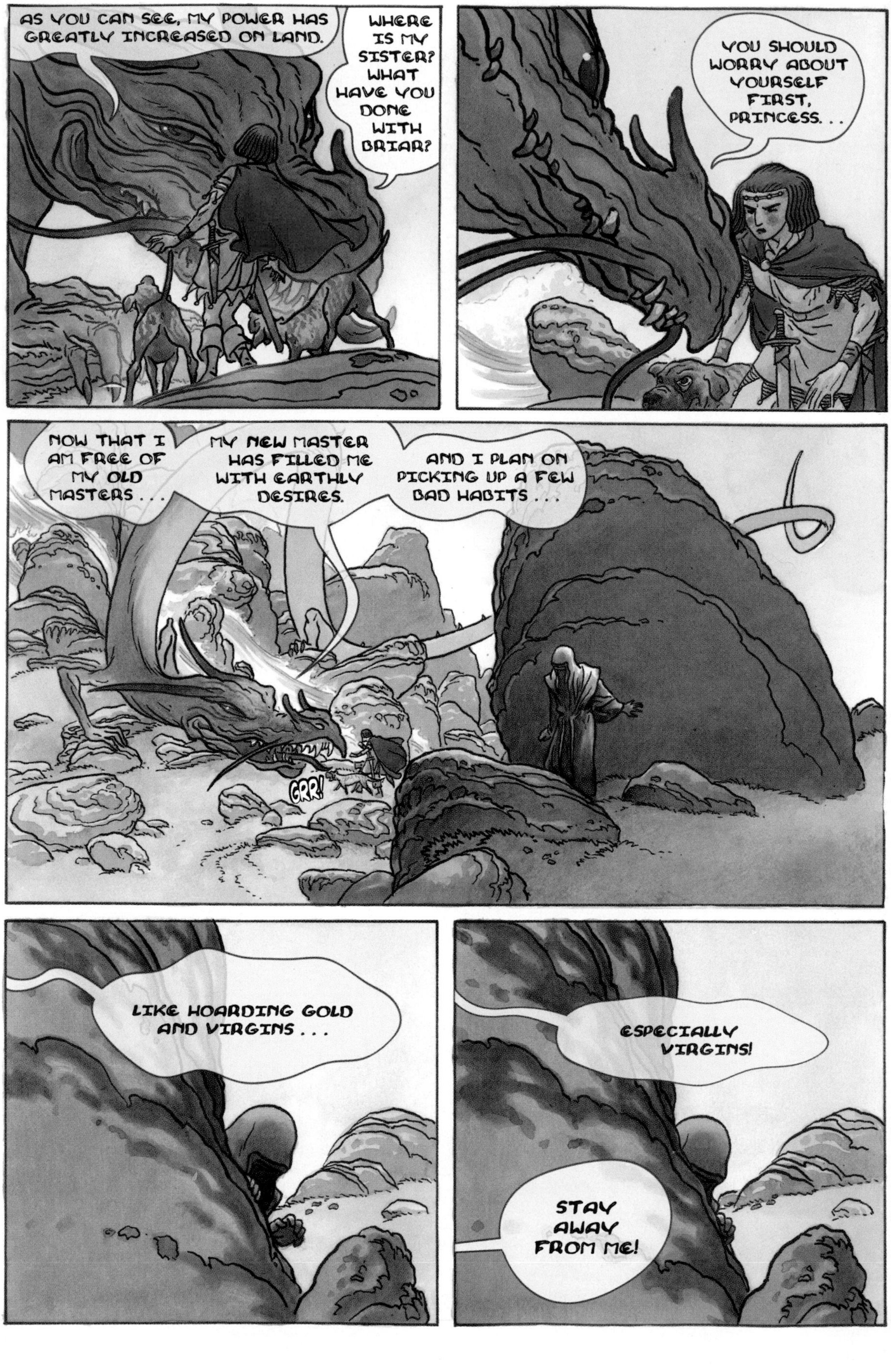
AS YOU CAN SEE, MY POWER HAS GREATLY INCREASED ON LAND.
WHERE IS MY SISTER? WHAT HAVE YOU DONE WITH BRIAR?
YOU SHOULD WORRY ABOUT YOURSELF FIRST, PRINCESS. . .
NOW THAT I AM FREE OF MY OLD MASTERS . . .
MY NEW MASTER HAS FILLED ME WITH EARTHLY DESIRES.
AND I PLAN ON PICKING UP A FEW BAD HABITS . . .
GRR!
LIKE HOARDING GOLD AND VIRGINS . . .
ESPECIALLY VIRGINS!
STAY AWAY FROM ME!

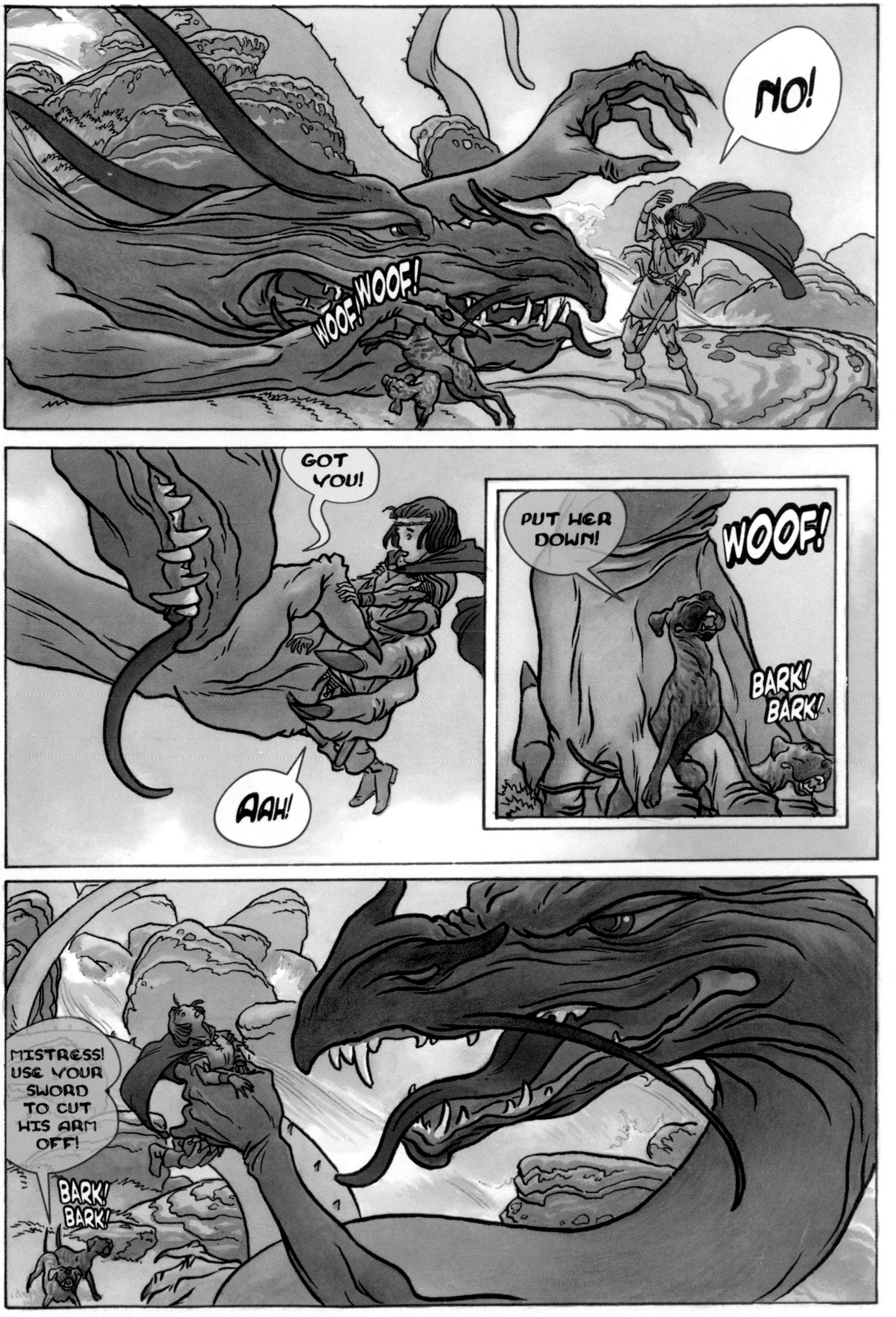
NO!
WOOF! WOOF!
GOT YOU!
AAH!
PUT HER DOWN!
WOOF!
BARK! BARK!
MISTRESS! USE YOUR SWORD TO CUT HIS ARM OFF!
BARK! BARK!

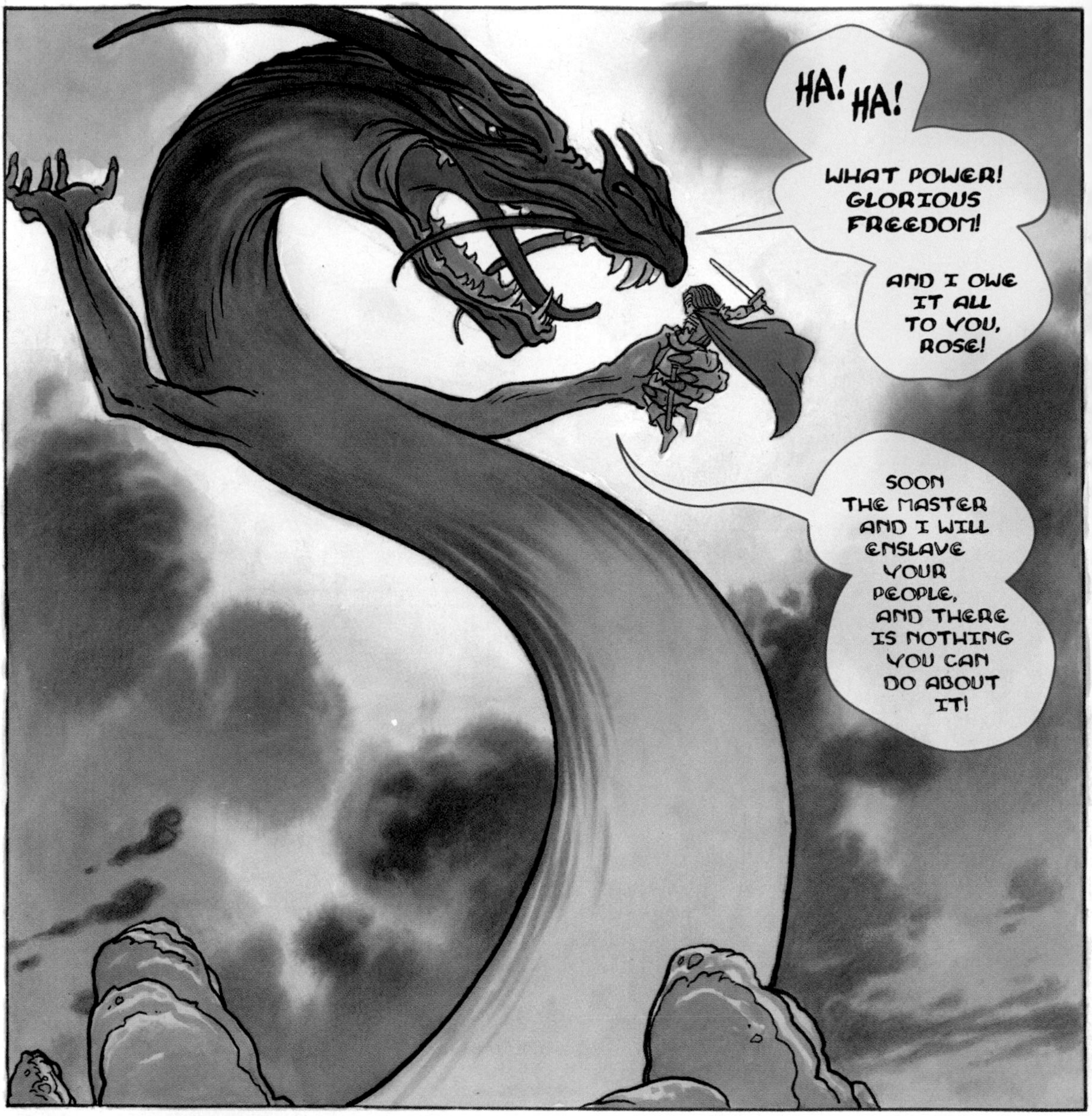
HA! HA!
WHAT POWER! GLORIOUS FREEDOM!
AND I OWE IT ALL TO YOU, ROSE!
SOON THE MASTER AND I WILL ENSLAVE YOUR PEOPLE, AND THERE IS NOTHING YOU CAN DO ABOUT IT!

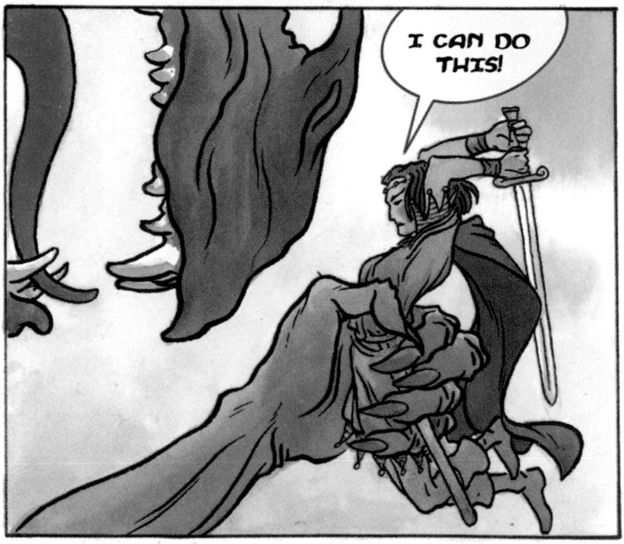
I CAN DO THIS!

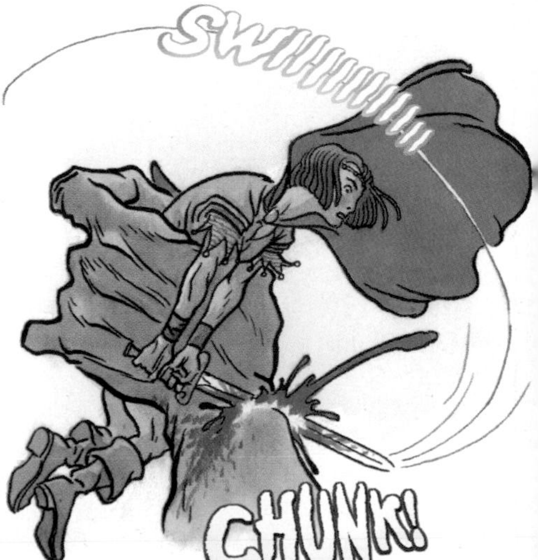
SWIIIIIIIII
CHUNK!

CHUNK!

!

THWAK!

POP
RIP!

AAAAAAAAAAAAAAAAA

WHUMP!

GET UP!
GET UP!

☆ GASP! ☆

SHE'S
HURT!

NO. ☆ GASP ☆,
WIND KNOCKED OUT--

GET
THIS THING
OFF ME--

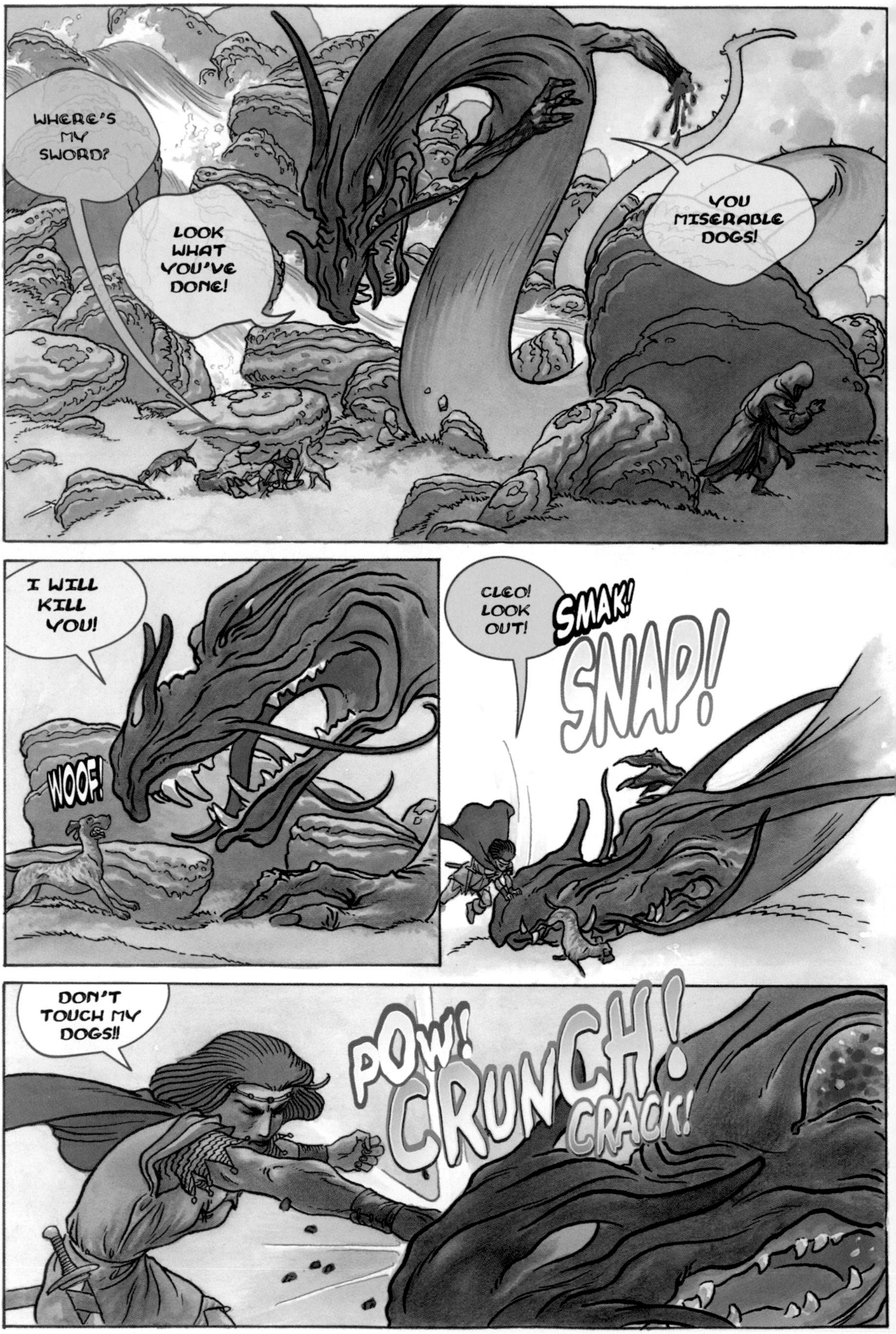

WHERE'S MY SWORD?
LOOK WHAT YOU'VE DONE!
YOU MISERABLE DOGS!
I WILL KILL YOU!
WOOF!
CLEO! LOOK OUT!
SMAK!
SNAP!
DON'T TOUCH MY DOGS!!
POW!
CRUNCH!
CRACK!

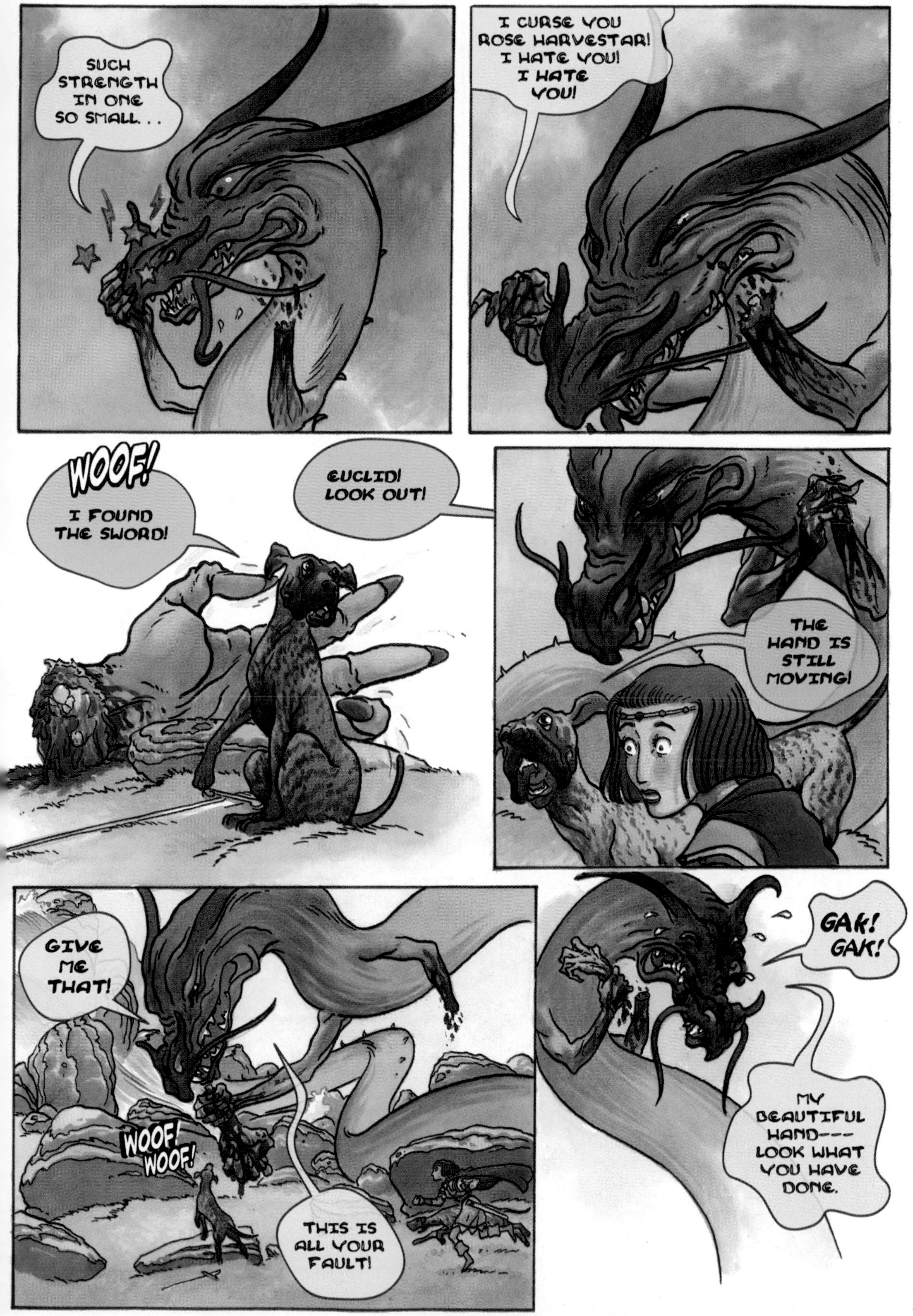
SUCH STRENGTH IN ONE SO SMALL. . .
I CURSE YOU ROSE HARVESTAR! I HATE YOU! I HATE YOU!
WOOF!
I FOUND THE SWORD!
EUCLID! LOOK OUT!
THE HAND IS STILL MOVING!
GIVE ME THAT!
WOOF! WOOF!
THIS IS ALL YOUR FAULT!
GAK! GAK!
MY BEAUTIFUL HAND--- LOOK WHAT YOU HAVE DONE.

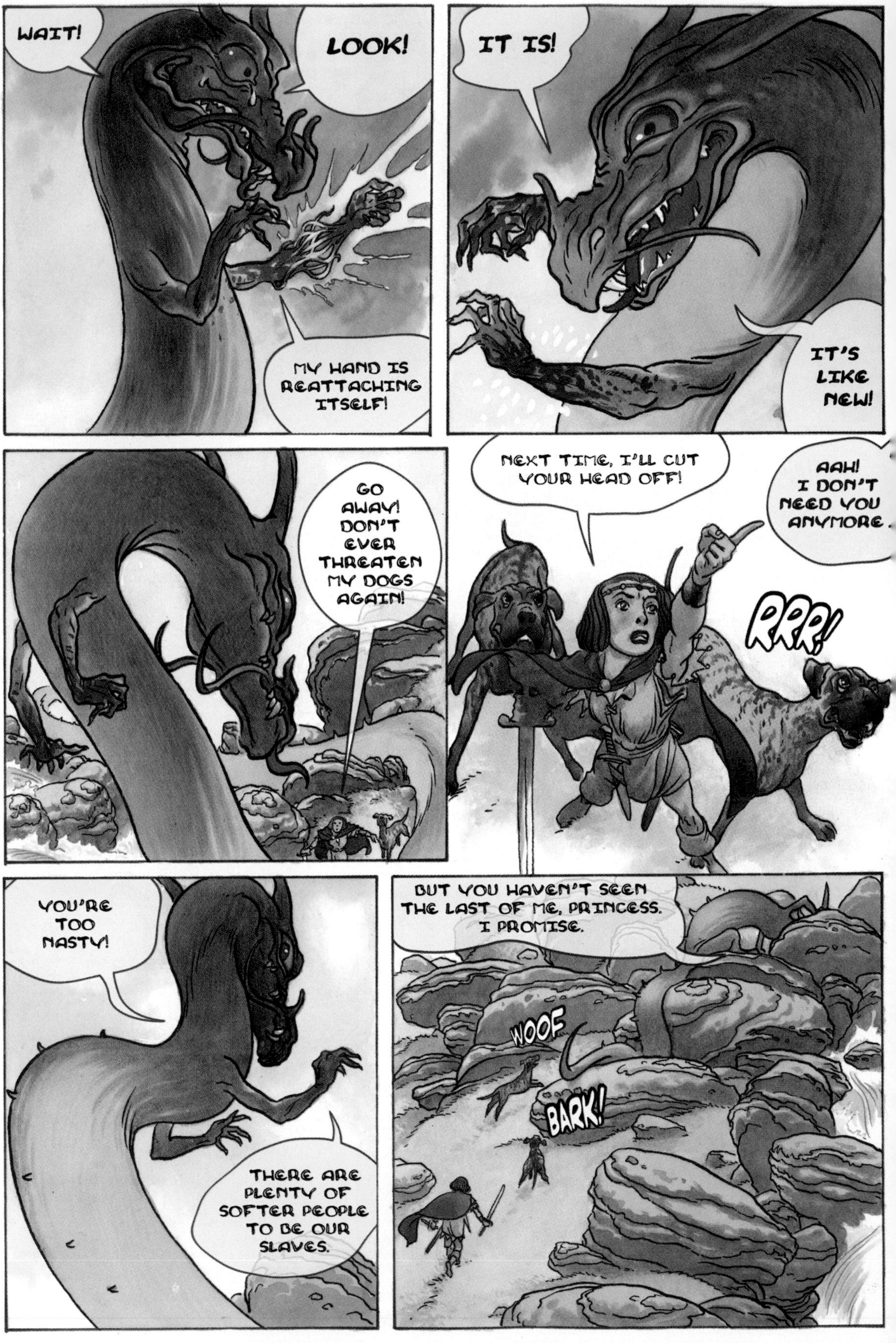
WAIT!
LOOK!
MY HAND IS REATTACHING ITSELF!
IT IS!
IT'S LIKE NEW!
GO AWAY! DON'T EVER THREATEN MY DOGS AGAIN!
NEXT TIME, I'LL CUT YOUR HEAD OFF!
AAH! I DON'T NEED YOU ANYMORE.
RRR!
YOU'RE TOO NASTY!
THERE ARE PLENTY OF SOFTER PEOPLE TO BE OUR SLAVES.
BUT YOU HAVEN'T SEEN THE LAST OF ME, PRINCESS. I PROMISE.
WOOF
BARK!

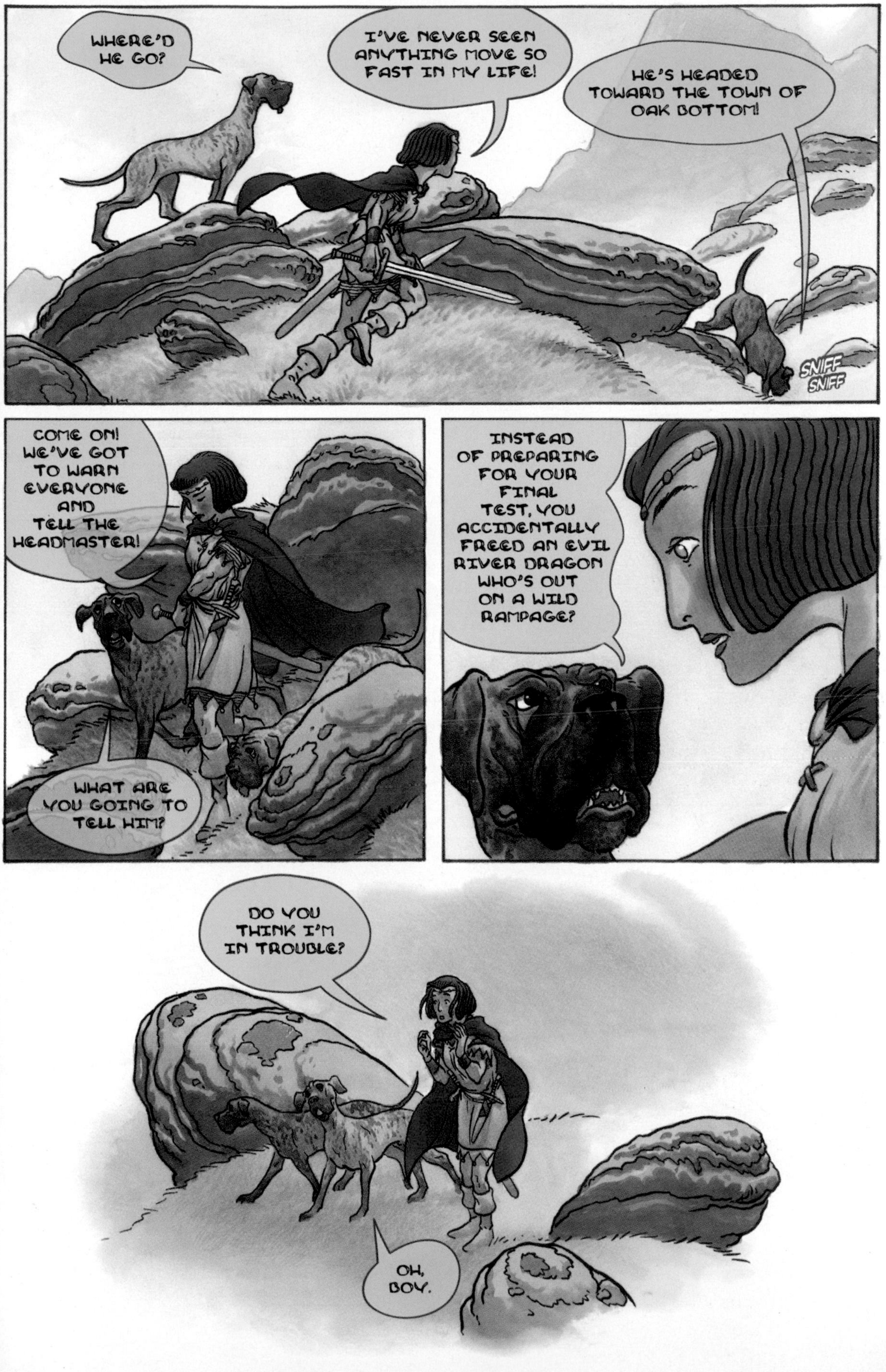
WHERE'D HE GO?
I'VE NEVER SEEN ANYTHING MOVE SO FAST IN MY LIFE!
HE'S HEADED TOWARD THE TOWN OF OAK BOTTOM!
SNIFF SNIFF
COME ON! WE'VE GOT TO WARN EVERYONE AND TELL THE HEADMASTER!
WHAT ARE YOU GOING TO TELL HIM?
INSTEAD OF PREPARING FOR YOUR FINAL TEST, YOU ACCIDENTALLY FREED AN EVIL RIVER DRAGON WHO'S OUT ON A WILD RAMPAGE?
DO YOU THINK I'M IN TROUBLE?
OH, BOY.

THE
WARNING

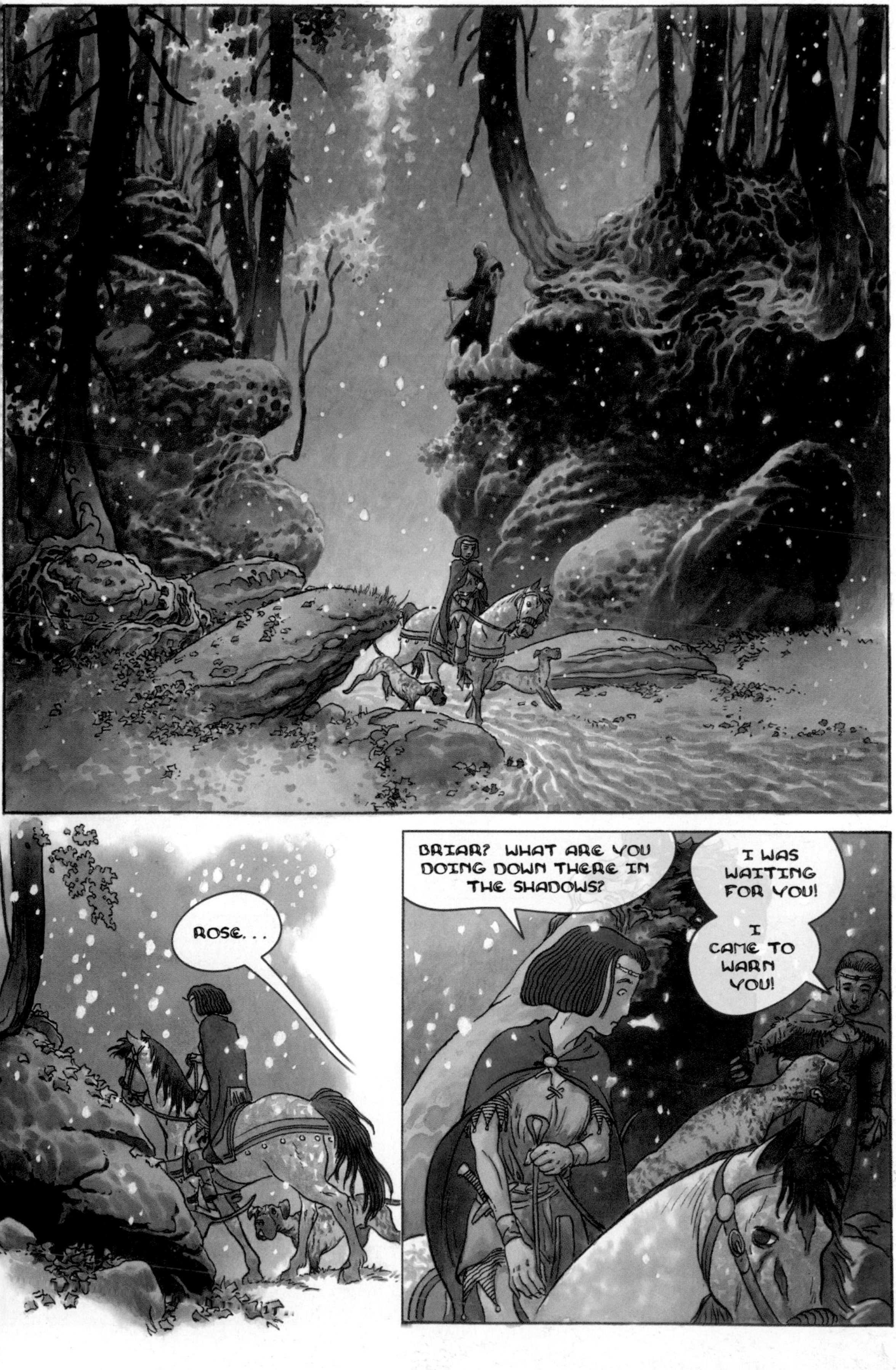
ROSE. . .
BRIAR? WHAT ARE YOU DOING DOWN THERE IN THE SHADOWS?
I WAS WAITING FOR YOU!
I CAME TO WARN YOU!

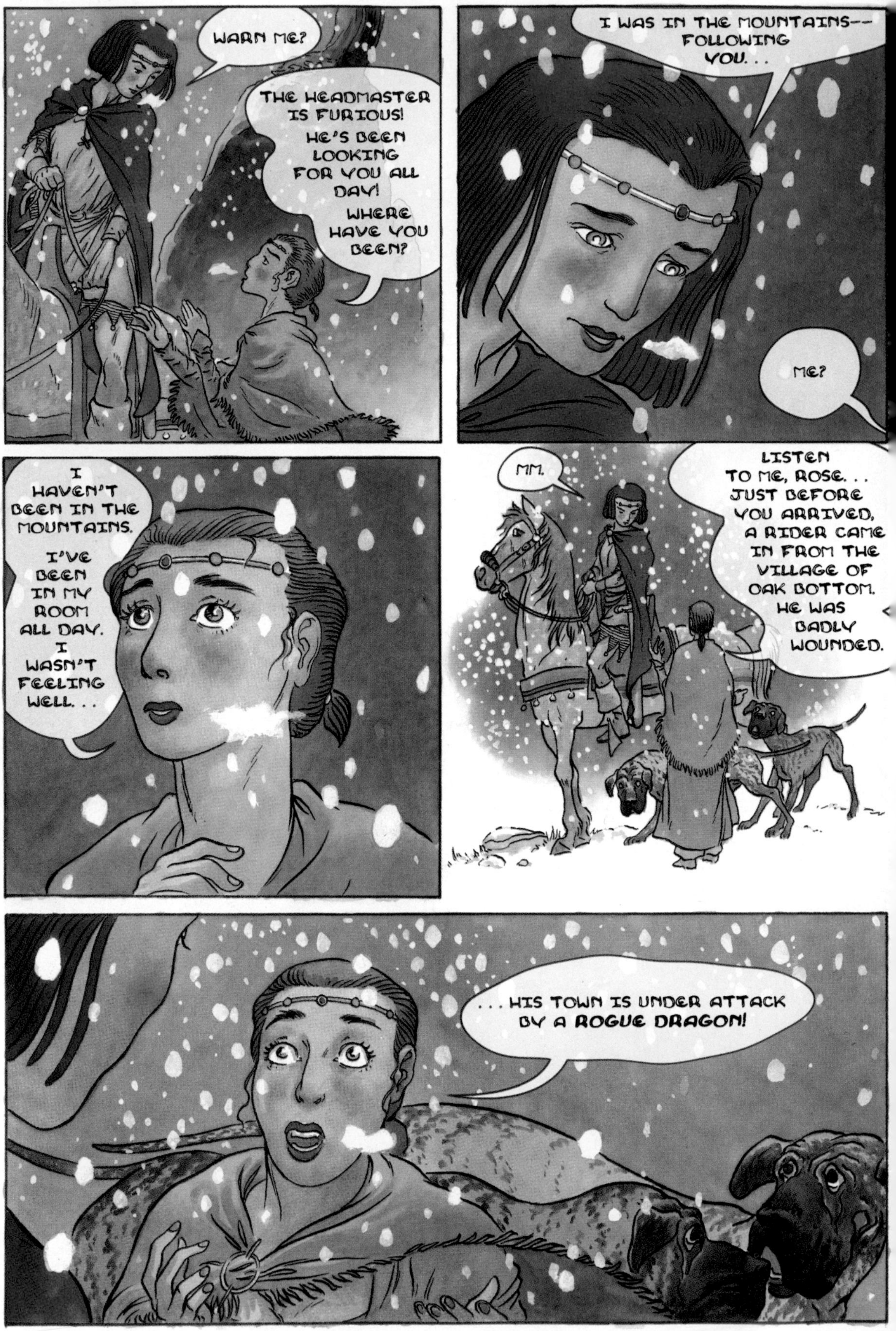
WARN ME?
THE HEADMASTER IS FURIOUS! HE'S BEEN LOOKING FOR YOU ALL DAY! WHERE HAVE YOU BEEN?
I WAS IN THE MOUNTAINS-- FOLLOWING YOU. . .
ME?
I HAVEN'T BEEN IN THE MOUNTAINS. I'VE BEEN IN MY ROOM ALL DAY. I WASN'T FEELING WELL. . .
MM.
LISTEN TO ME, ROSE. . . JUST BEFORE YOU ARRIVED, A RIDER CAME IN FROM THE VILLAGE OF OAK BOTTOM. HE WAS BADLY WOUNDED.
. . . HIS TOWN IS UNDER ATTACK BY A ROGUE DRAGON!

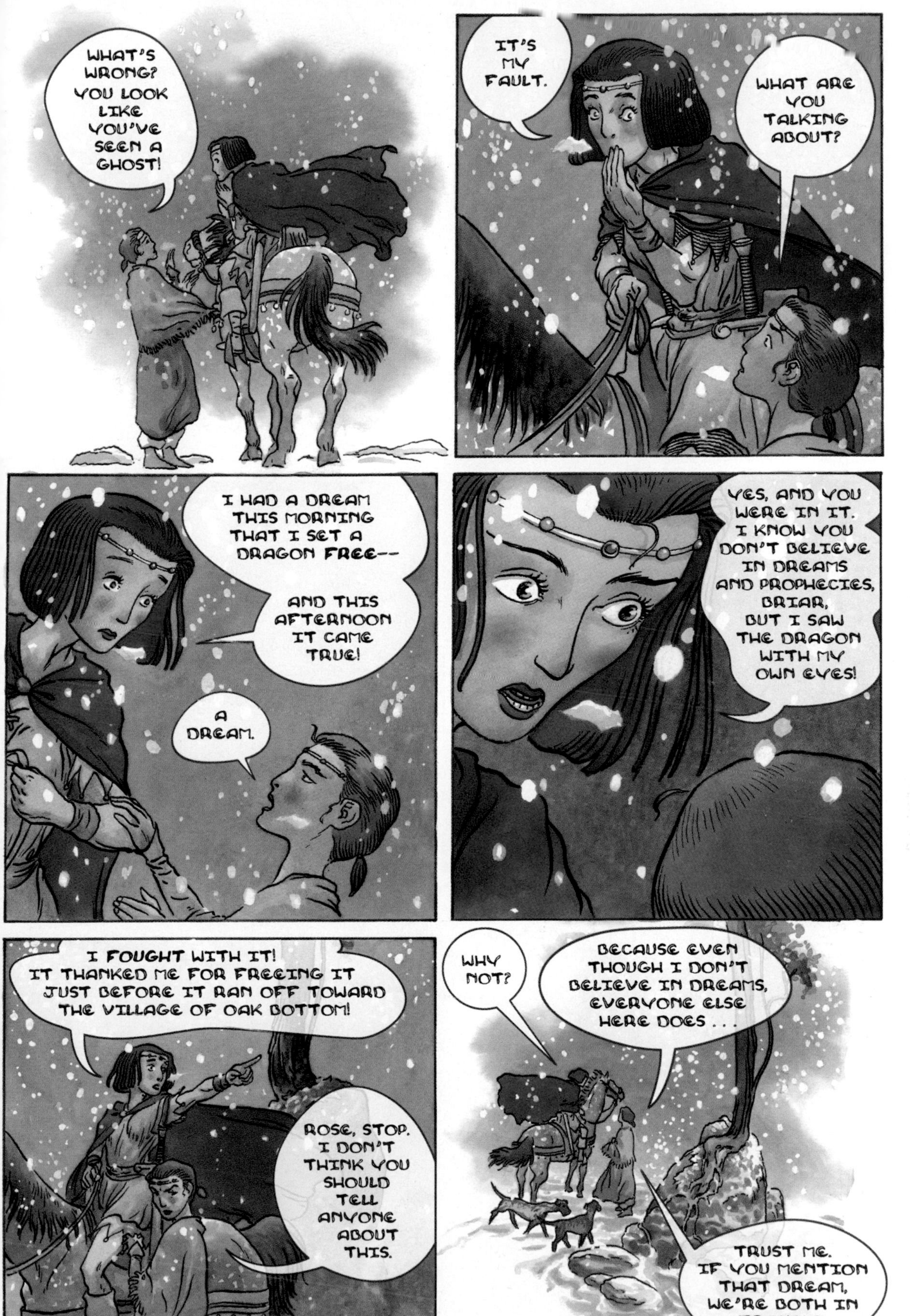
WHAT'S WRONG? YOU LOOK LIKE YOU'VE SEEN A GHOST!
IT'S MY FAULT.
WHAT ARE YOU TALKING ABOUT?
I HAD A DREAM THIS MORNING THAT I SET A DRAGON FREE--
AND THIS AFTERNOON IT CAME TRUE!
A DREAM.
YES, AND YOU WERE IN IT. I KNOW YOU DON'T BELIEVE IN DREAMS AND PROPHECIES, BRIAR, BUT I SAW THE DRAGON WITH MY OWN EYES!
I FOUGHT WITH IT! IT THANKED ME FOR FREEING IT JUST BEFORE IT RAN OFF TOWARD THE VILLAGE OF OAK BOTTOM!
ROSE, STOP. I DON'T THINK YOU SHOULD TELL ANYONE ABOUT THIS.
WHY NOT?
BECAUSE EVEN THOUGH I DON'T BELIEVE IN DREAMS, EVERYONE ELSE HERE DOES . . .
TRUST ME. IF YOU MENTION THAT DREAM, WE'RE BOTH IN TROUBLE.

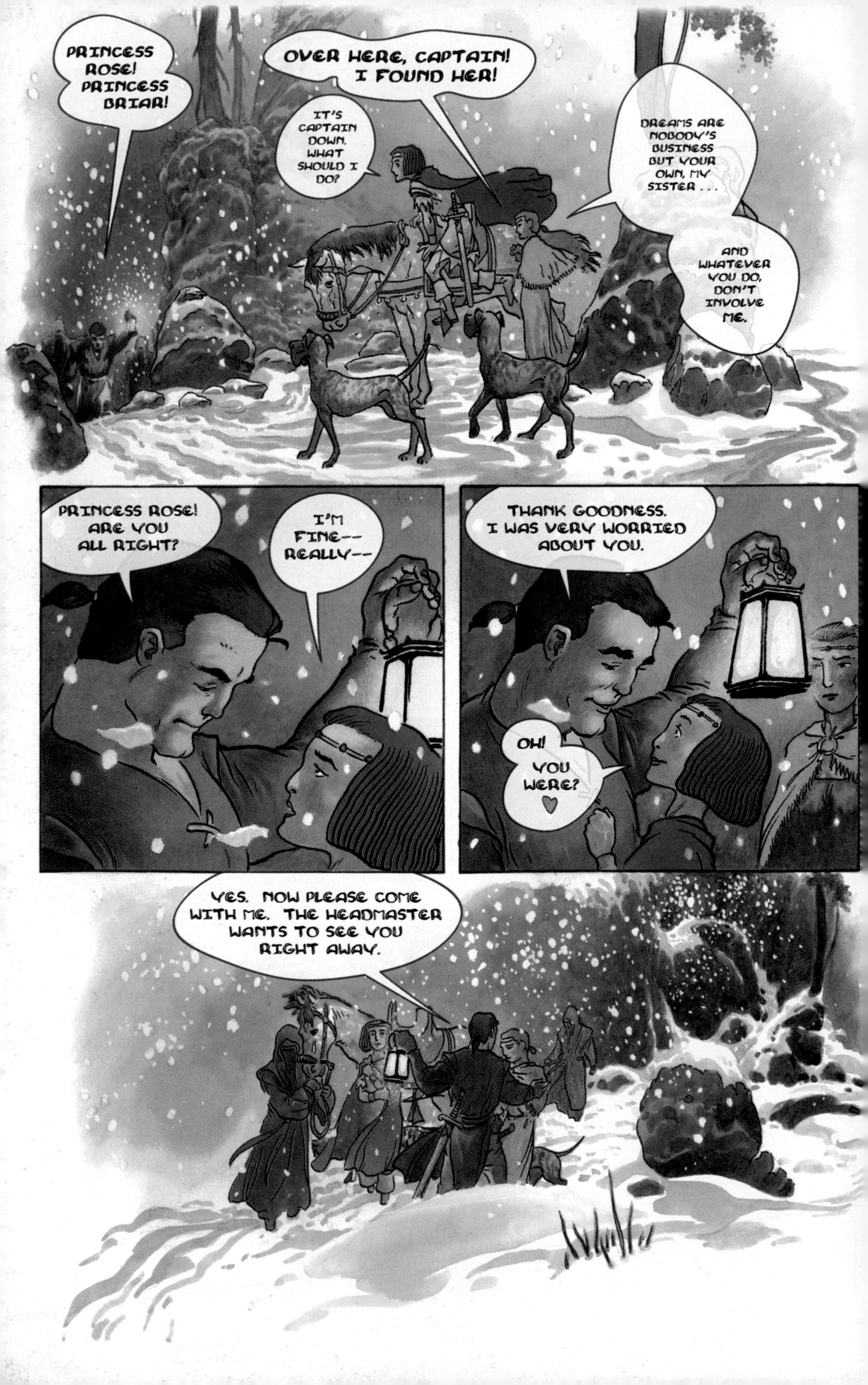

PRINCESS ROSE! PRINCESS BRIAR!
OVER HERE, CAPTAIN! I FOUND HER!
IT'S CAPTAIN DOWN. WHAT SHOULD I DO?
DREAMS ARE NOBODY'S BUSINESS BUT YOUR OWN, MY SISTER . . .
AND WHATEVER YOU DO, DON'T INVOLVE ME.
PRINCESS ROSE! ARE YOU ALL RIGHT?
I'M FINE-- REALLY--
THANK GOODNESS. I WAS VERY WORRIED ABOUT YOU.
OH! YOU WERE? ♥
YES. NOW PLEASE COME WITH ME. THE HEADMASTER WANTS TO SEE YOU RIGHT AWAY.

THE
CAVE

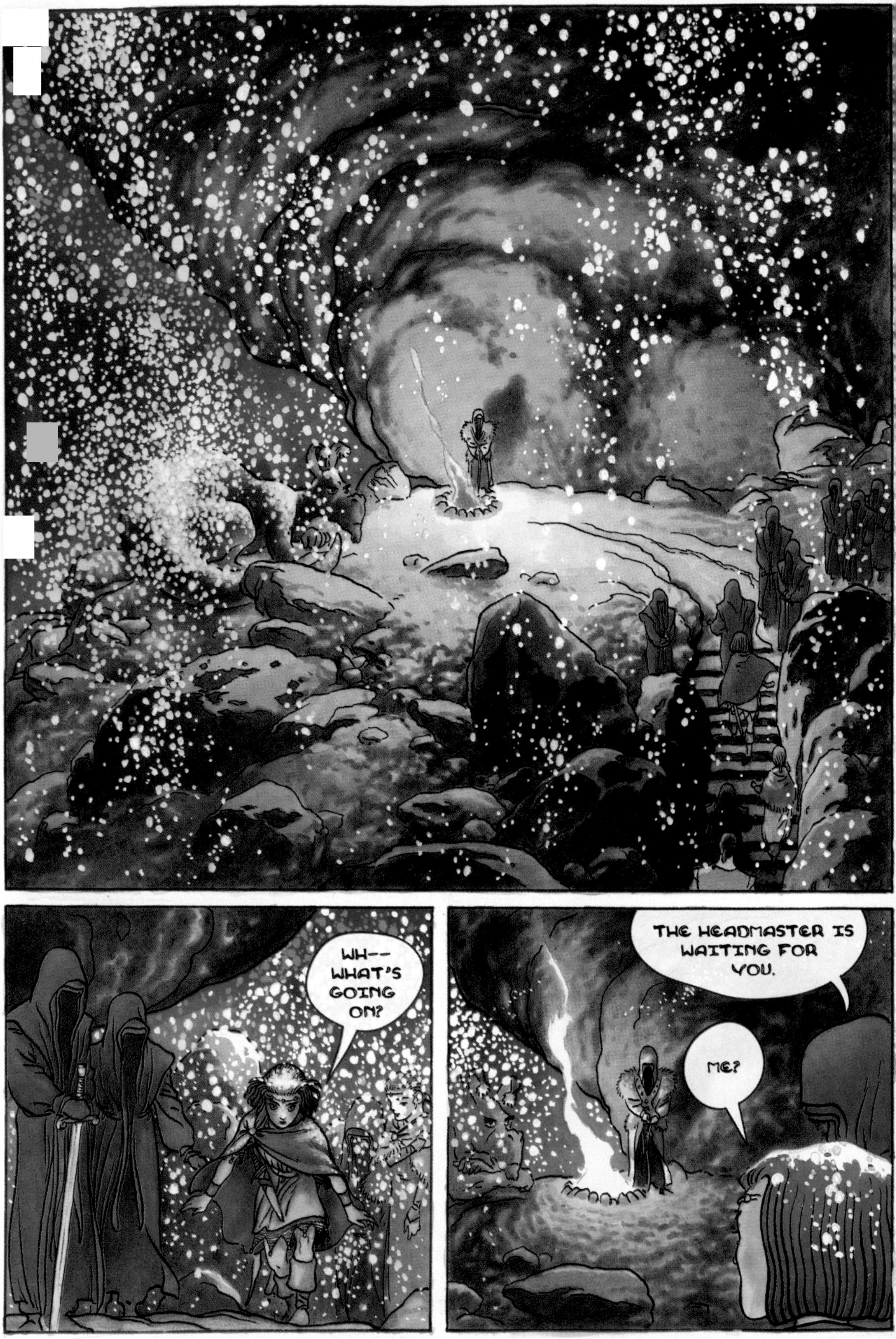
WH-- WHAT'S GOING ON?
THE HEADMASTER IS WAITING FOR YOU.
ME?

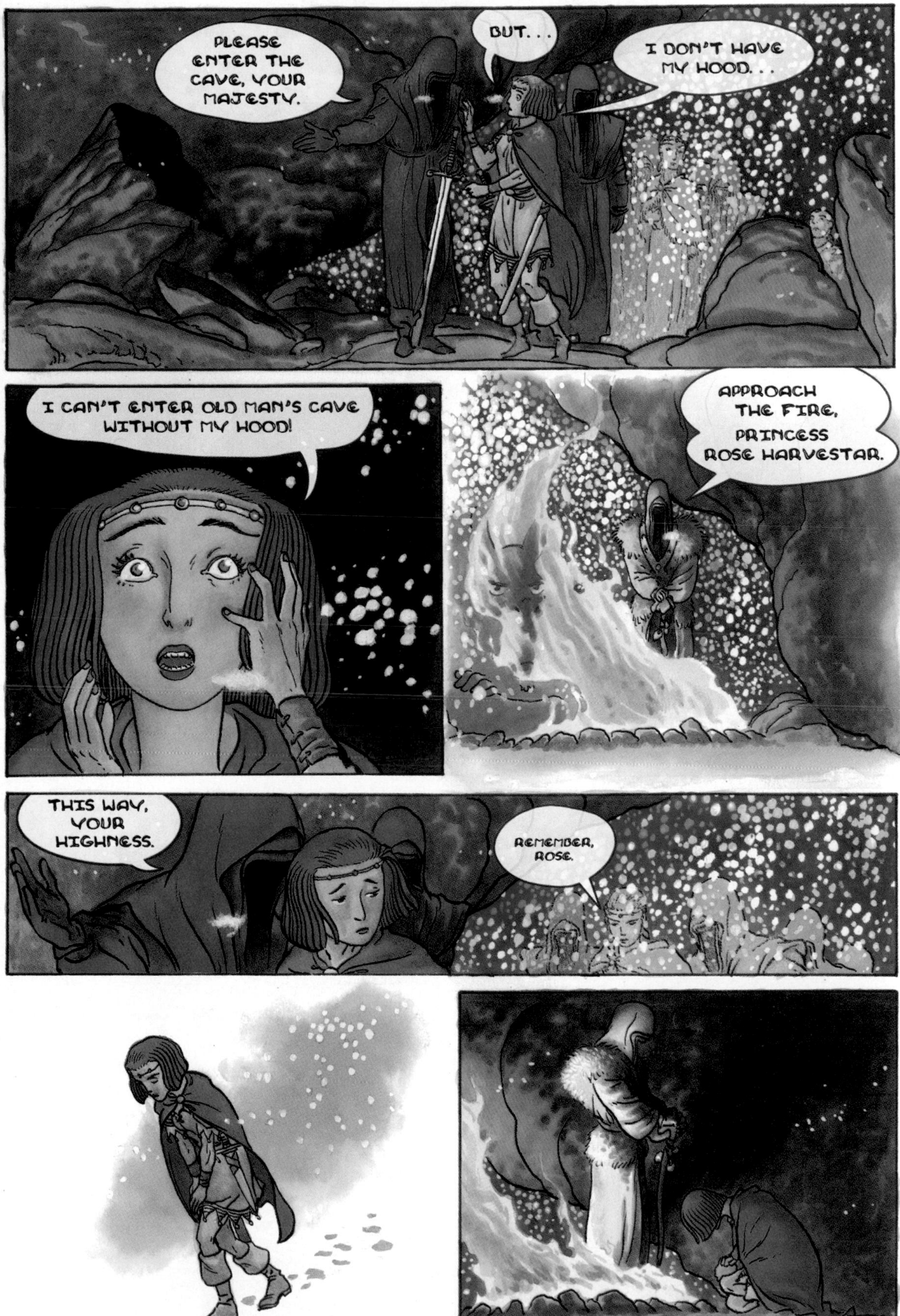
PLEASE ENTER THE CAVE, YOUR MAJESTY.
BUT. . .
I DON'T HAVE MY HOOD. . .
I CAN'T ENTER OLD MAN'S CAVE WITHOUT MY HOOD!
APPROACH THE FIRE, PRINCESS ROSE HARVESTAR.
THIS WAY, YOUR HIGHNESS.
REMEMBER, ROSE.

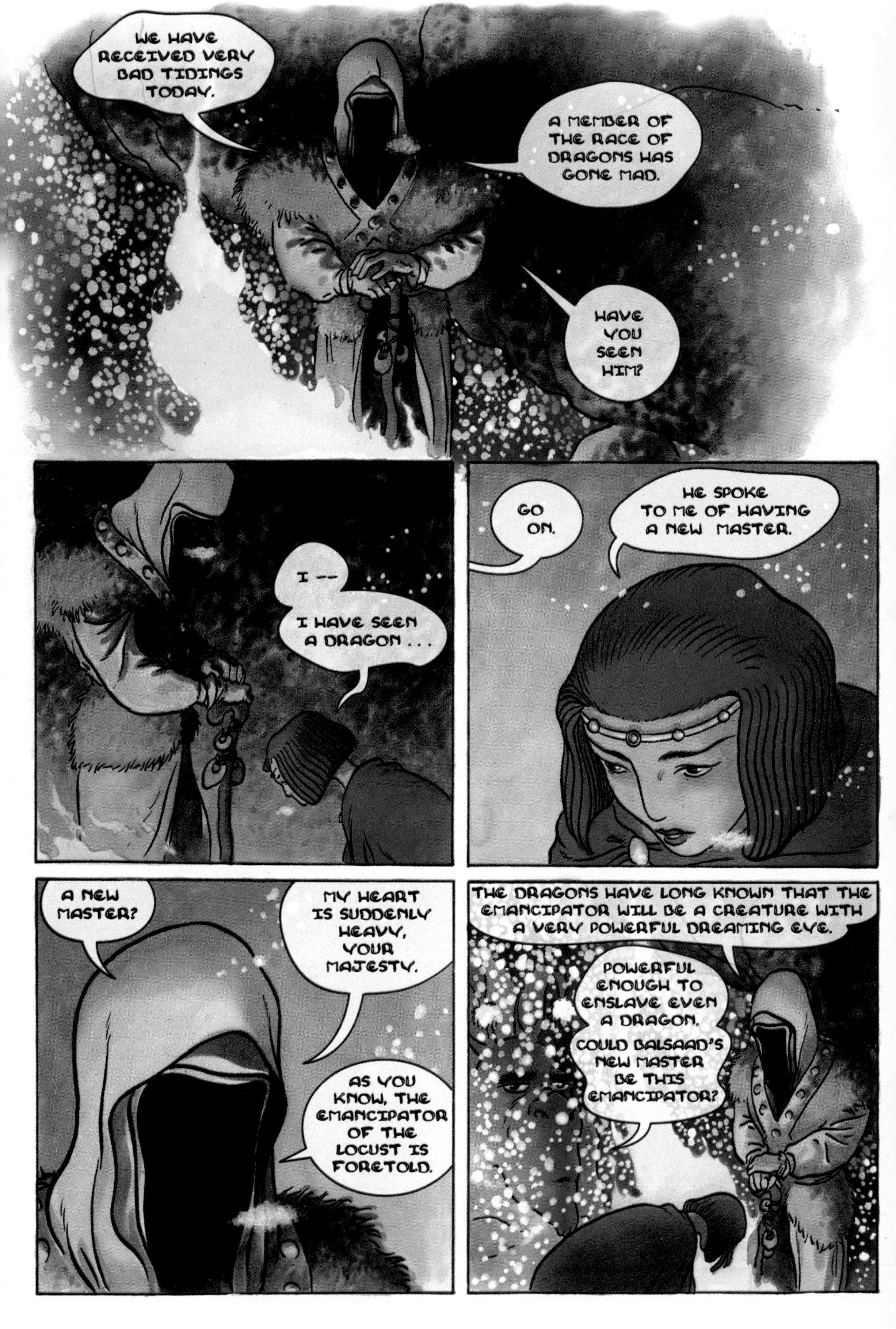
WE HAVE RECEIVED VERY BAD TIDINGS TODAY.
A MEMBER OF THE RACE OF DRAGONS HAS GONE MAD.
HAVE YOU SEEN HIM?
I --
I HAVE SEEN A DRAGON . . .
GO ON.
HE SPOKE TO ME OF HAVING A NEW MASTER.
A NEW MASTER?
MY HEART IS SUDDENLY HEAVY, YOUR MAJESTY.
AS YOU KNOW, THE EMANCIPATOR OF THE LOCUST IS FORETOLD.
THE DRAGONS HAVE LONG KNOWN THAT THE EMANCIPATOR WILL BE A CREATURE WITH A VERY POWERFUL DREAMING EYE.
POWERFUL ENOUGH TO ENSLAVE EVEN A DRAGON.
COULD BALSAAD'S NEW MASTER BE THIS EMANCIPATOR?

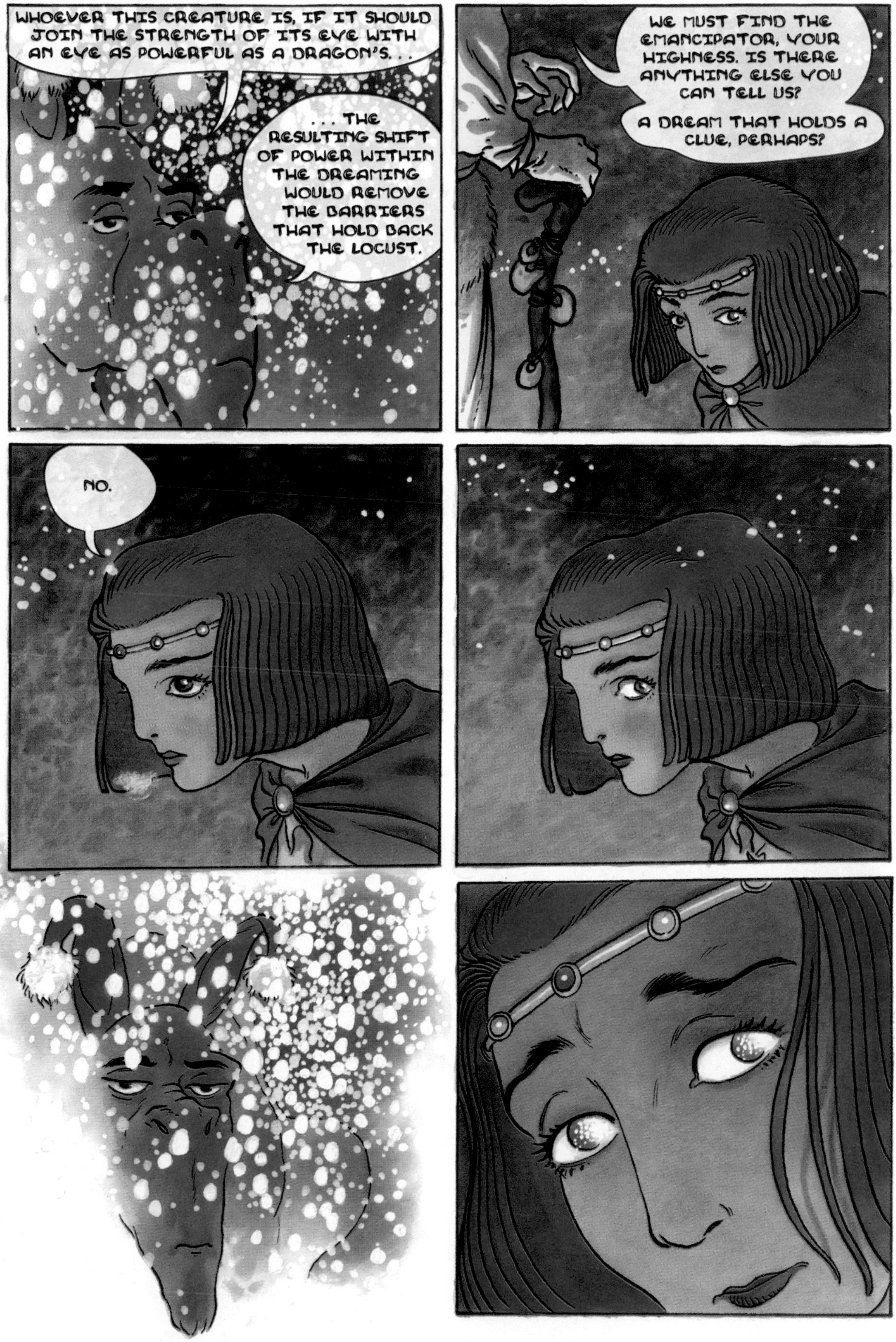
WHOEVER THIS CREATURE IS, IF IT SHOULD JOIN THE STRENGTH OF ITS EYE WITH AN EYE AS POWERFUL AS A DRAGON'S. . .
. . . THE RESULTING SHIFT OF POWER WITHIN THE DREAMING WOULD REMOVE THE BARRIERS THAT HOLD BACK THE LOCUST.
WE MUST FIND THE EMANCIPATOR, YOUR HIGHNESS. IS THERE ANYTHING ELSE YOU CAN TELL US?
A DREAM THAT HOLDS A CLUE, PERHAPS?
NO.

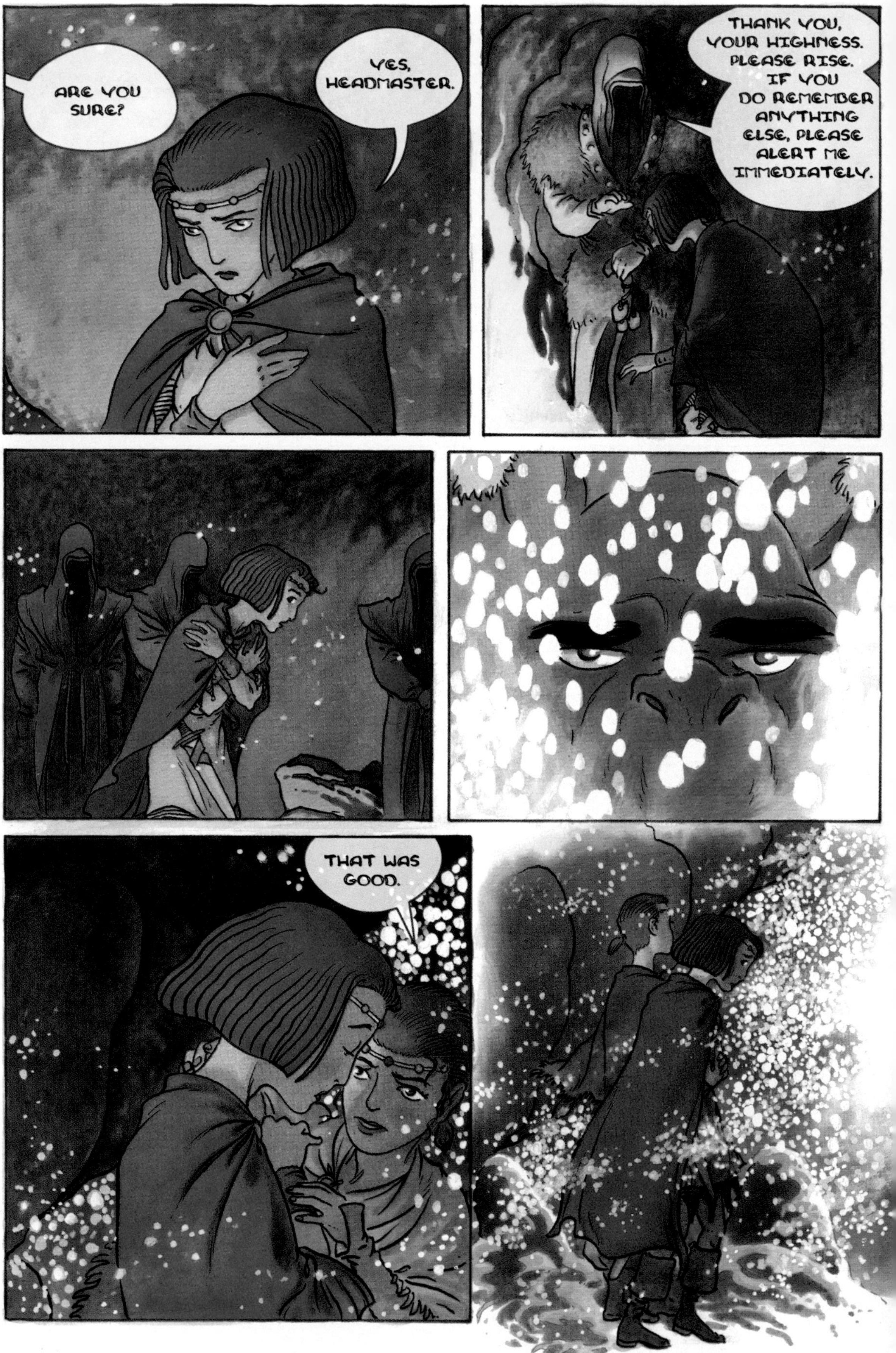
ARE YOU SURE?
YES, HEADMASTER.
THANK YOU, YOUR HIGHNESS. PLEASE RISE. IF YOU DO REMEMBER ANYTHING ELSE, PLEASE ALERT ME IMMEDIATELY.
THAT WAS GOOD.

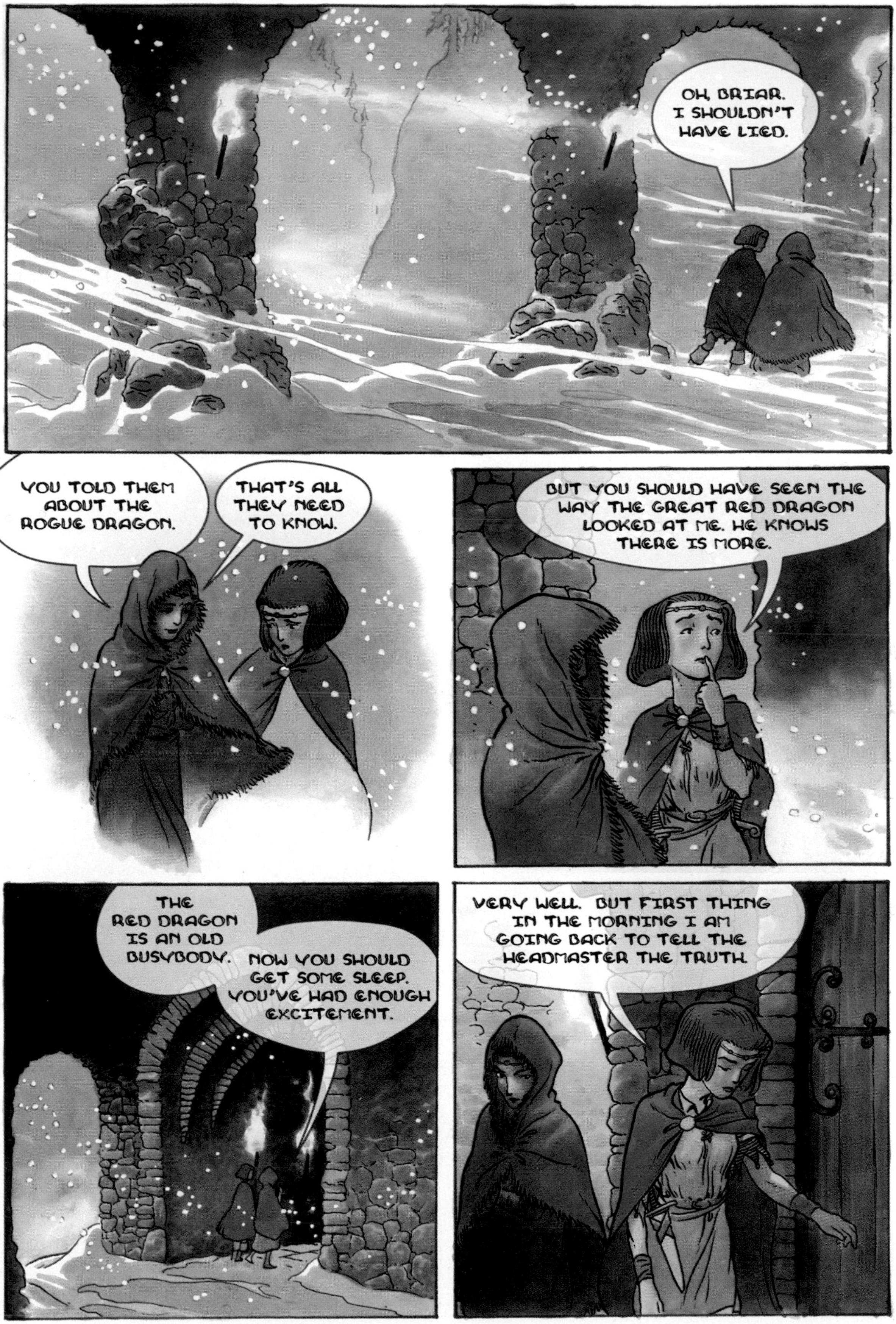
OH, BRIAR. I SHOULDN'T HAVE LIED.
YOU TOLD THEM ABOUT THE ROGUE DRAGON.
THAT'S ALL THEY NEED TO KNOW.
BUT YOU SHOULD HAVE SEEN THE WAY THE GREAT RED DRAGON LOOKED AT ME. HE KNOWS THERE IS MORE.
THE RED DRAGON IS AN OLD BUSYBODY.
NOW YOU SHOULD GET SOME SLEEP. YOU'VE HAD ENOUGH EXCITEMENT.
VERY WELL. BUT FIRST THING IN THE MORNING I AM GOING BACK TO TELL THE HEADMASTER THE TRUTH.

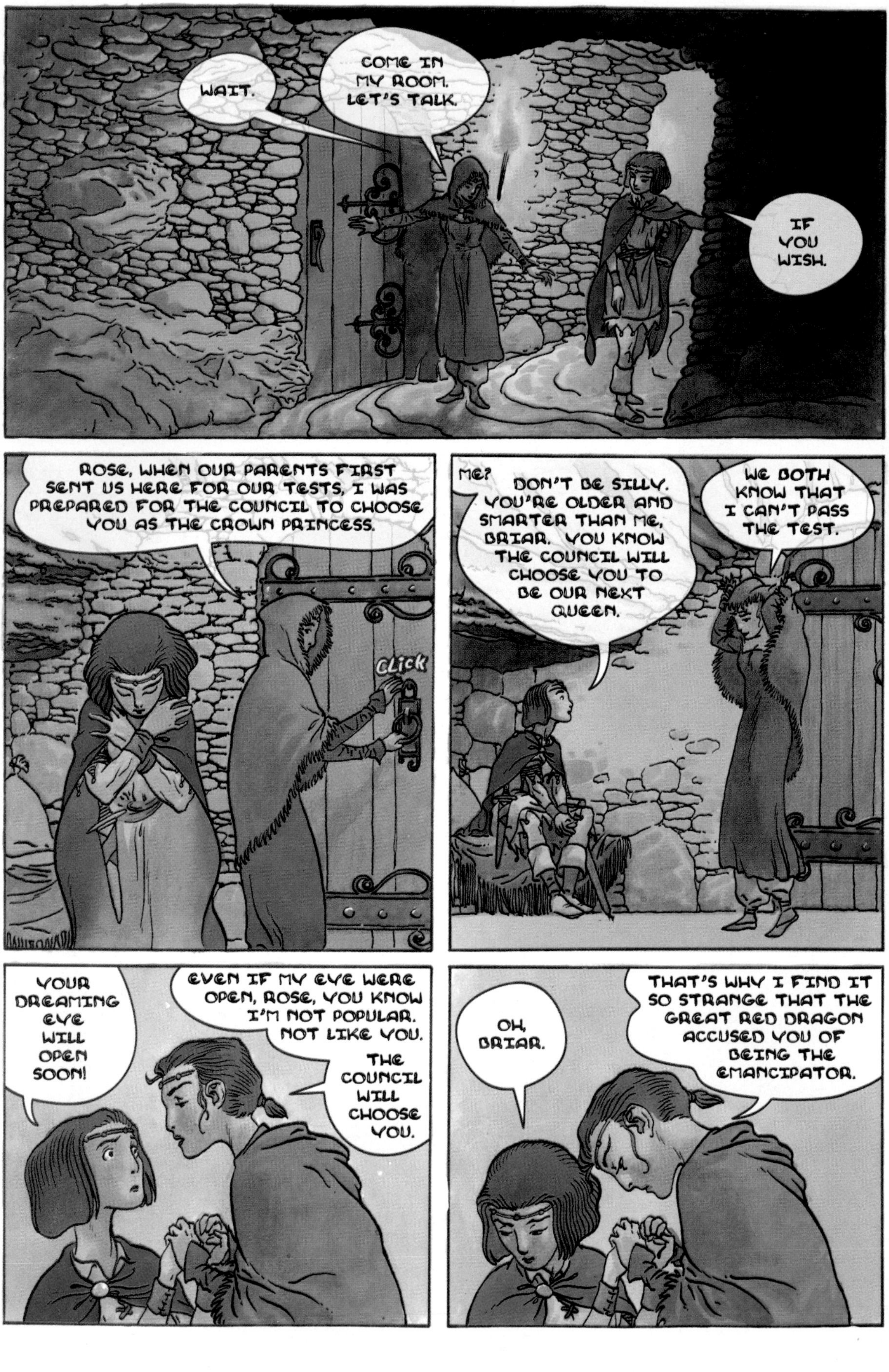
WAIT.
COME IN MY ROOM. LET'S TALK.
IF YOU WISH.
ROSE, WHEN OUR PARENTS FIRST SENT US HERE FOR OUR TESTS, I WAS PREPARED FOR THE COUNCIL TO CHOOSE YOU AS THE CROWN PRINCESS.
CLICK
ME?
DON'T BE SILLY. YOU'RE OLDER AND SMARTER THAN ME, BRIAR. YOU KNOW THE COUNCIL WILL CHOOSE YOU TO BE OUR NEXT QUEEN.
WE BOTH KNOW THAT I CAN'T PASS THE TEST.
YOUR DREAMING EYE WILL OPEN SOON!
EVEN IF MY EYE WERE OPEN, ROSE, YOU KNOW I'M NOT POPULAR. NOT LIKE YOU.
THE COUNCIL WILL CHOOSE YOU.
OH, BRIAR.
THAT'S WHY I FIND IT SO STRANGE THAT THE GREAT RED DRAGON ACCUSED YOU OF BEING THE EMANCIPATOR.

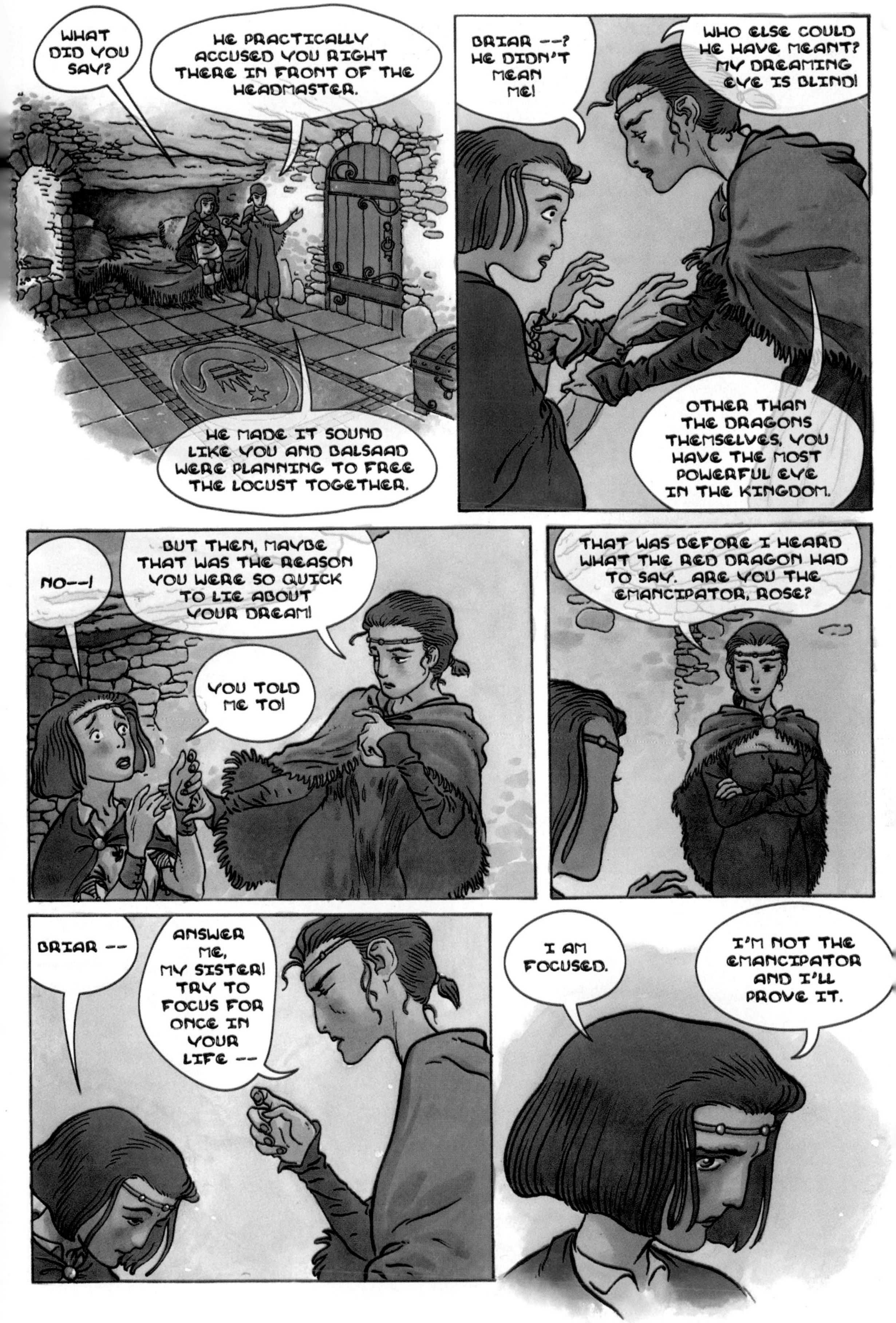
WHAT DID YOU SAY?
HE PRACTICALLY ACCUSED YOU RIGHT THERE IN FRONT OF THE HEADMASTER.
HE MADE IT SOUND LIKE YOU AND BALSAAD WERE PLANNING TO FREE THE LOCUST TOGETHER.
BRIAR --? HE DIDN'T MEAN ME!
WHO ELSE COULD HE HAVE MEANT? MY DREAMING EYE IS BLIND!
OTHER THAN THE DRAGONS THEMSELVES, YOU HAVE THE MOST POWERFUL EYE IN THE KINGDOM.
NO--!
BUT THEN, MAYBE THAT WAS THE REASON YOU WERE SO QUICK TO LIE ABOUT YOUR DREAM!
YOU TOLD ME TO!
THAT WAS BEFORE I HEARD WHAT THE RED DRAGON HAD TO SAY. ARE YOU THE EMANCIPATOR, ROSE?
BRIAR --
ANSWER ME, MY SISTER! TRY TO FOCUS FOR ONCE IN YOUR LIFE --
I AM FOCUSED.
I'M NOT THE EMANCIPATOR AND I'LL PROVE IT.

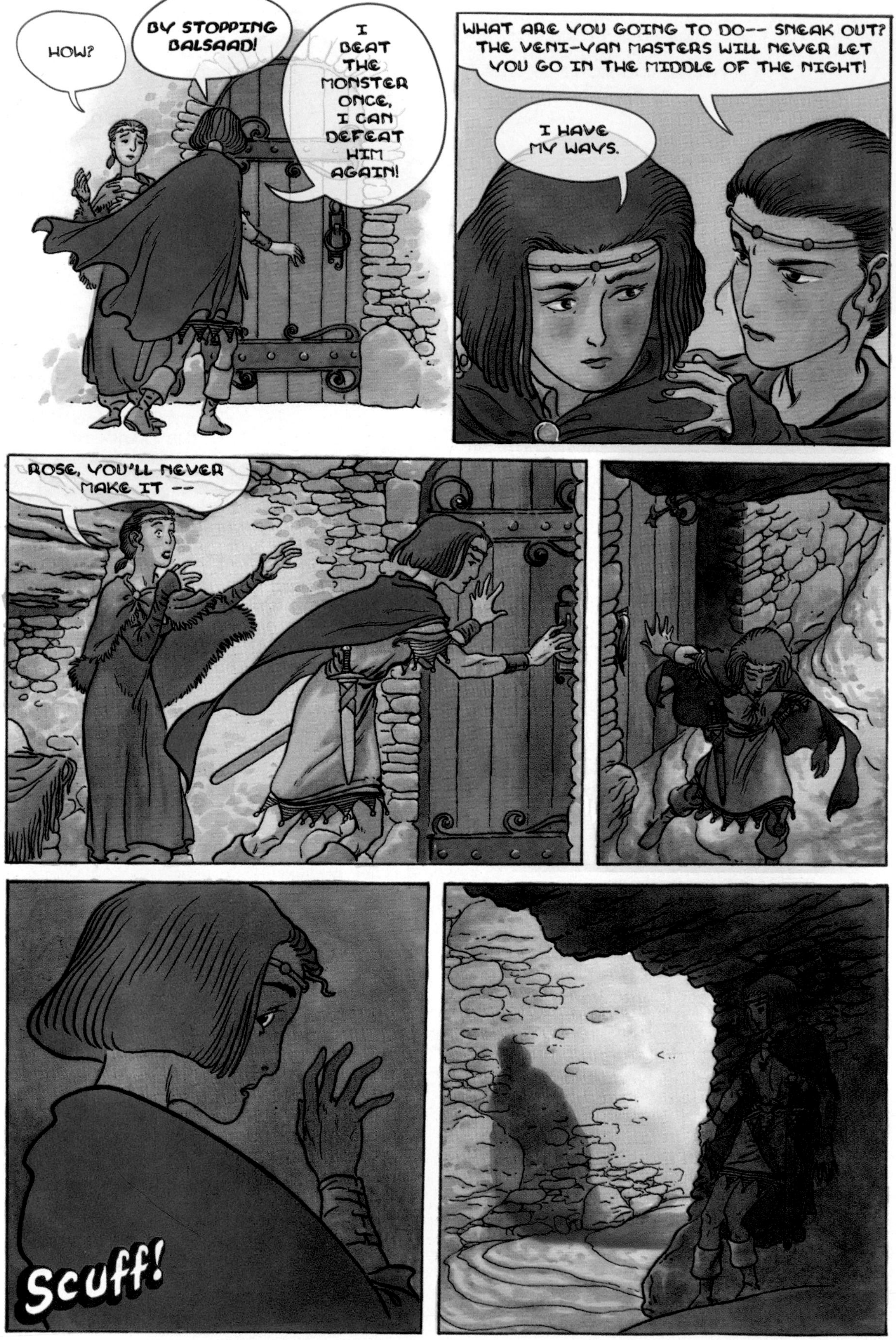
HOW?
BY STOPPING BALSAAD!
I BEAT THE MONSTER ONCE, I CAN DEFEAT HIM AGAIN!
WHAT ARE YOU GOING TO DO-- SNEAK OUT? THE VENI-YAN MASTERS WILL NEVER LET YOU GO IN THE MIDDLE OF THE NIGHT!
I HAVE MY WAYS.
ROSE, YOU'LL NEVER MAKE IT --
Scuff!

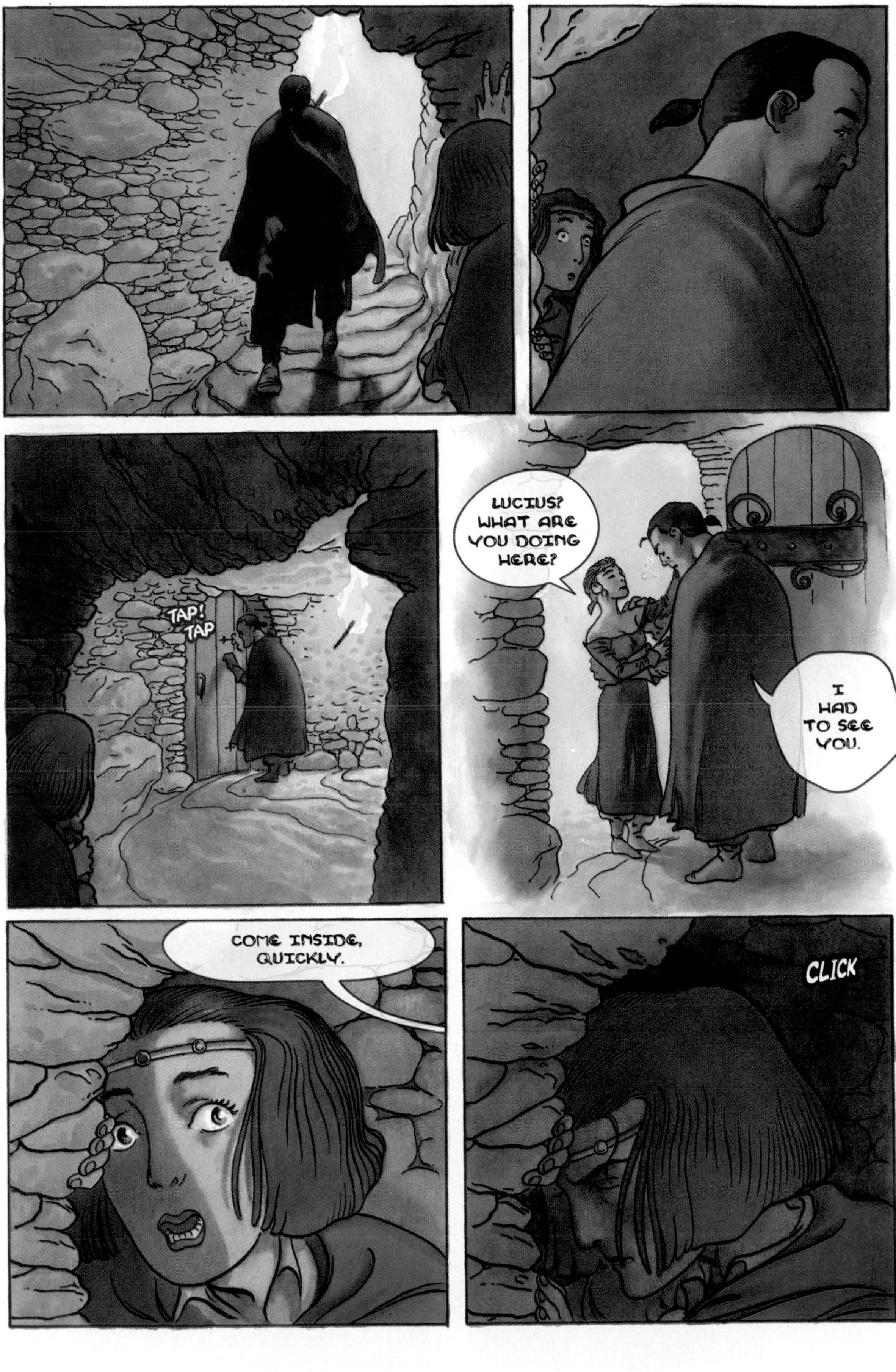
TAP! TAP
LUCIUS? WHAT ARE YOU DOING HERE?
I HAD TO SEE YOU.
COME INSIDE, QUICKLY.
CLICK

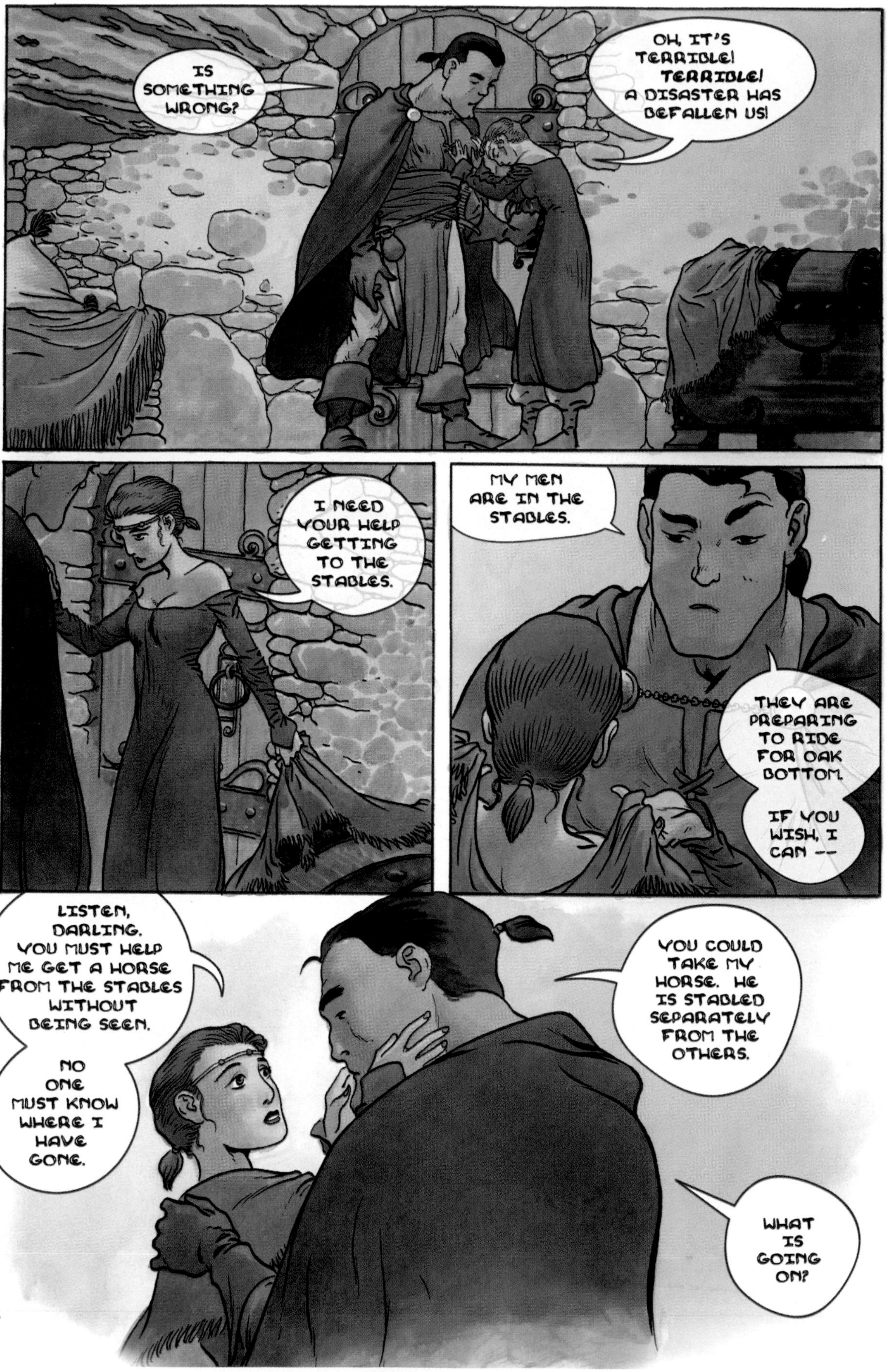
IS SOMETHING WRONG?
OH, IT'S TERRIBLE! TERRIBLE! A DISASTER HAS BEFALLEN US!
I NEED YOUR HELP GETTING TO THE STABLES.
MY MEN ARE IN THE STABLES.
THEY ARE PREPARING TO RIDE FOR OAK BOTTOM.
IF YOU WISH, I CAN --
LISTEN, DARLING. YOU MUST HELP ME GET A HORSE FROM THE STABLES WITHOUT BEING SEEN.
NO ONE MUST KNOW WHERE I HAVE GONE.
YOU COULD TAKE MY HORSE. HE IS STABLED SEPARATELY FROM THE OTHERS.
WHAT IS GOING ON?

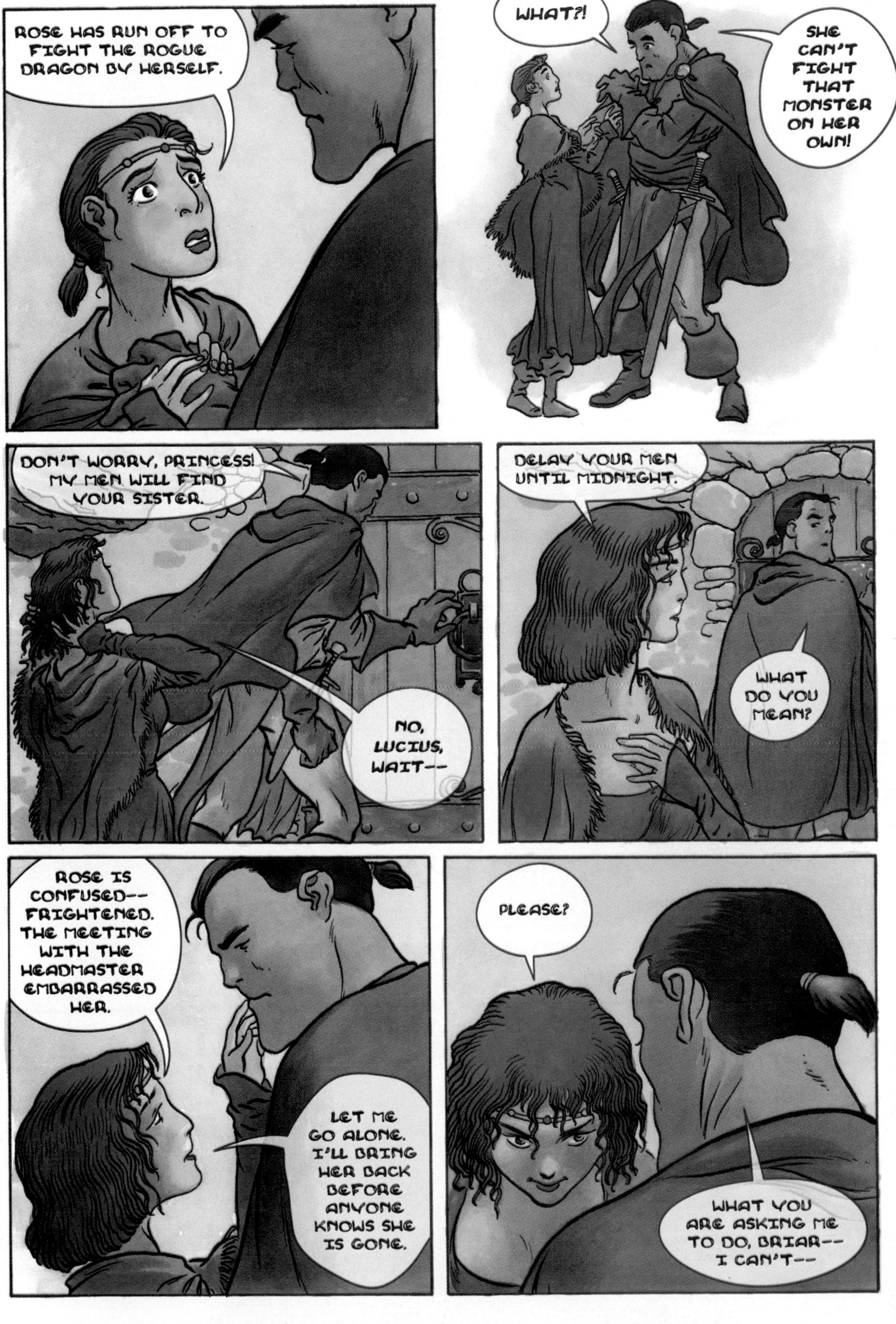
ROSE HAS RUN OFF TO FIGHT THE ROGUE DRAGON BY HERSELF.
WHAT?!
SHE CAN'T FIGHT THAT MONSTER ON HER OWN!
DON'T WORRY, PRINCESS! MY MEN WILL FIND YOUR SISTER.
NO, LUCIUS, WAIT--
DELAY YOUR MEN UNTIL MIDNIGHT.
WHAT DO YOU MEAN?
ROSE IS CONFUSED-- FRIGHTENED. THE MEETING WITH THE HEADMASTER EMBARRASSED HER.
LET ME GO ALONE. I'LL BRING HER BACK BEFORE ANYONE KNOWS SHE IS GONE.
PLEASE?
WHAT YOU ARE ASKING ME TO DO, BRIAR-- I CAN'T--

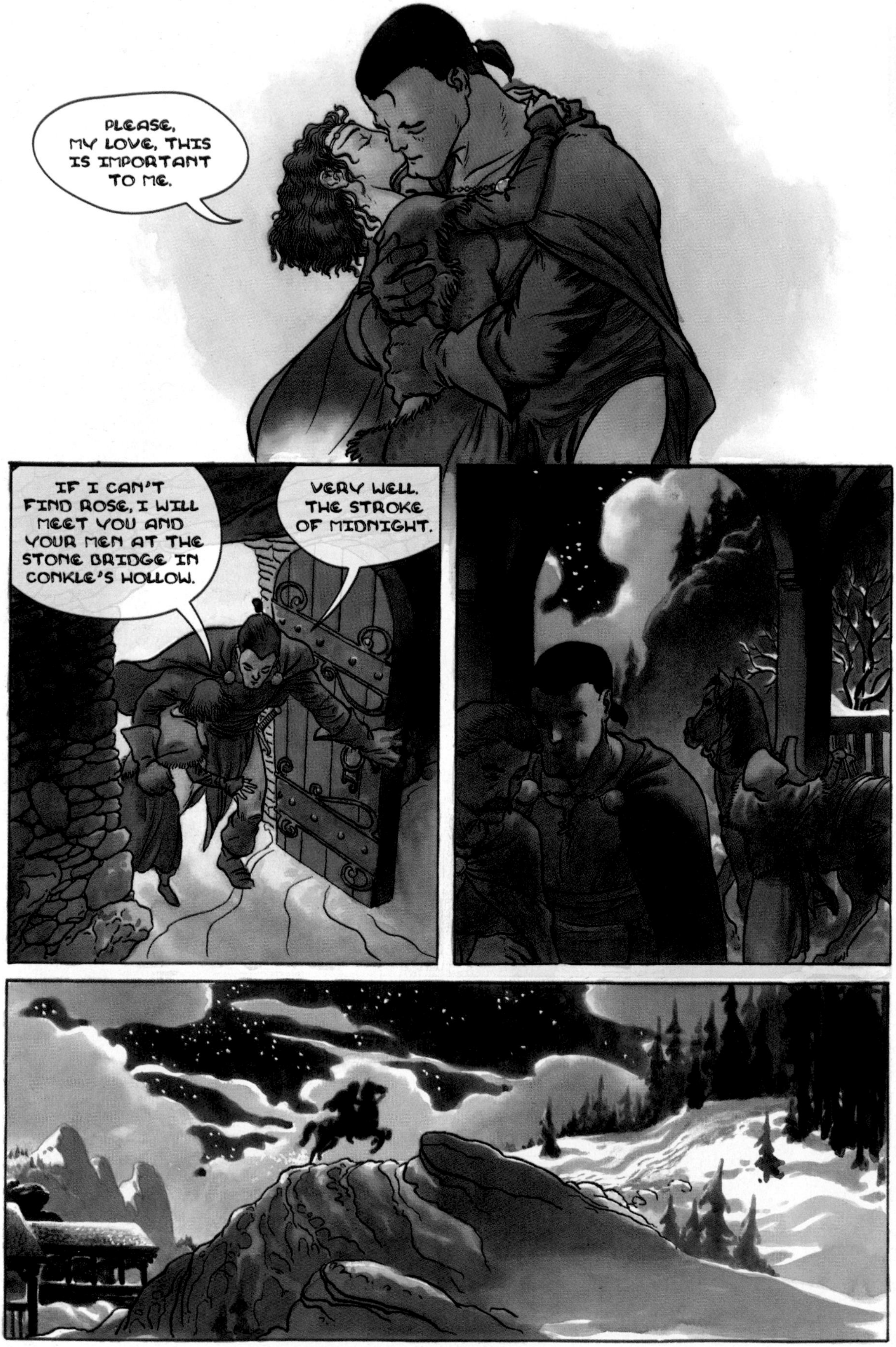
PLEASE, MY LOVE, THIS IS IMPORTANT TO ME.
IF I CAN'T FIND ROSE, I WILL MEET YOU AND YOUR MEN AT THE STONE BRIDGE IN CONKLE'S HOLLOW.
VERY WELL. THE STROKE OF MIDNIGHT.

INTO
THE
NIGHT...

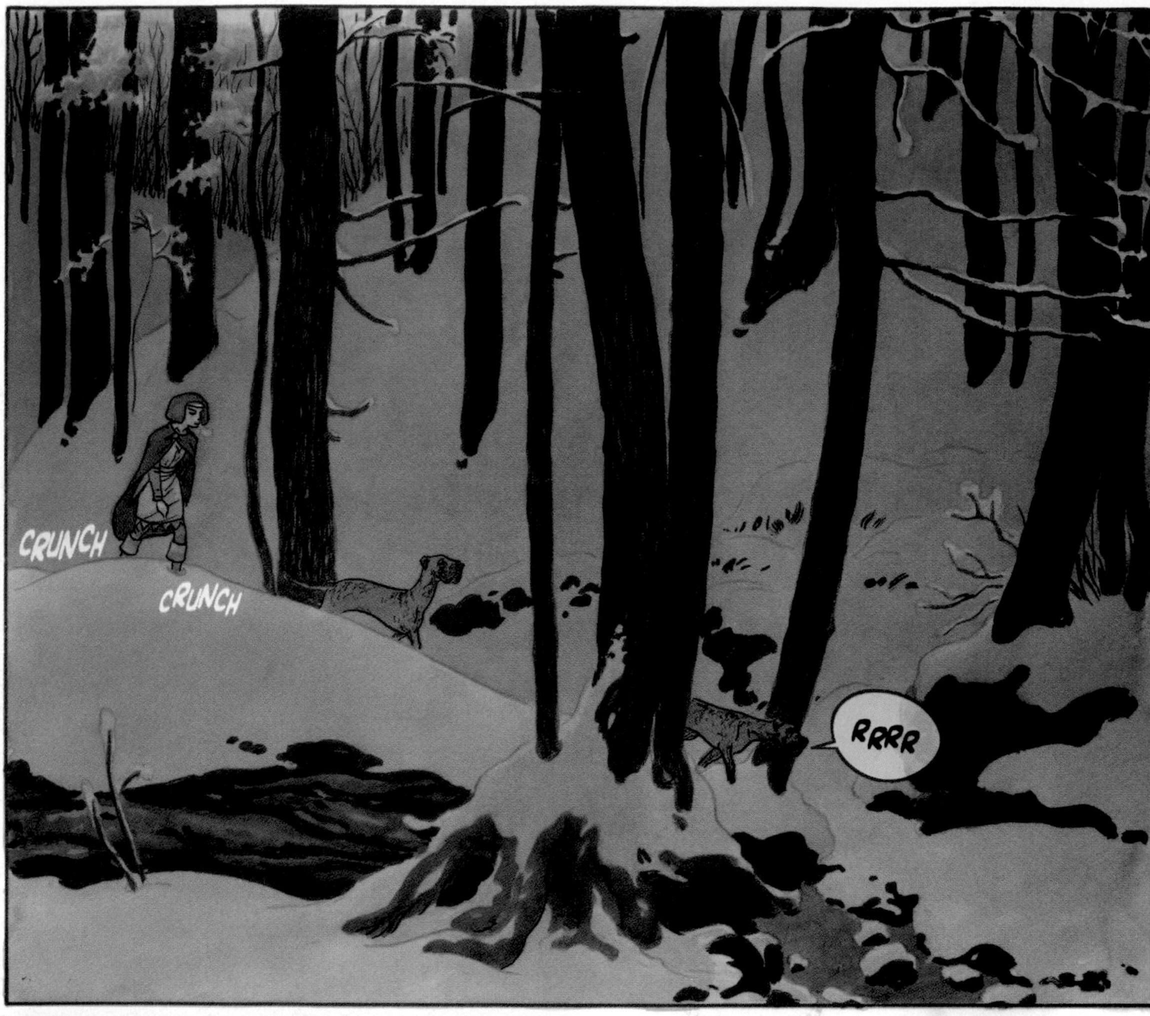
CRUNCH
CRUNCH
RRRR

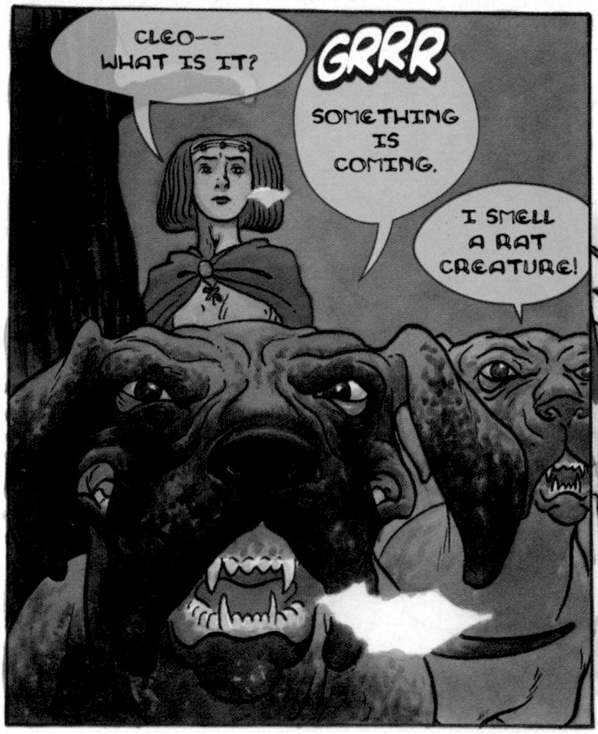
CLEO-- WHAT IS IT?
GRRR
SOMETHING IS COMING.
I SMELL A RAT CREATURE!

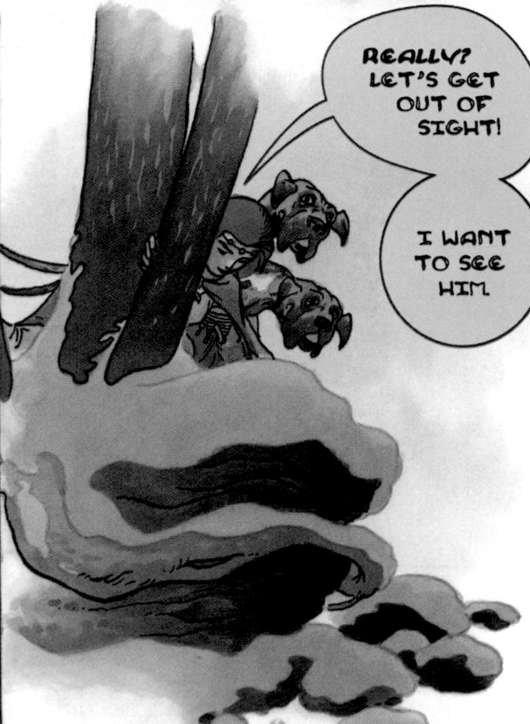
REALLY? LET'S GET OUT OF SIGHT!
I WANT TO SEE HIM.

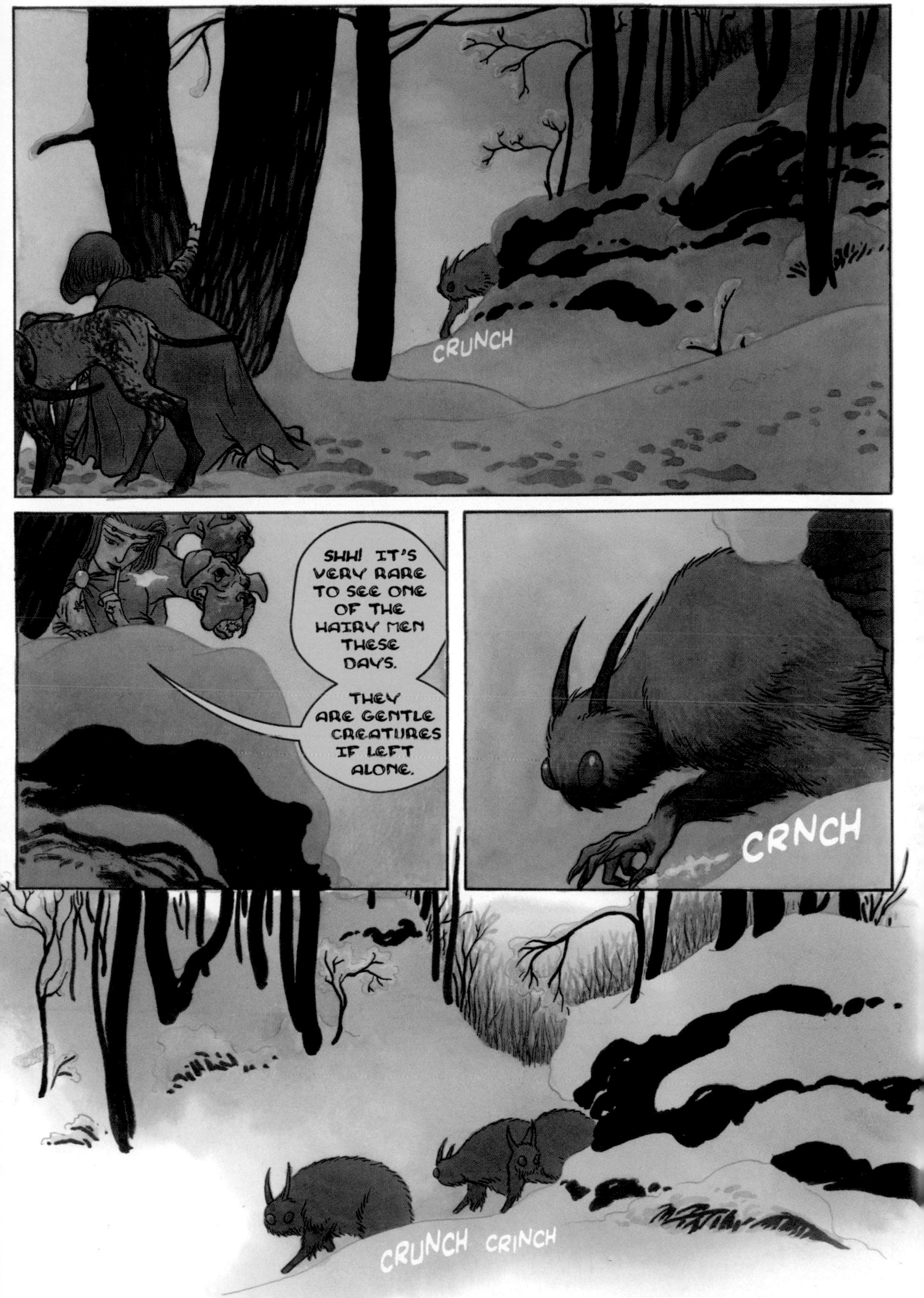
CRUNCH
SHH! IT'S VERY RARE TO SEE ONE OF THE HAIRY MEN THESE DAYS.
THEY ARE GENTLE CREATURES IF LEFT ALONE.
CRNCH
CRUNCH CRINCH

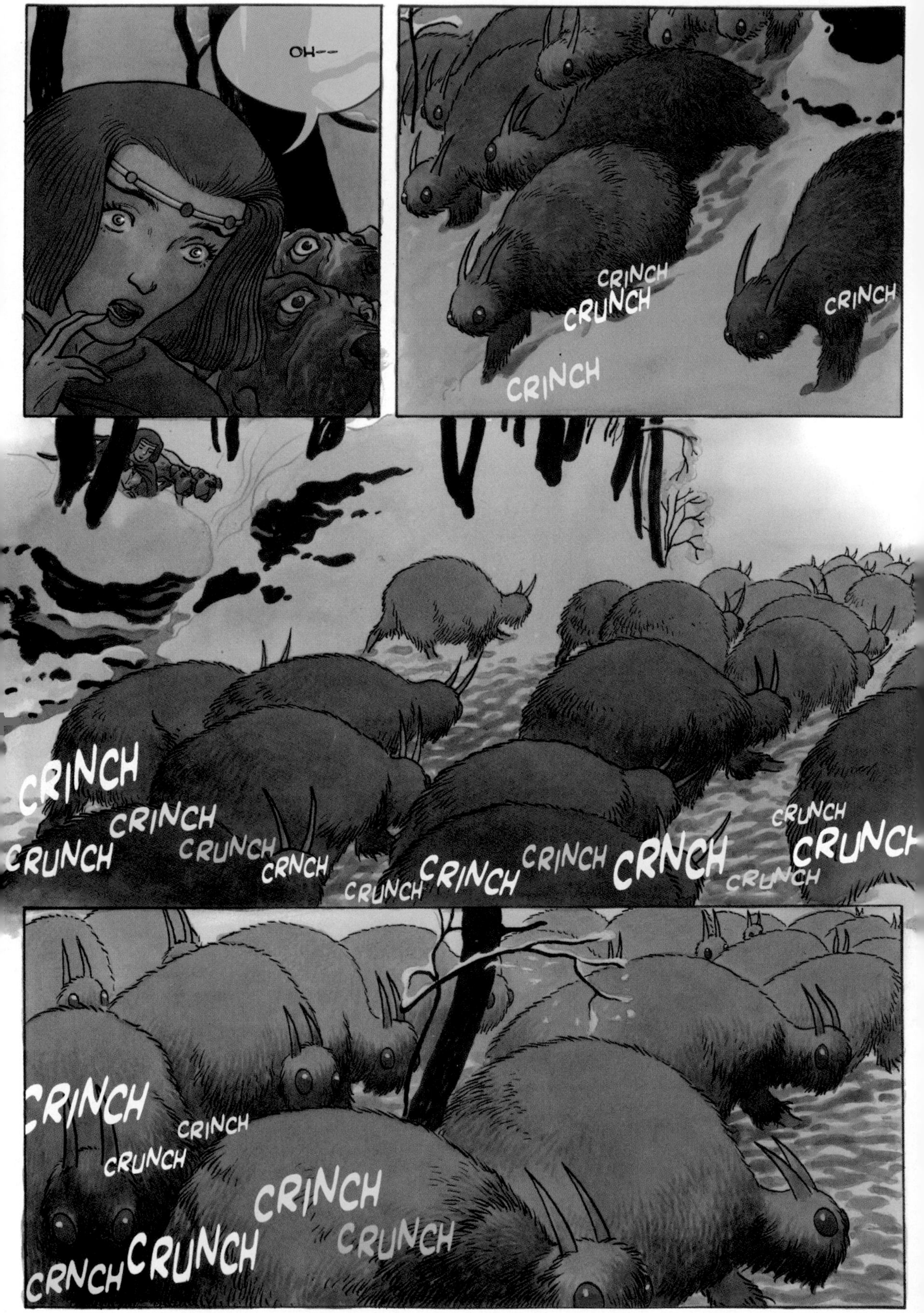
OH--
CRINCH
CRUNCH
CRINCH
CRINCH
CRINCH
CRINCH
CRUNCH
CRUNCH
CRNCH
CRUNCH
CRINCH
CRINCH
CRNCH
CRUNCH
CRUNCH
CRUNCH
CRINCH
CRINCH
CRUNCH
CRINCH
CRUNCH
CRNCH
CRUNCH

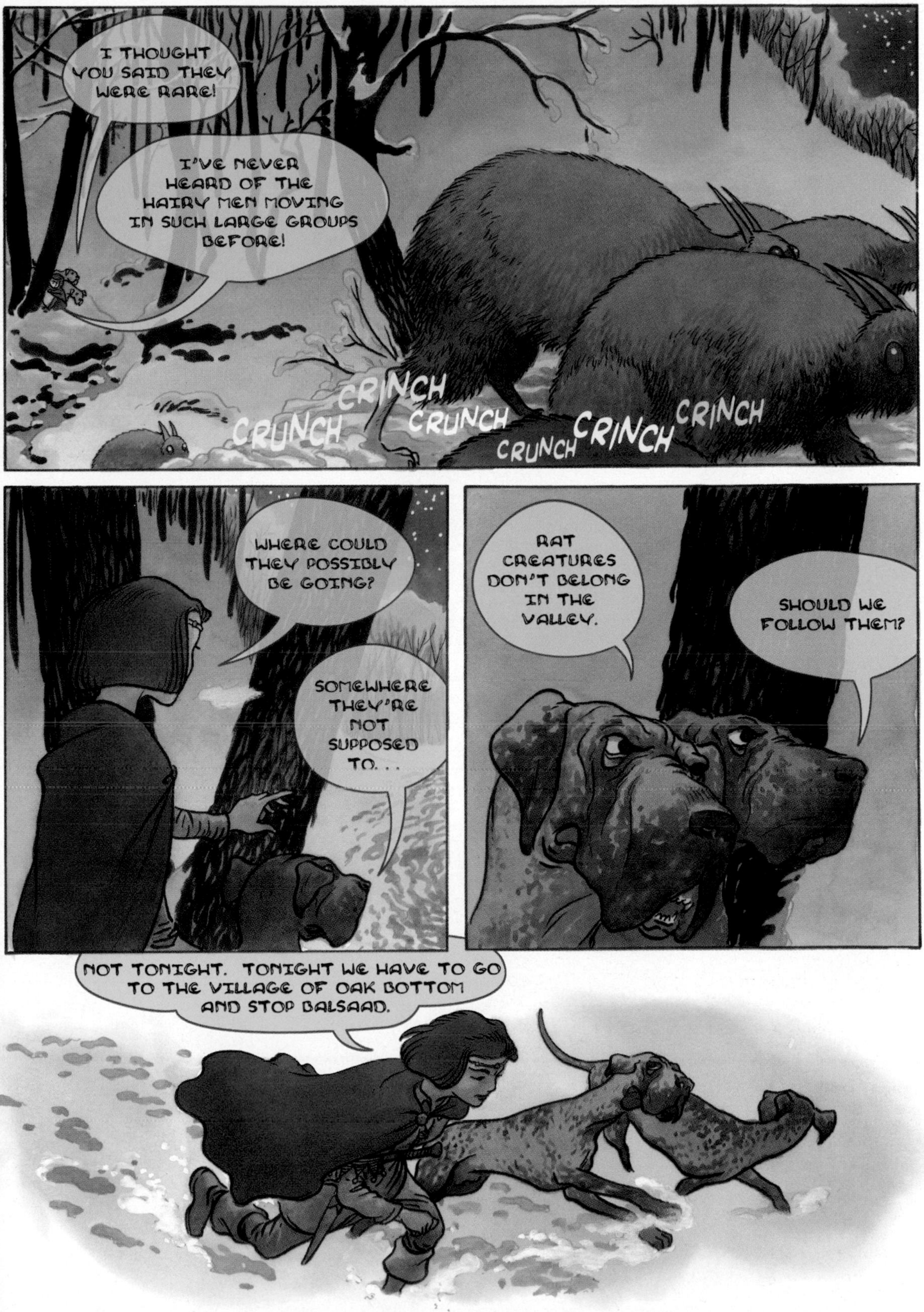
I THOUGHT YOU SAID THEY WERE RARE!
I'VE NEVER HEARD OF THE HAIRY MEN MOVING IN SUCH LARGE GROUPS BEFORE!
CRUNCH CRINCH CRUNCH CRUNCH CRINCH CRINCH
WHERE COULD THEY POSSIBLY BE GOING?
SOMEWHERE THEY'RE NOT SUPPOSED TO. . .
RAT CREATURES DON'T BELONG IN THE VALLEY.
SHOULD WE FOLLOW THEM?
NOT TONIGHT. TONIGHT WE HAVE TO GO TO THE VILLAGE OF OAK BOTTOM AND STOP BALSAAD.

The Master Calls

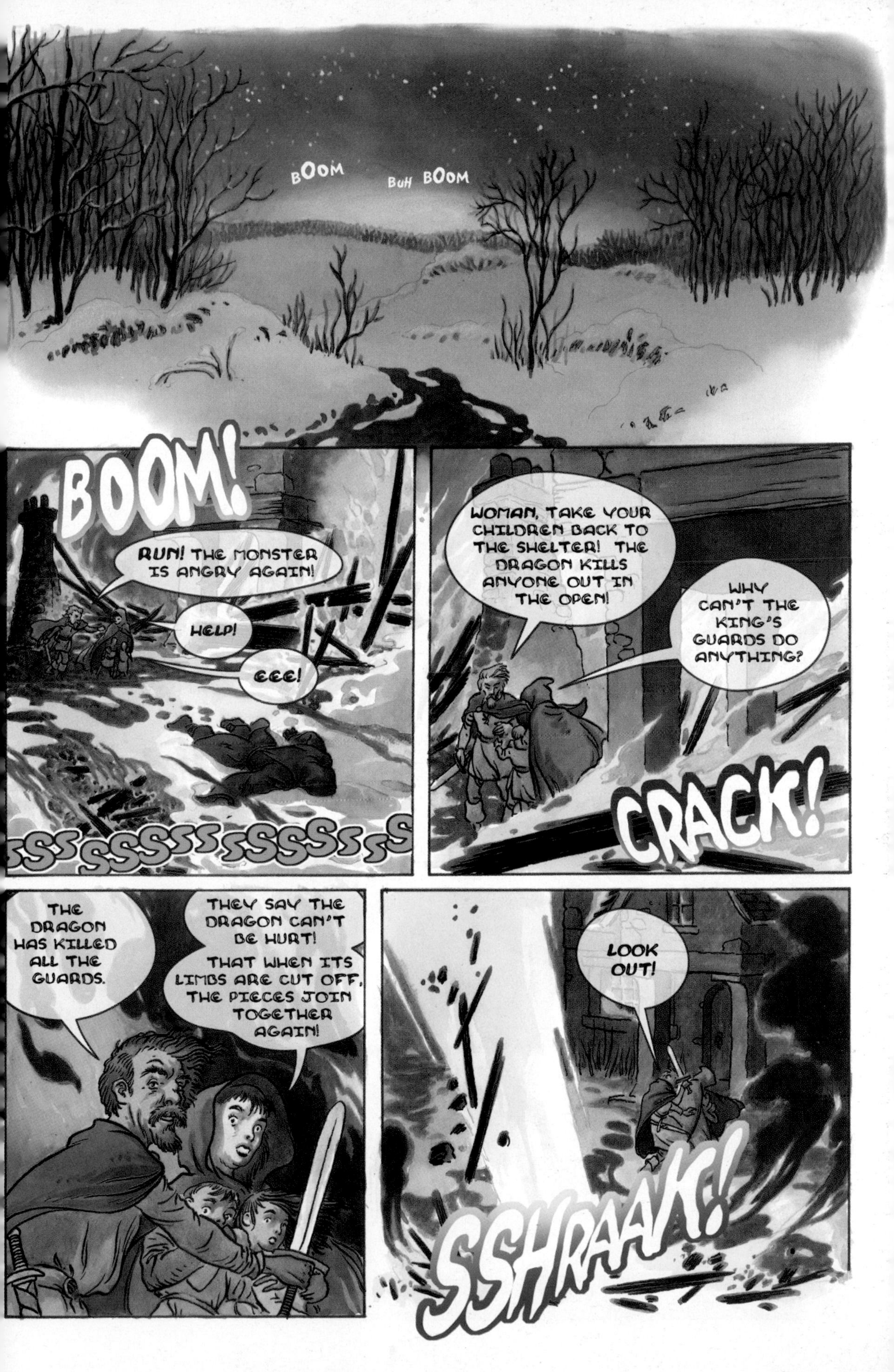
bOOM
BuH bOOM
BOOM!
RUN! THE MONSTER IS ANGRY AGAIN!
HELP!
EEE!
SSSSSSSSSSSSSSS
WOMAN, TAKE YOUR CHILDREN BACK TO THE SHELTER! THE DRAGON KILLS ANYONE OUT IN THE OPEN!
WHY CAN'T THE KING'S GUARDS DO ANYTHING?
CRACK!
THE DRAGON HAS KILLED ALL THE GUARDS.
THEY SAY THE DRAGON CAN'T BE HURT!
THAT WHEN ITS LIMBS ARE CUT OFF, THE PIECES JOIN TOGETHER AGAIN!
LOOK OUT!
SSHRAAK!

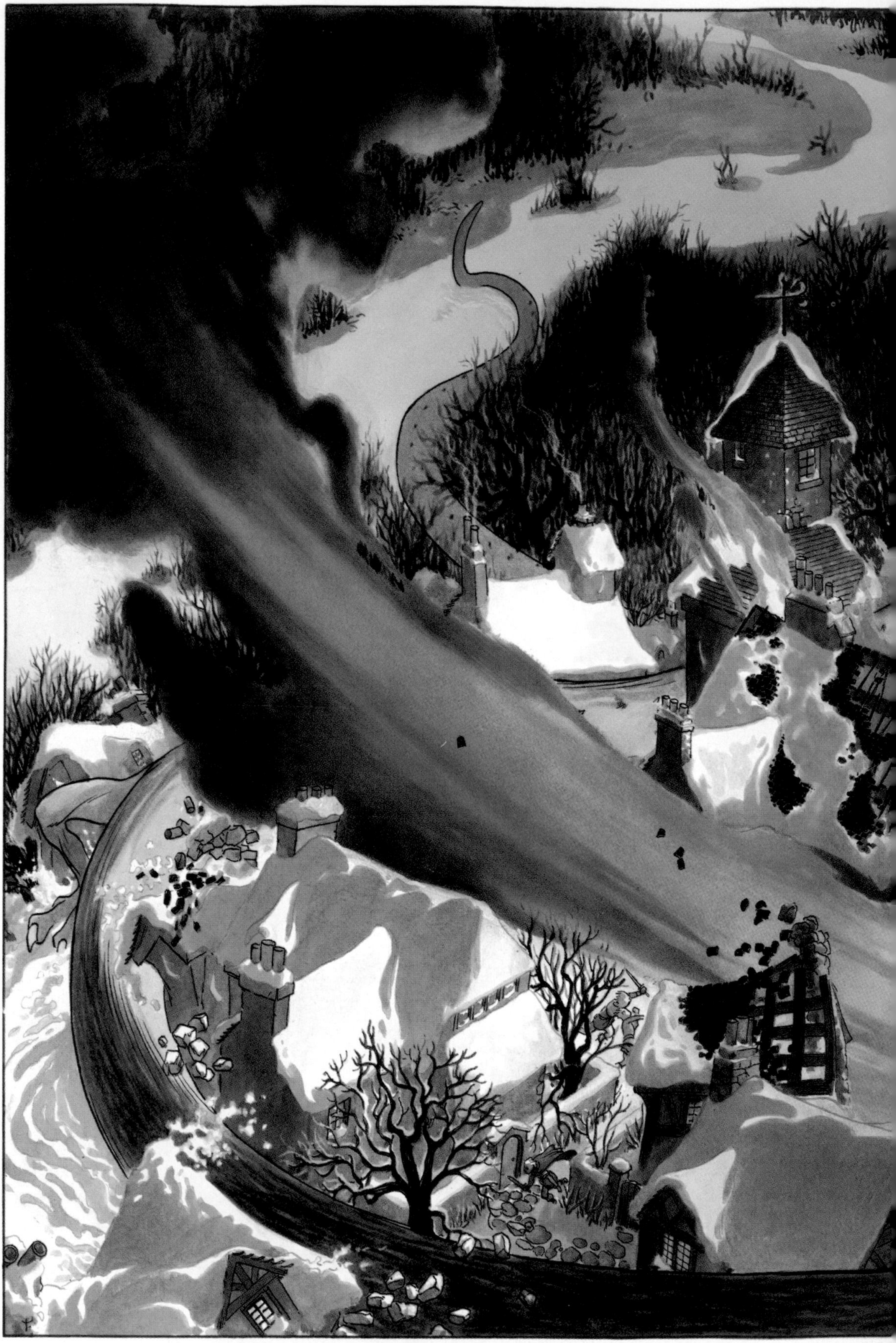

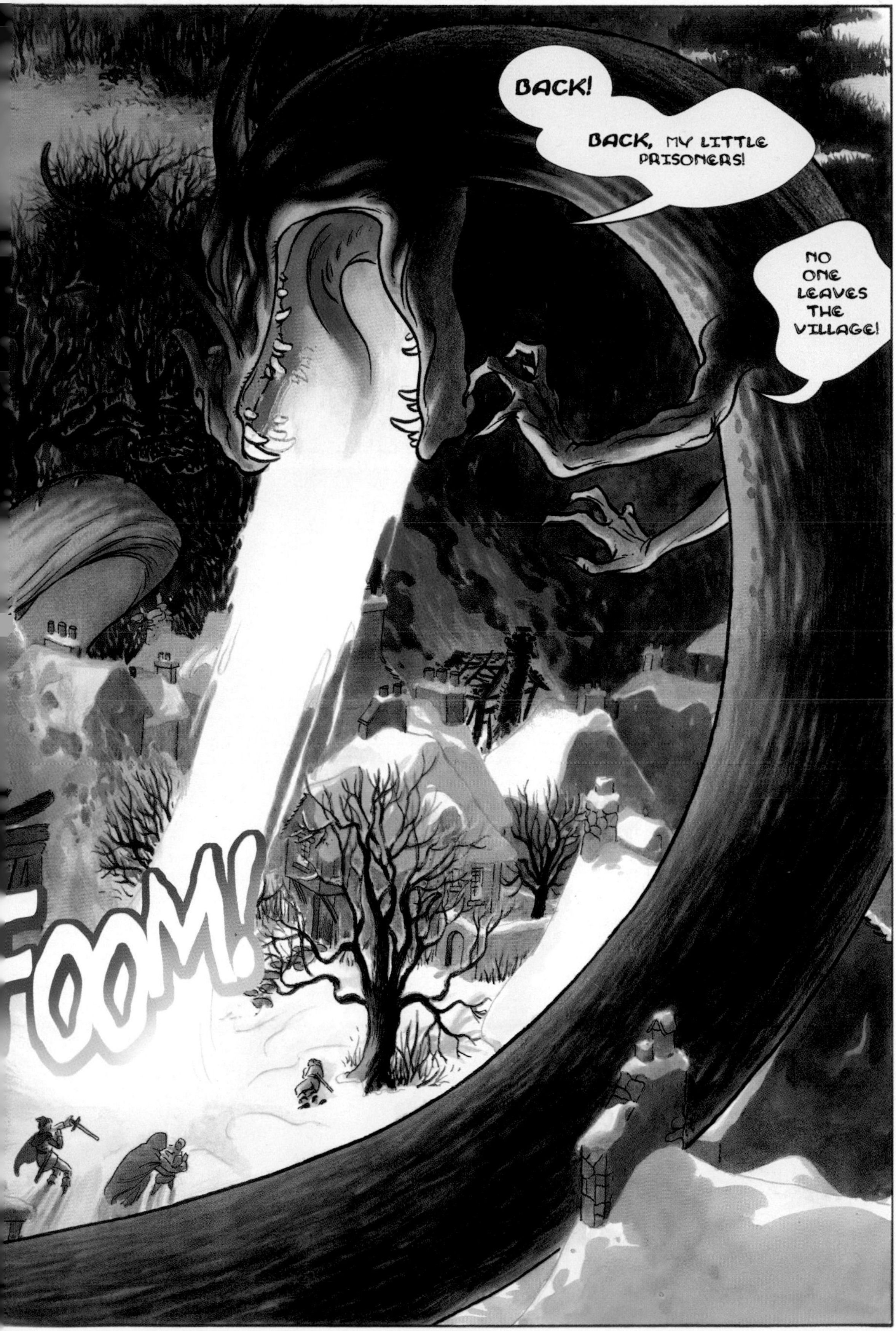
BACK!
BACK, MY LITTLE PRISONERS!
NO ONE LEAVES THE VILLAGE!
FOOM!

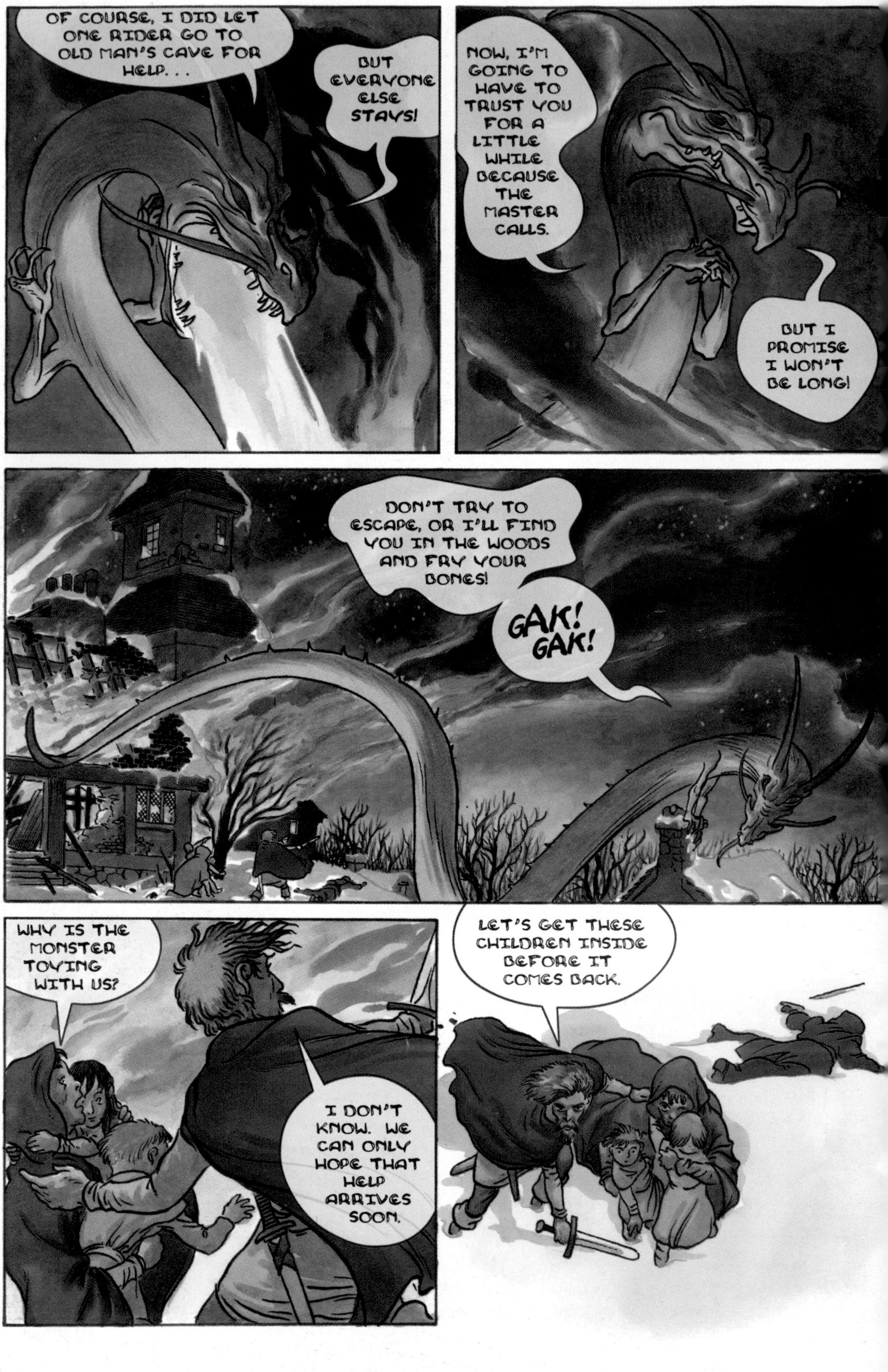
OF COURSE, I DID LET ONE RIDER GO TO OLD MAN'S CAVE FOR HELP. . .
BUT EVERYONE ELSE STAYS!
NOW, I'M GOING TO HAVE TO TRUST YOU FOR A LITTLE WHILE BECAUSE THE MASTER CALLS.
BUT I PROMISE I WON'T BE LONG!
DON'T TRY TO ESCAPE, OR I'LL FIND YOU IN THE WOODS AND FRY YOUR BONES!
GAK! GAK!
WHY IS THE MONSTER TOYING WITH US?
I DON'T KNOW. WE CAN ONLY HOPE THAT HELP ARRIVES SOON.
LET'S GET THESE CHILDREN INSIDE BEFORE IT COMES BACK.

The Pact

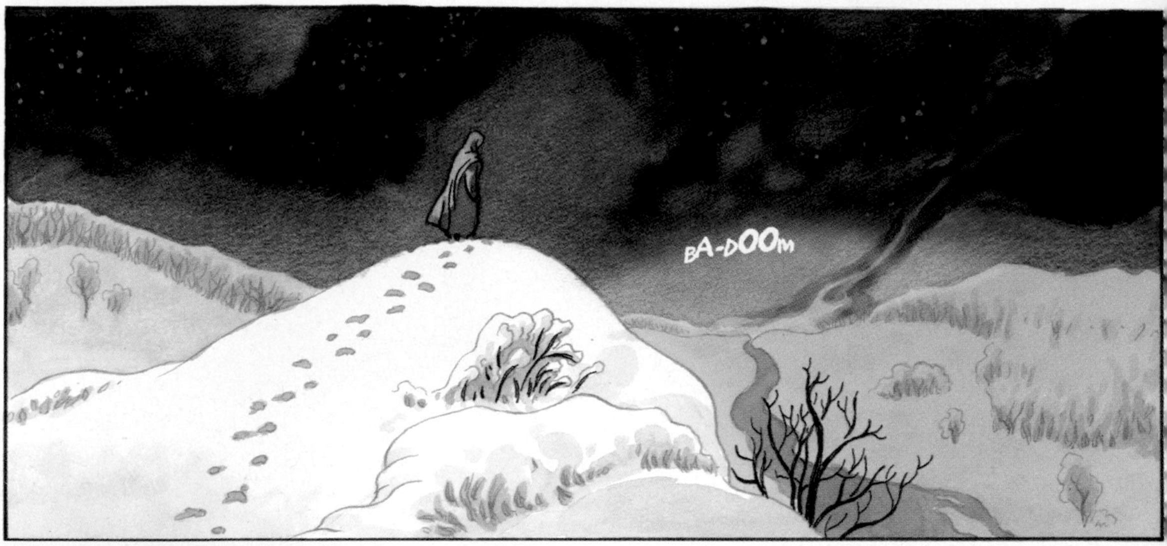
BA-DOOM

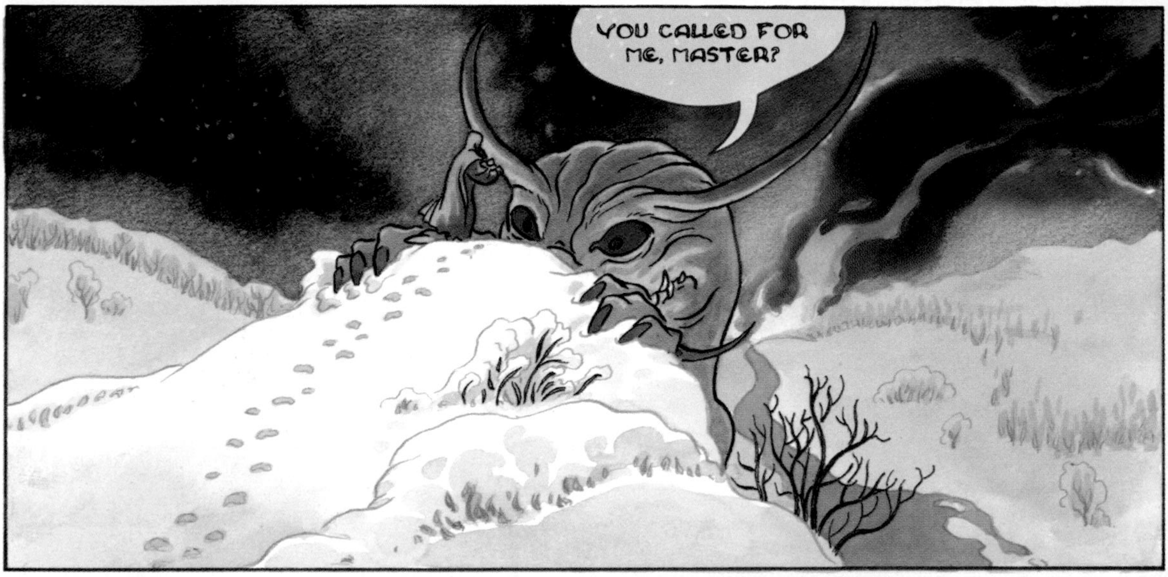
YOU CALLED FOR ME, MASTER?

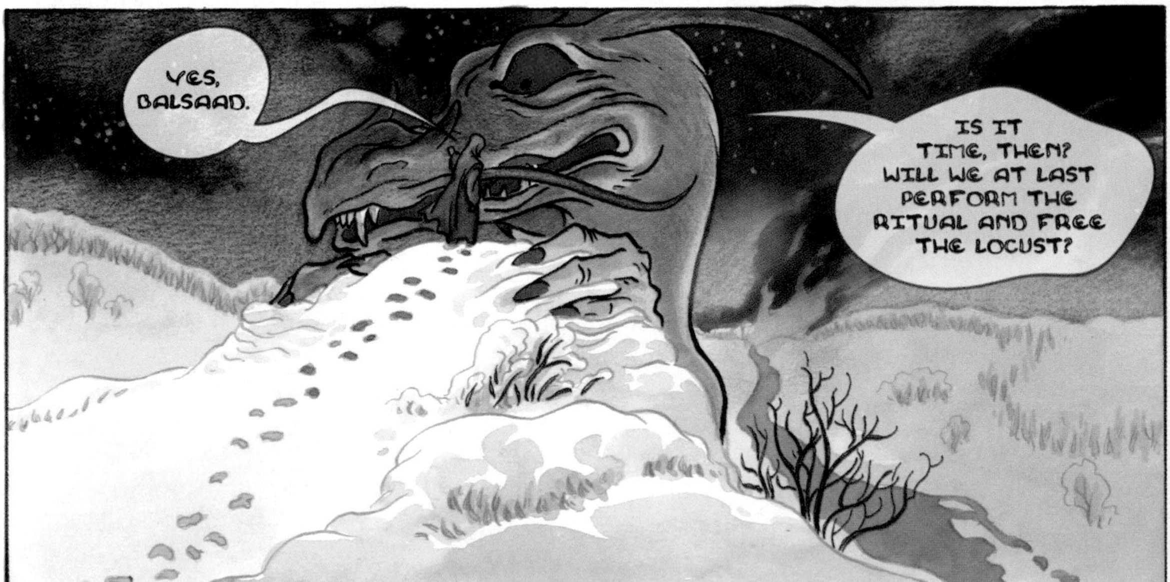
YES, BALSAAD.
IS IT TIME, THEN? WILL WE AT LAST PERFORM THE RITUAL AND FREE THE LOCUST?

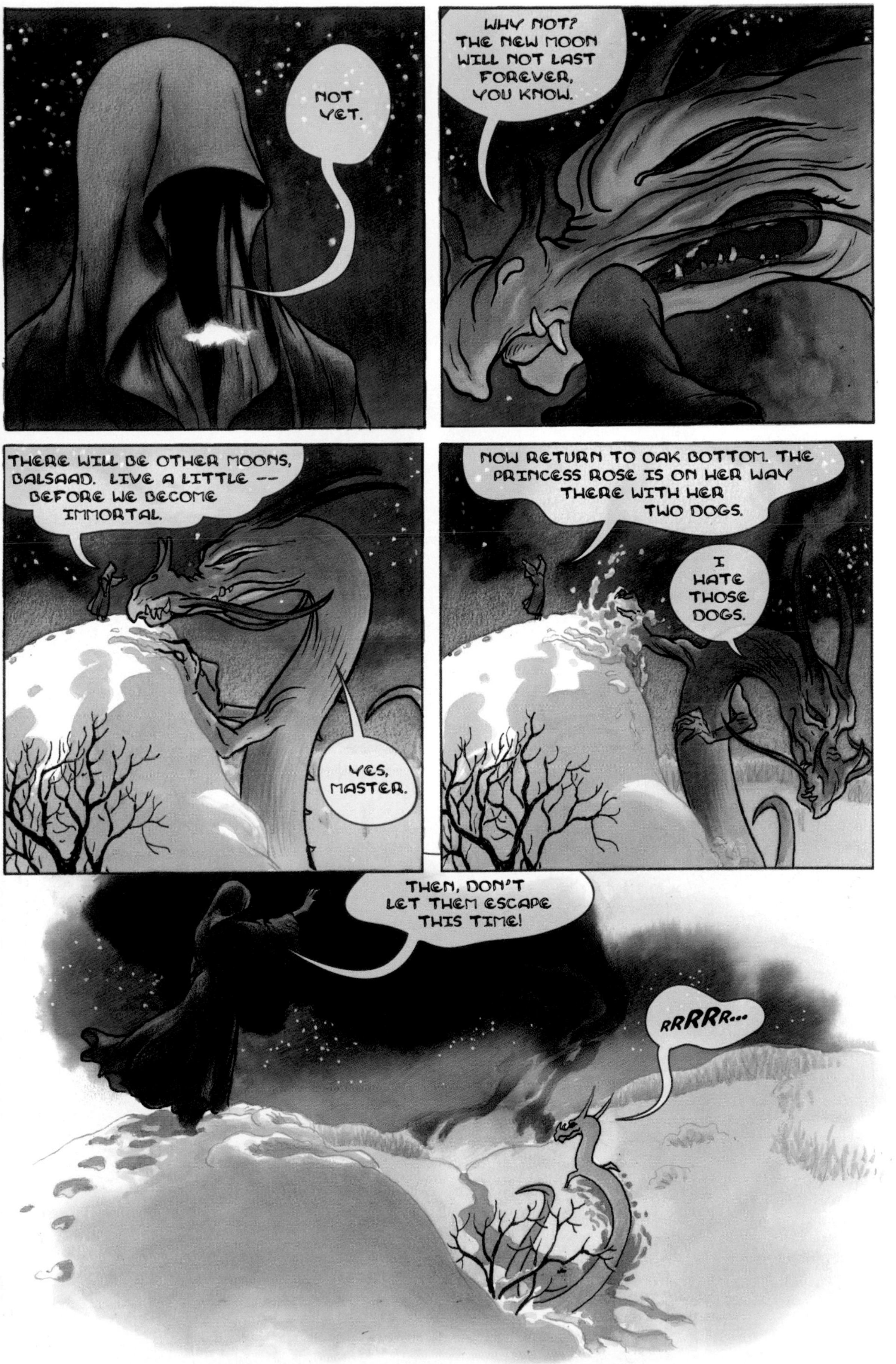
NOT YET.
WHY NOT? THE NEW MOON WILL NOT LAST FOREVER, YOU KNOW.
THERE WILL BE OTHER MOONS, BALSAAD. LIVE A LITTLE -- BEFORE WE BECOME IMMORTAL.
YES, MASTER.
NOW RETURN TO OAK BOTTOM. THE PRINCESS ROSE IS ON HER WAY THERE WITH HER TWO DOGS.
I HATE THOSE DOGS.
THEN, DON'T LET THEM ESCAPE THIS TIME!
RRRRR...

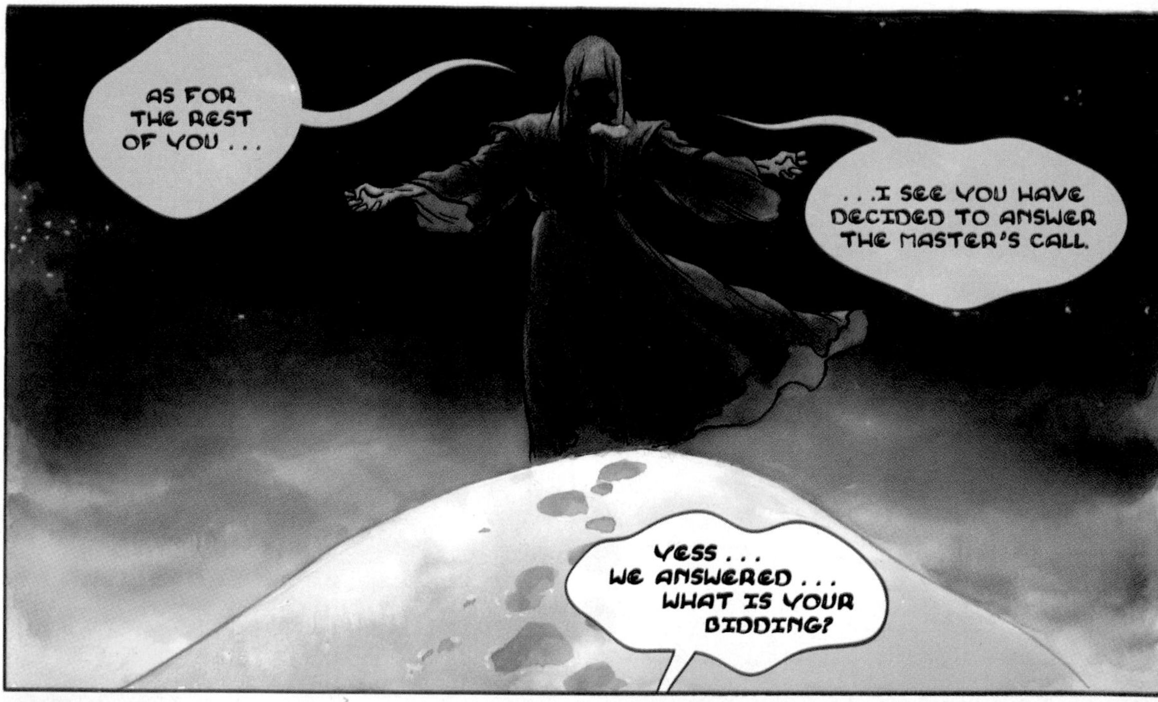
AS FOR THE REST OF YOU . . .
. . .I SEE YOU HAVE DECIDED TO ANSWER THE MASTER'S CALL.
YESS . . . WE ANSWERED . . . WHAT IS YOUR BIDDING?

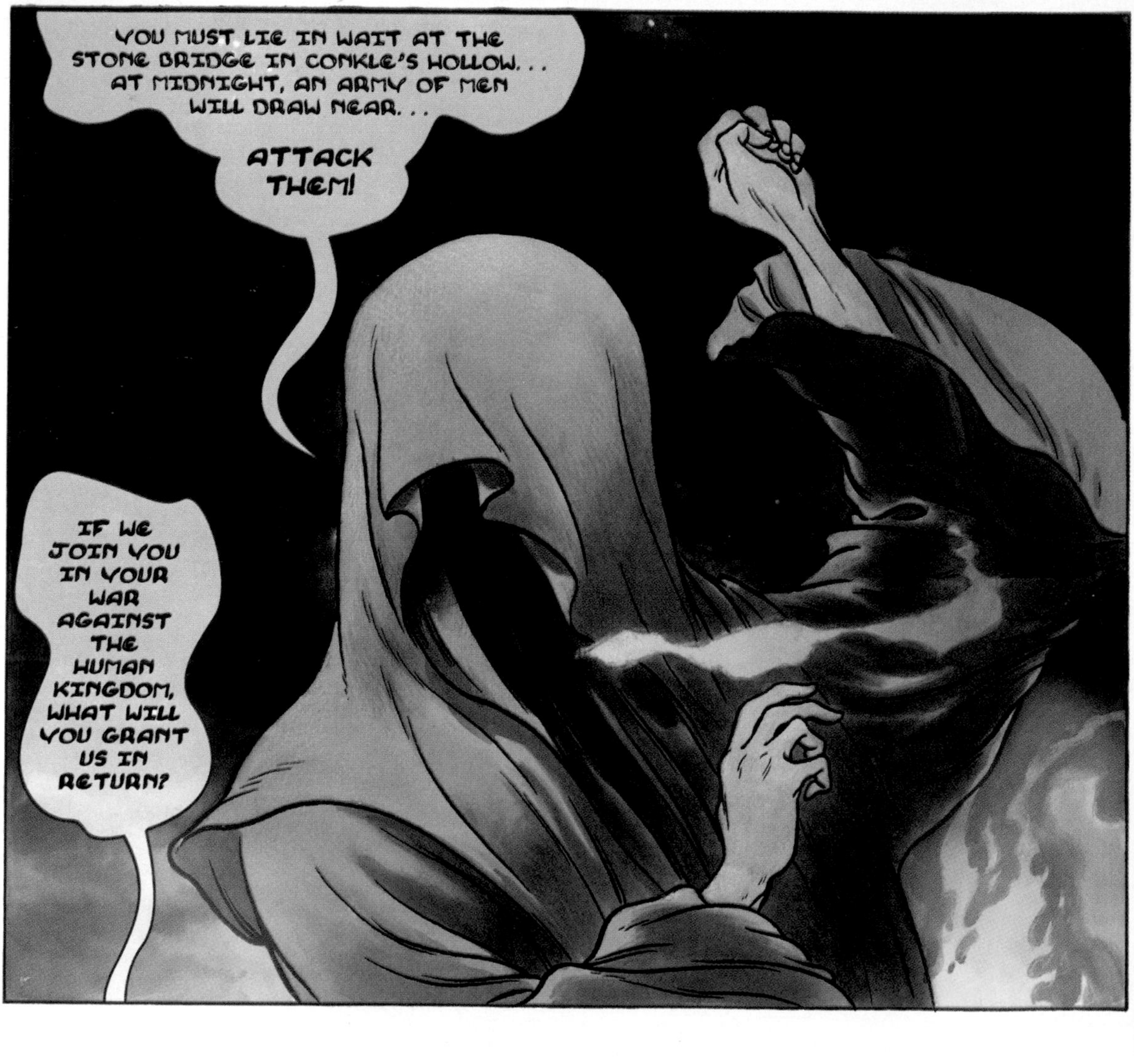
YOU MUST LIE IN WAIT AT THE STONE BRIDGE IN CONKLE'S HOLLOW. . . AT MIDNIGHT, AN ARMY OF MEN WILL DRAW NEAR. . .
ATTACK THEM!
IF WE JOIN YOU IN YOUR WAR AGAINST THE HUMAN KINGDOM, WHAT WILL YOU GRANT US IN RETURN?

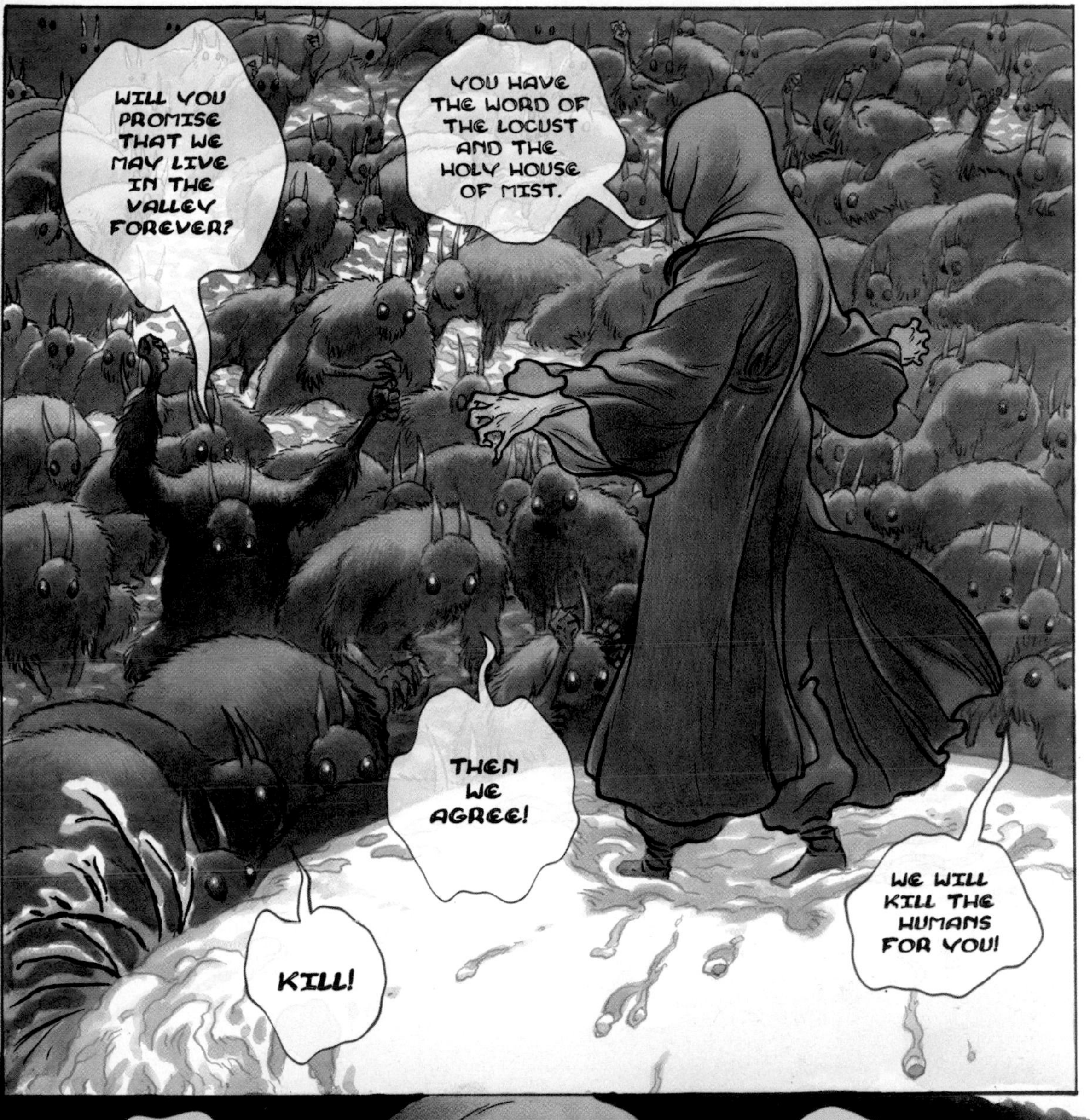
WILL YOU PROMISE THAT WE MAY LIVE IN THE VALLEY FOREVER?
YOU HAVE THE WORD OF THE LOCUST AND THE HOLY HOUSE OF MIST.
THEN WE AGREE!
KILL!
WE WILL KILL THE HUMANS FOR YOU!
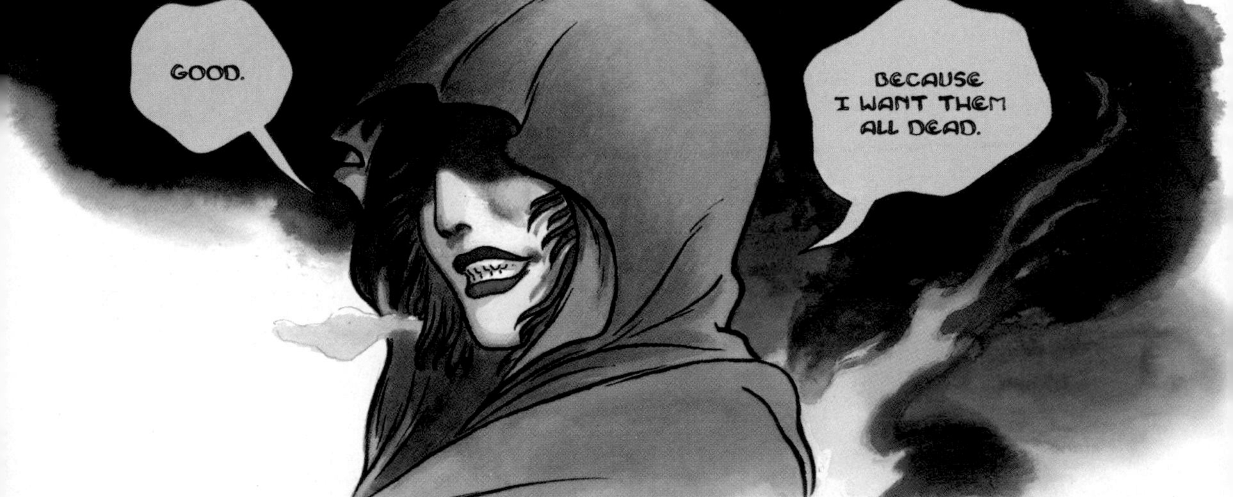
GOOD.
BECAUSE I WANT THEM ALL DEAD.

FROZEN

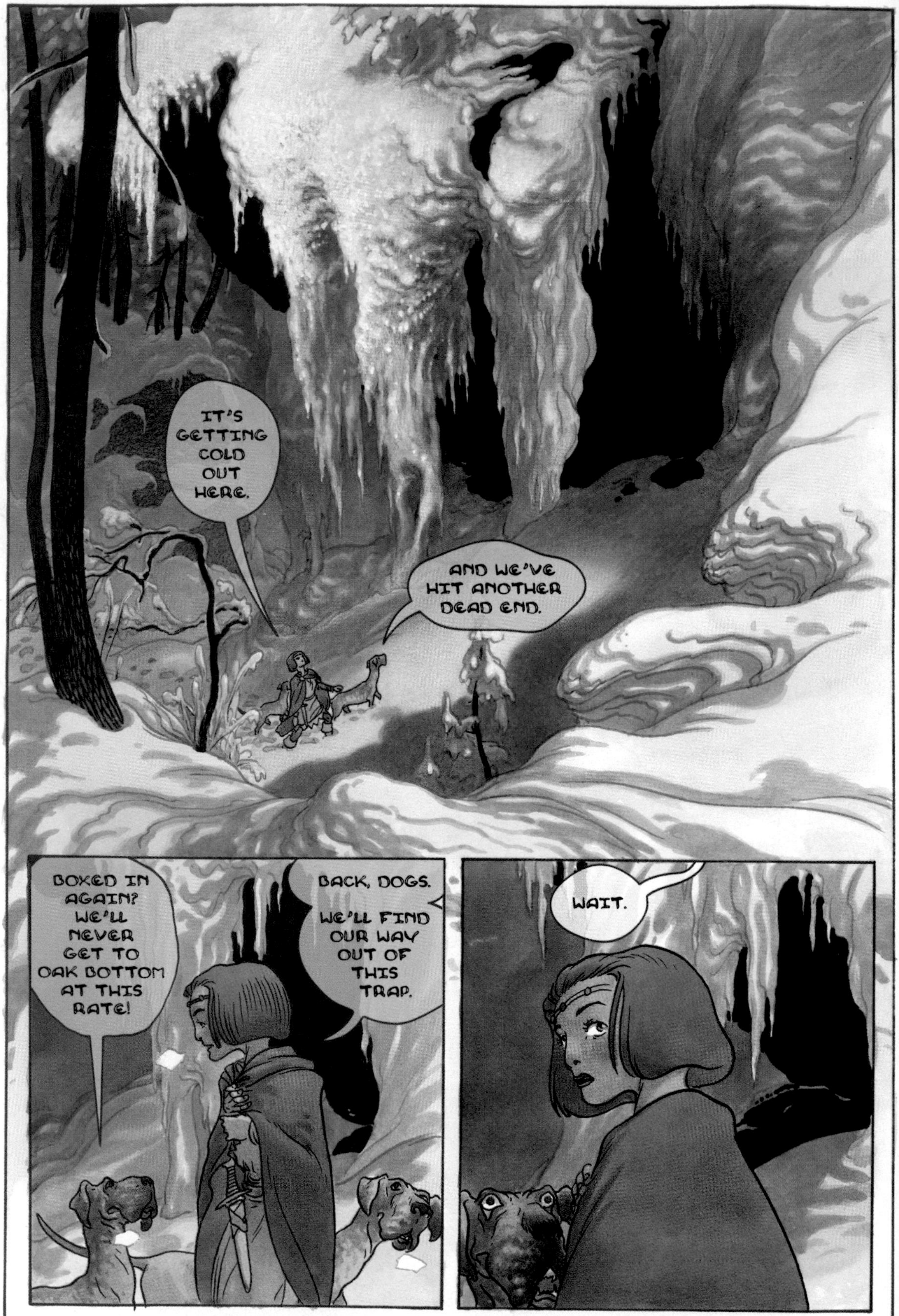
IT'S GETTING COLD OUT HERE.
AND WE'VE HIT ANOTHER DEAD END.
BOXED IN AGAIN? WE'LL NEVER GET TO OAK BOTTOM AT THIS RATE!
BACK, DOGS.
WE'LL FIND OUR WAY OUT OF THIS TRAP.
WAIT.

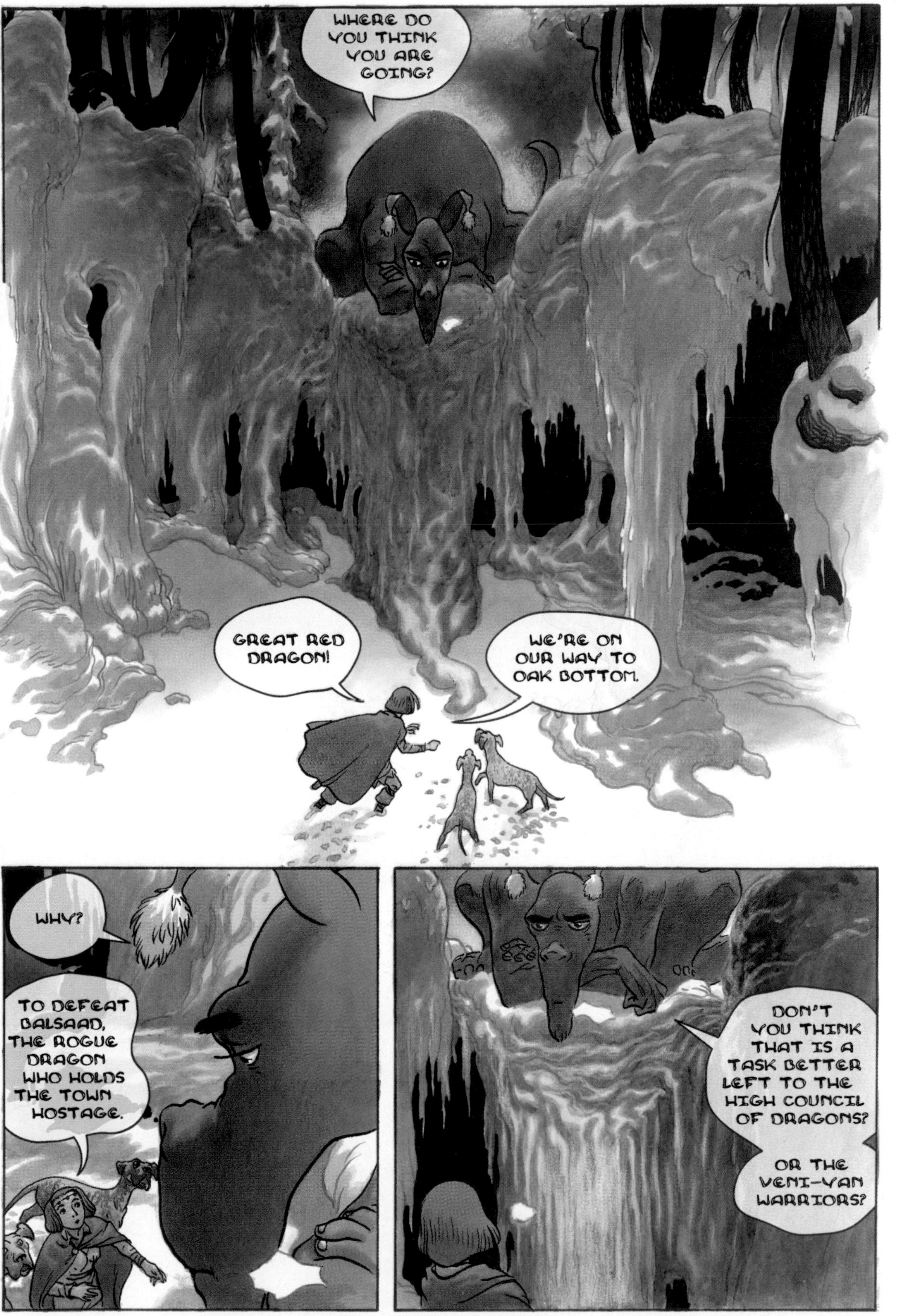
WHERE DO YOU THINK YOU ARE GOING?
GREAT RED DRAGON!
WE'RE ON OUR WAY TO OAK BOTTOM.
WHY?
TO DEFEAT BALSAAD, THE ROGUE DRAGON WHO HOLDS THE TOWN HOSTAGE.
DON'T YOU THINK THAT IS A TASK BETTER LEFT TO THE HIGH COUNCIL OF DRAGONS?
OR THE VENI-YAN WARRIORS?

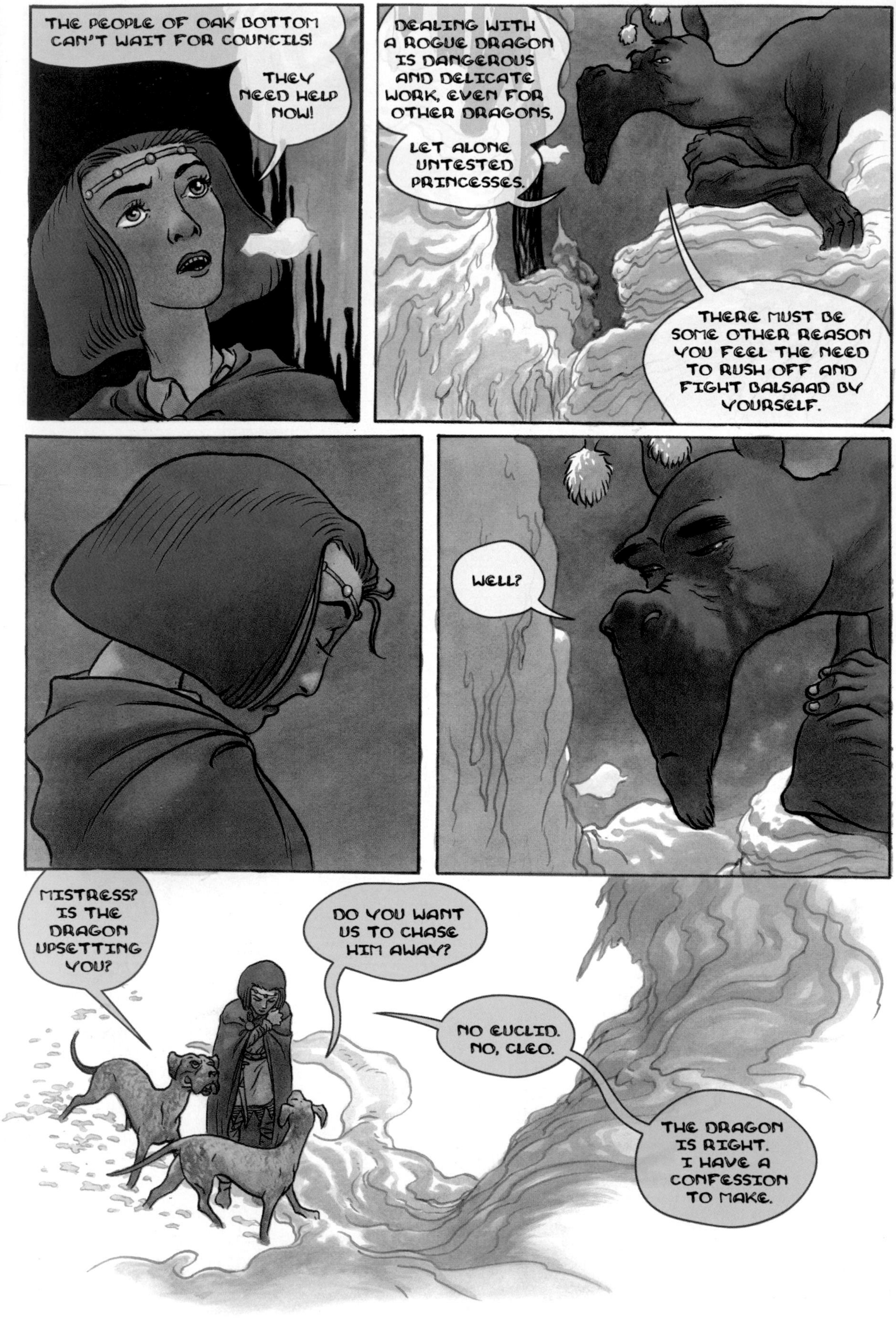
THE PEOPLE OF OAK BOTTOM CAN'T WAIT FOR COUNCILS!
THEY NEED HELP NOW!
DEALING WITH A ROGUE DRAGON IS DANGEROUS AND DELICATE WORK, EVEN FOR OTHER DRAGONS,
LET ALONE UNTESTED PRINCESSES.
THERE MUST BE SOME OTHER REASON YOU FEEL THE NEED TO RUSH OFF AND FIGHT BALSAAD BY YOURSELF.
WELL?
MISTRESS? IS THE DRAGON UPSETTING YOU?
DO YOU WANT US TO CHASE HIM AWAY?
NO EUCLID. NO, CLEO.
THE DRAGON IS RIGHT. I HAVE A CONFESSION TO MAKE.

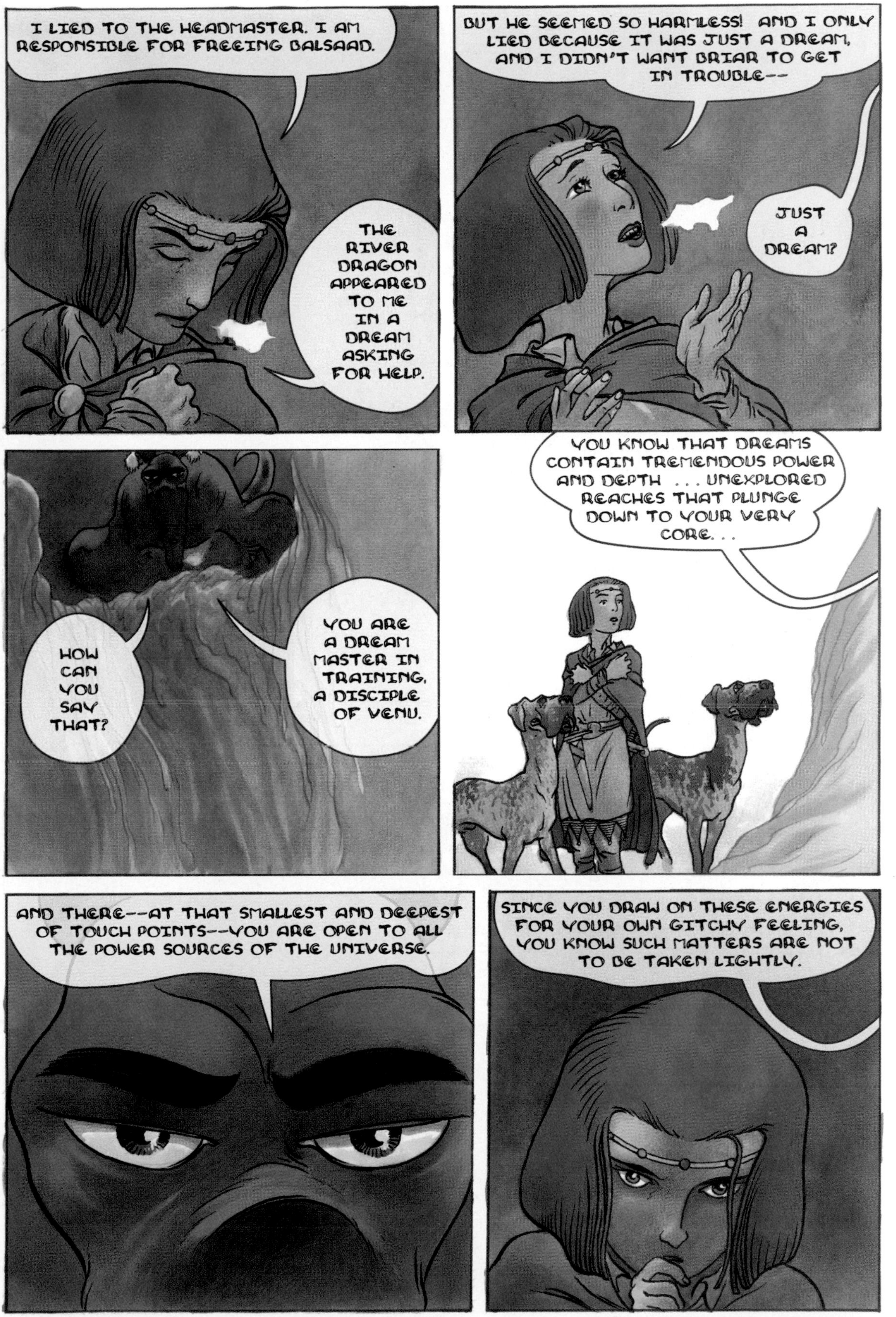
I LIED TO THE HEADMASTER. I AM RESPONSIBLE FOR FREEING BALSAAD.
THE RIVER DRAGON APPEARED TO ME IN A DREAM ASKING FOR HELP.
BUT HE SEEMED SO HARMLESS! AND I ONLY LIED BECAUSE IT WAS JUST A DREAM, AND I DIDN'T WANT BRIAR TO GET IN TROUBLE--
JUST A DREAM?
HOW CAN YOU SAY THAT?
YOU ARE A DREAM MASTER IN TRAINING, A DISCIPLE OF VENU.
YOU KNOW THAT DREAMS CONTAIN TREMENDOUS POWER AND DEPTH . . . UNEXPLORED REACHES THAT PLUNGE DOWN TO YOUR VERY CORE. . .
AND THERE--AT THAT SMALLEST AND DEEPEST OF TOUCH POINTS--YOU ARE OPEN TO ALL THE POWER SOURCES OF THE UNIVERSE.
SINCE YOU DRAW ON THESE ENERGIES FOR YOUR OWN GITCHY FEELING, YOU KNOW SUCH MATTERS ARE NOT TO BE TAKEN LIGHTLY.

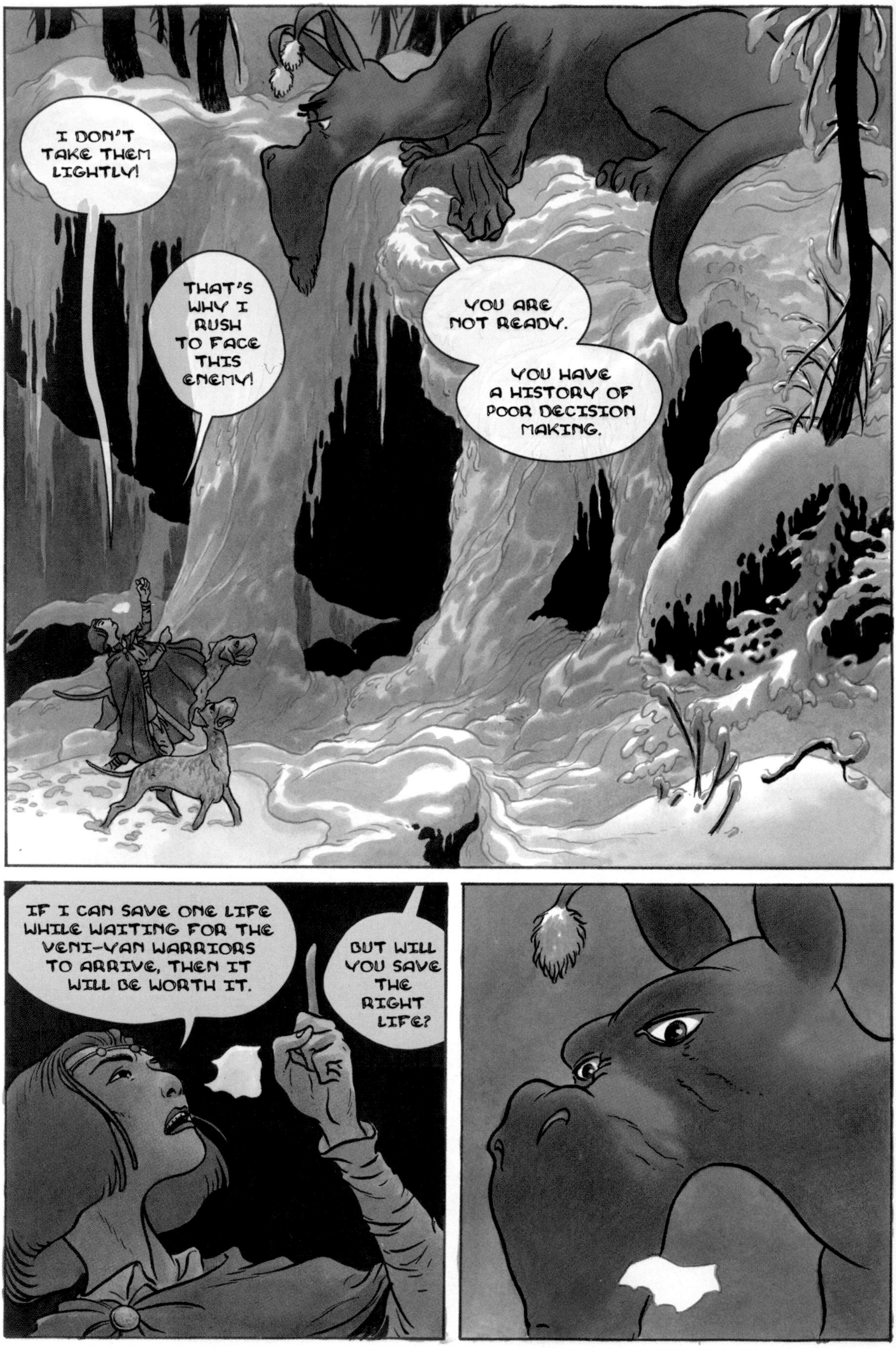
I DON'T TAKE THEM LIGHTLY!
THAT'S WHY I RUSH TO FACE THIS ENEMY!
YOU ARE NOT READY.
YOU HAVE A HISTORY OF POOR DECISION MAKING.
IF I CAN SAVE ONE LIFE WHILE WAITING FOR THE VENI-YAN WARRIORS TO ARRIVE, THEN IT WILL BE WORTH IT.
BUT WILL YOU SAVE THE RIGHT LIFE?

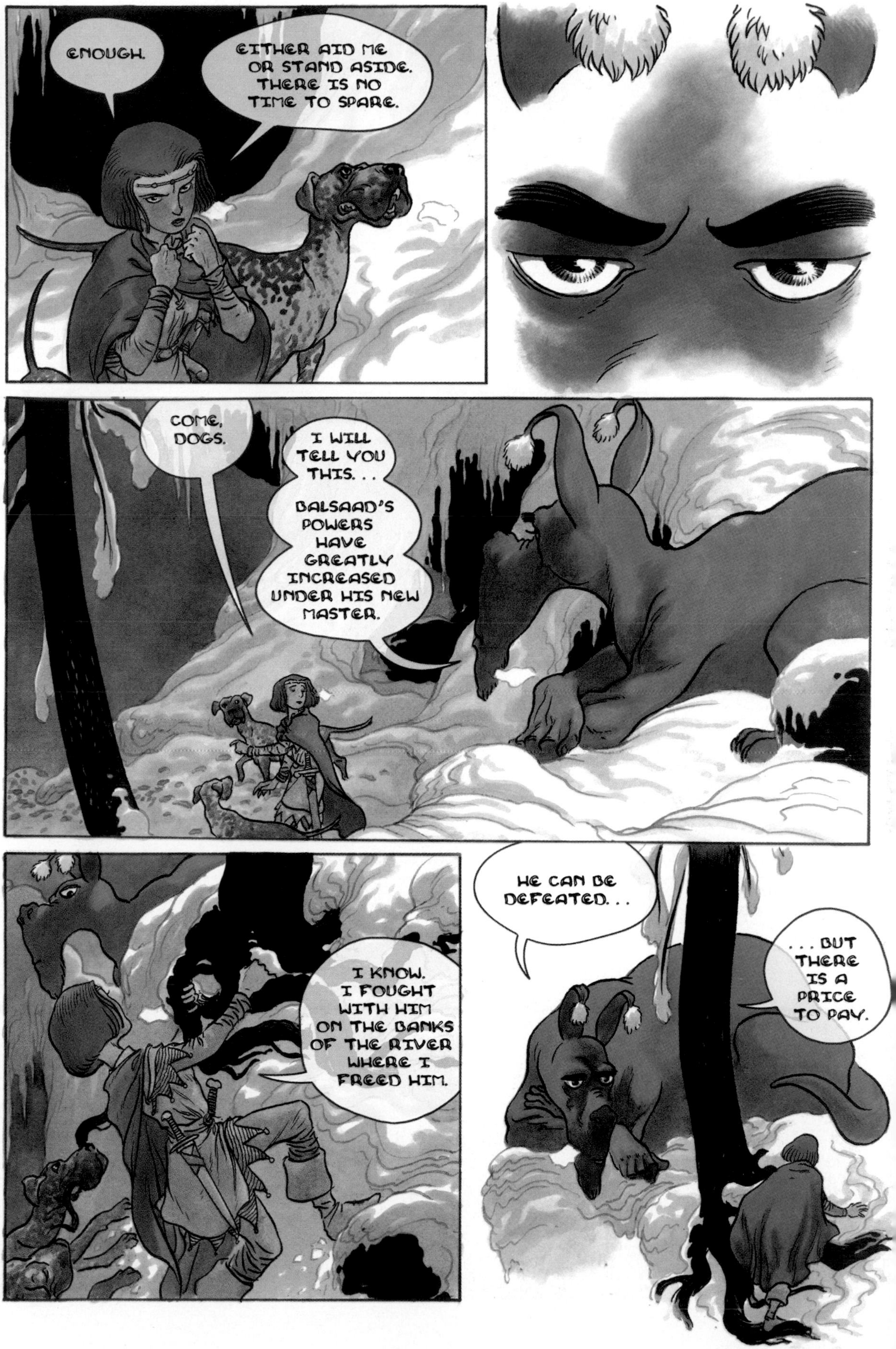
ENOUGH.
EITHER AID ME OR STAND ASIDE. THERE IS NO TIME TO SPARE.
COME, DOGS.
I WILL TELL YOU THIS. . .
BALSAAD'S POWERS HAVE GREATLY INCREASED UNDER HIS NEW MASTER.
I KNOW. I FOUGHT WITH HIM ON THE BANKS OF THE RIVER WHERE I FREED HIM.
HE CAN BE DEFEATED. . .
. . . BUT THERE IS A PRICE TO PAY.

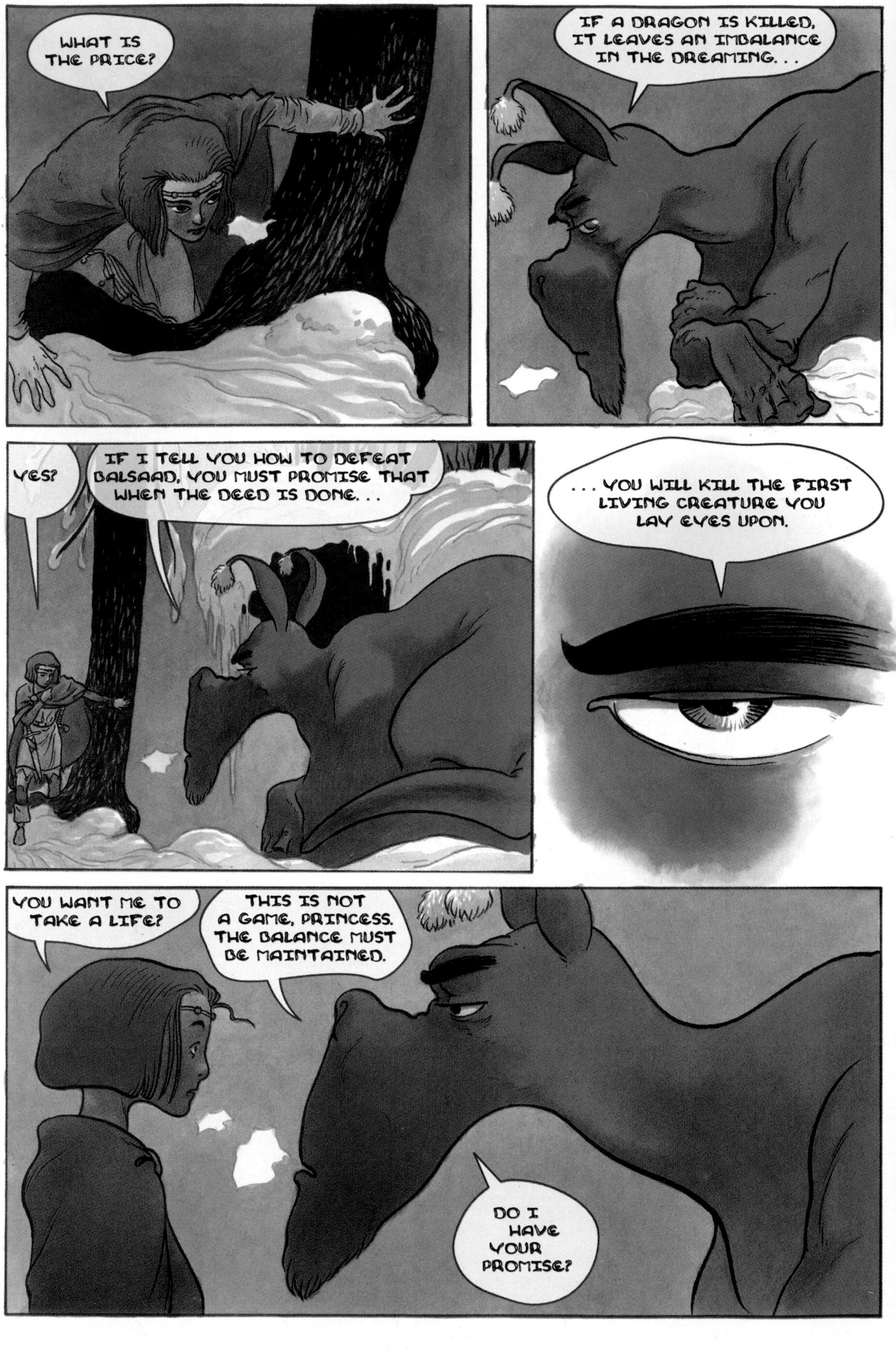
WHAT IS THE PRICE?
IF A DRAGON IS KILLED, IT LEAVES AN IMBALANCE IN THE DREAMING...
YES?
IF I TELL YOU HOW TO DEFEAT BALSAAD, YOU MUST PROMISE THAT WHEN THE DEED IS DONE...
...YOU WILL KILL THE FIRST LIVING CREATURE YOU LAY EYES UPON.
YOU WANT ME TO TAKE A LIFE?
THIS IS NOT A GAME, PRINCESS. THE BALANCE MUST BE MAINTAINED.
DO I HAVE YOUR PROMISE?

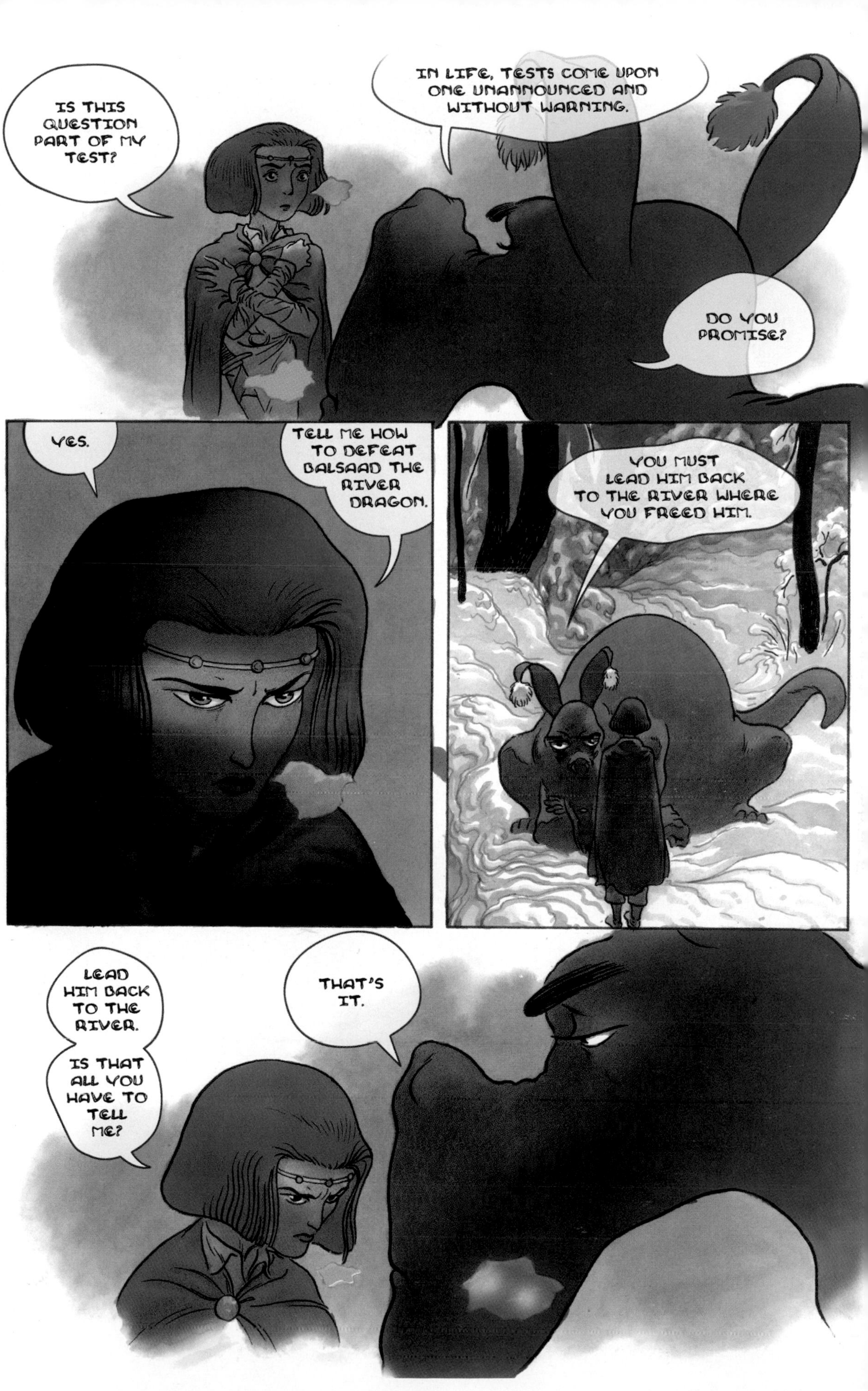
IS THIS QUESTION PART OF MY TEST?
IN LIFE, TESTS COME UPON ONE UNANNOUNCED AND WITHOUT WARNING.
DO YOU PROMISE?
YES.
TELL ME HOW TO DEFEAT BALSAAD THE RIVER DRAGON.
YOU MUST LEAD HIM BACK TO THE RIVER WHERE YOU FREED HIM.
LEAD HIM BACK TO THE RIVER.
IS THAT ALL YOU HAVE TO TELL ME?
THAT'S IT.

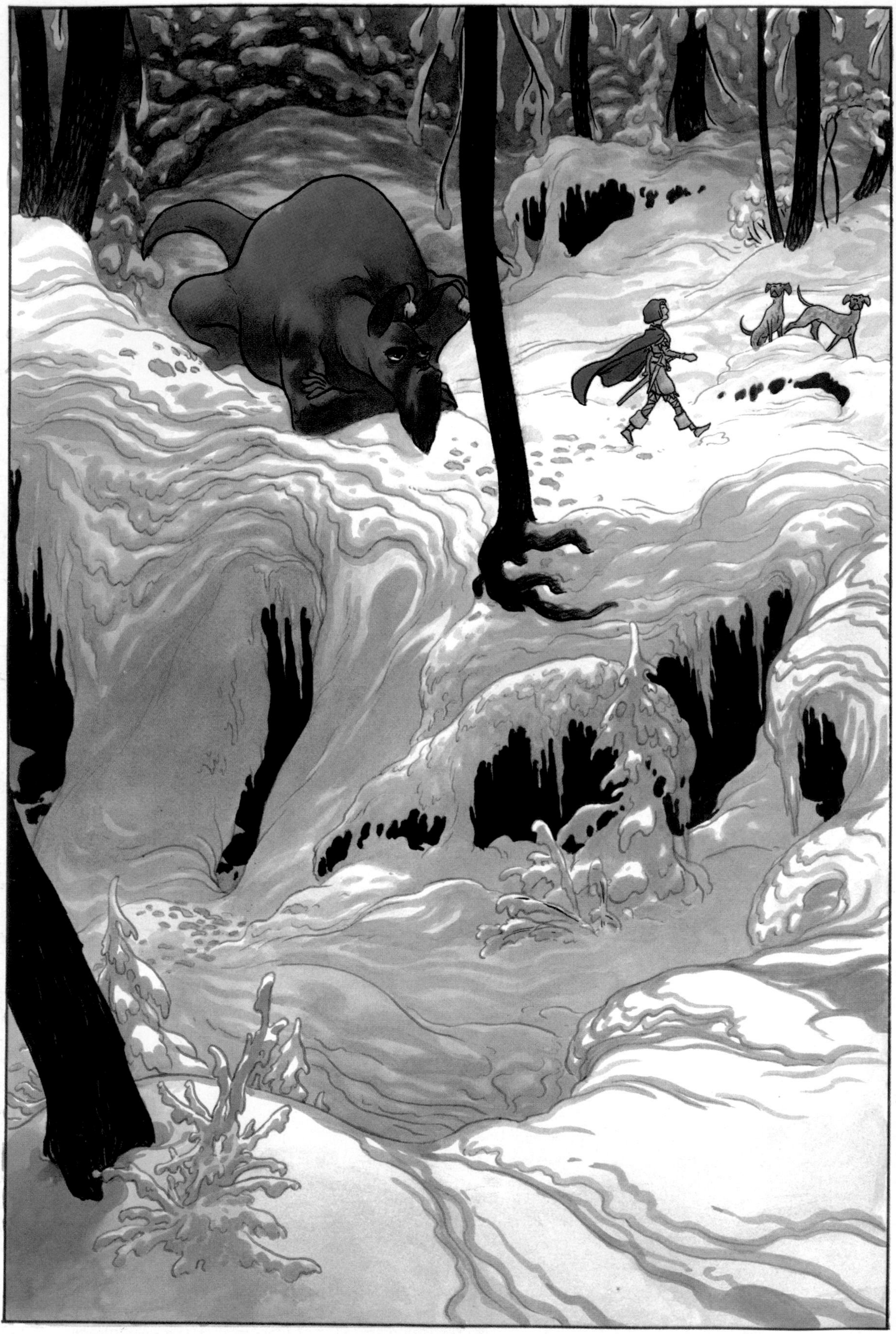

MIDNIGHT

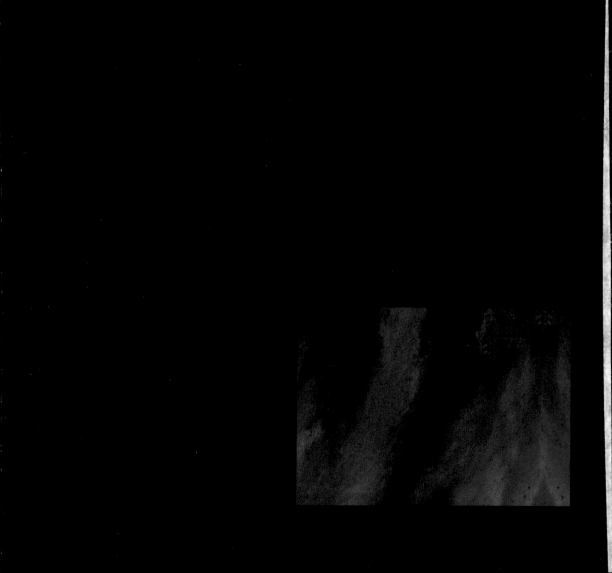

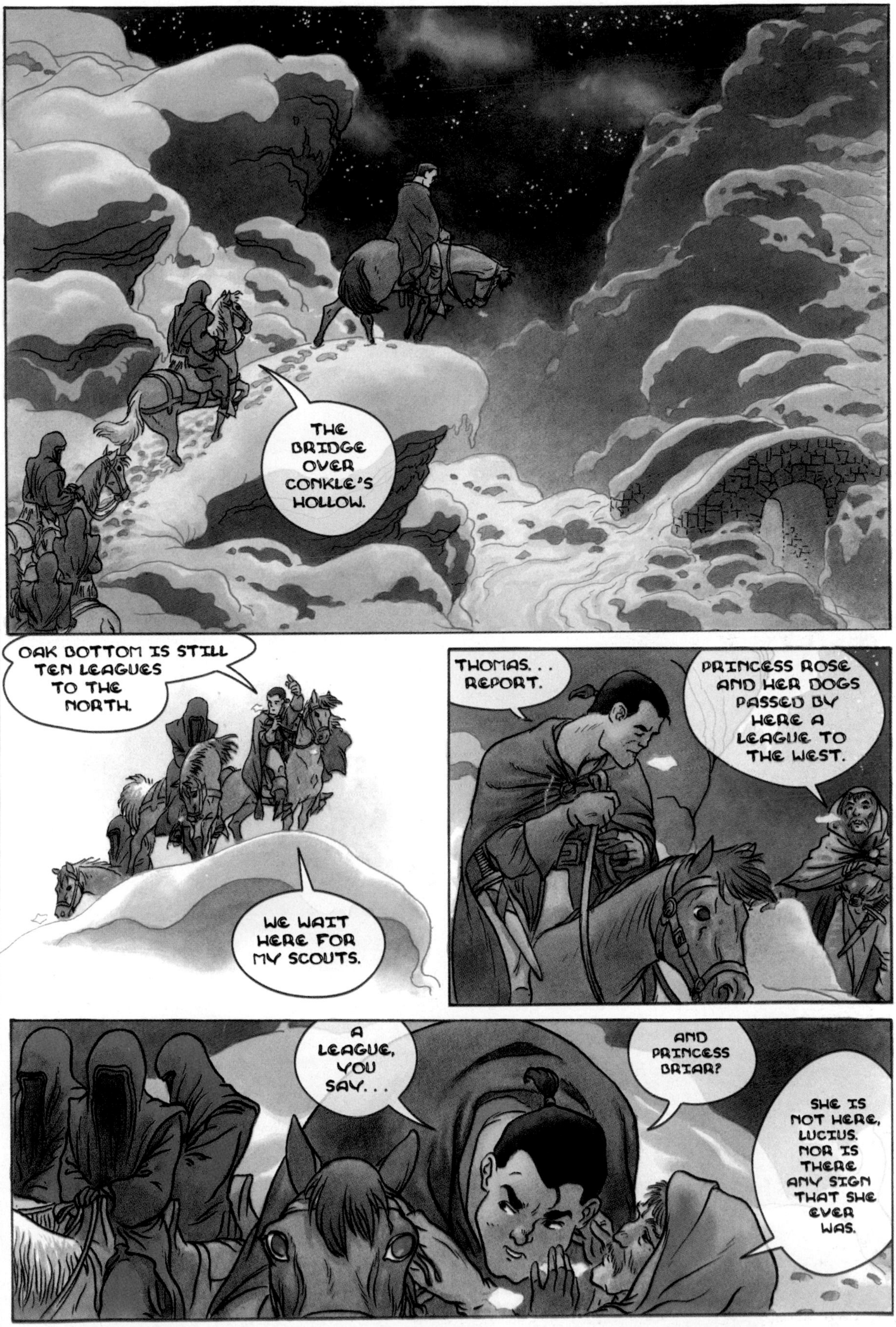
THE BRIDGE OVER CONKLE'S HOLLOW.
OAK BOTTOM IS STILL TEN LEAGUES TO THE NORTH.
WE WAIT HERE FOR MY SCOUTS.
THOMAS. . . REPORT.
PRINCESS ROSE AND HER DOGS PASSED BY HERE A LEAGUE TO THE WEST.
A LEAGUE, YOU SAY. . .
AND PRINCESS BRIAR?
SHE IS NOT HERE, LUCIUS. NOR IS THERE ANY SIGN THAT SHE EVER WAS.

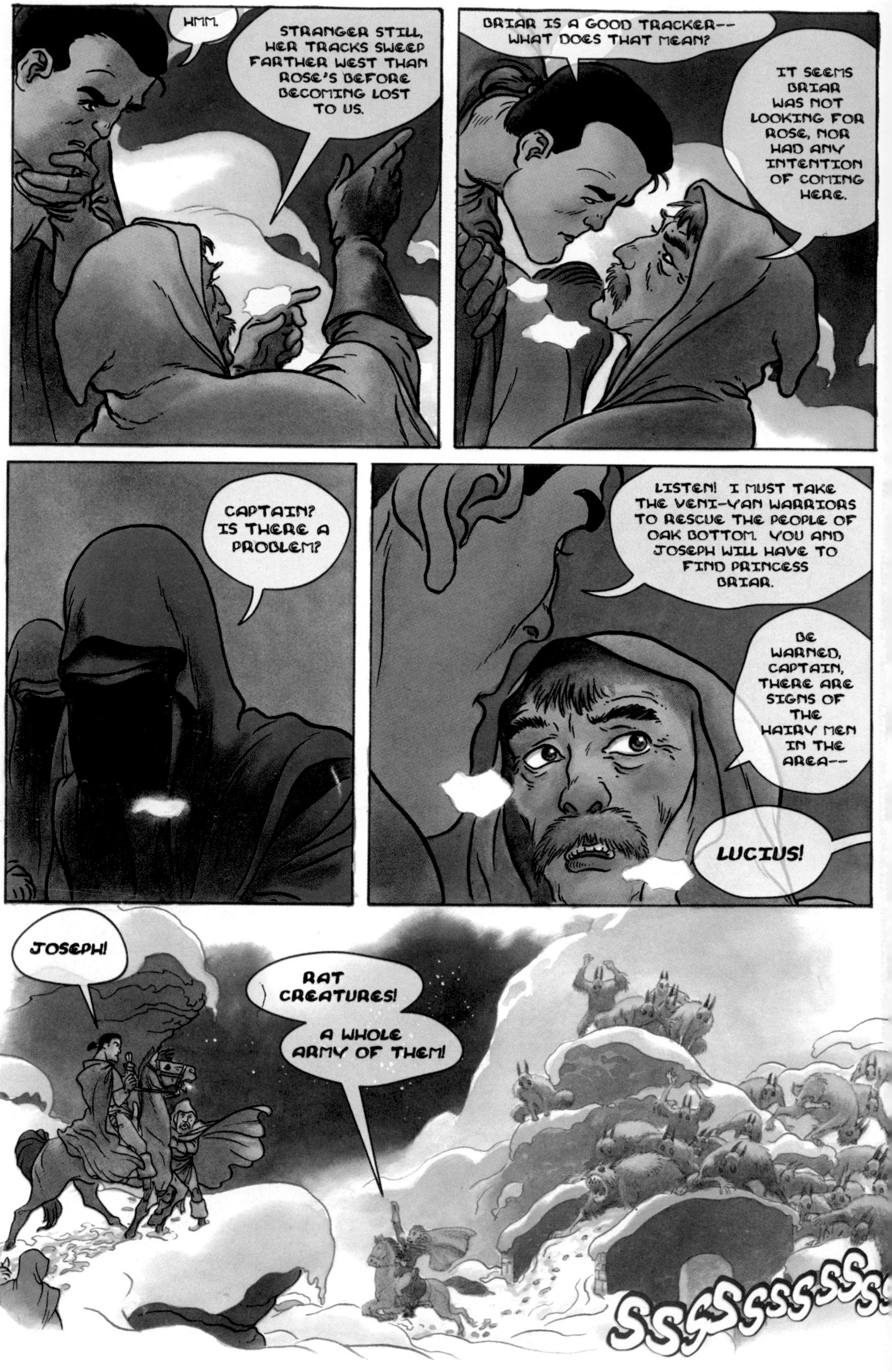
HMM.
STRANGER STILL, HER TRACKS SWEEP FARTHER WEST THAN ROSE'S BEFORE BECOMING LOST TO US.
BRIAR IS A GOOD TRACKER-- WHAT DOES THAT MEAN?
IT SEEMS BRIAR WAS NOT LOOKING FOR ROSE, NOR HAD ANY INTENTION OF COMING HERE.
CAPTAIN? IS THERE A PROBLEM?
LISTEN! I MUST TAKE THE VENI-YAN WARRIORS TO RESCUE THE PEOPLE OF OAK BOTTOM. YOU AND JOSEPH WILL HAVE TO FIND PRINCESS BRIAR.
BE WARNED, CAPTAIN, THERE ARE SIGNS OF THE HAIRY MEN IN THE AREA--
LUCIUS!
JOSEPH!
RAT CREATURES!
A WHOLE ARMY OF THEM!
SSSSSSSSSS

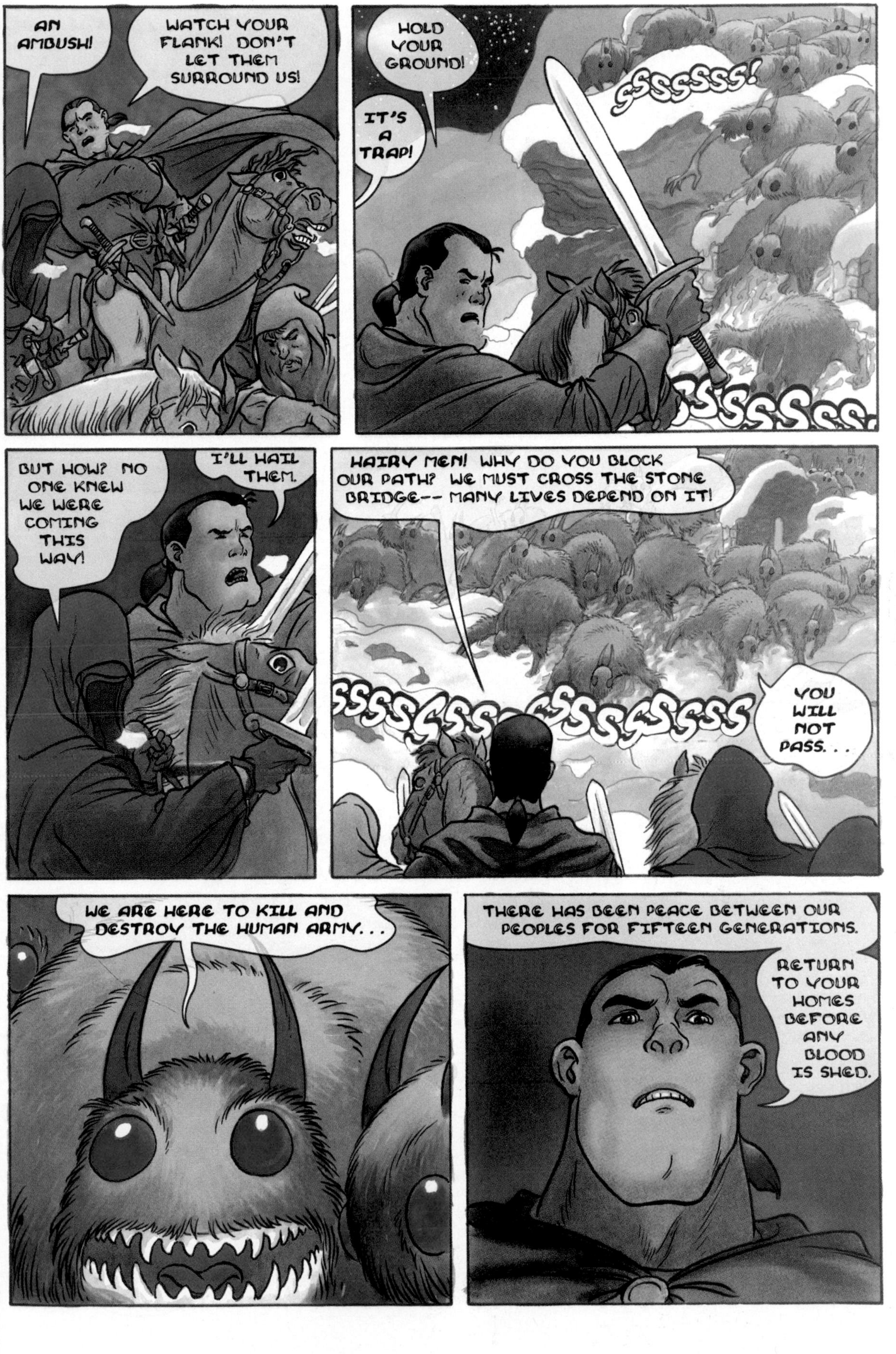
AN AMBUSH!
WATCH YOUR FLANK! DON'T LET THEM SURROUND US!
HOLD YOUR GROUND!
IT'S A TRAP!
SSSSSSS!
SSSSSSS
BUT HOW? NO ONE KNEW WE WERE COMING THIS WAY!
I'LL HAIL THEM.
HAIRY MEN! WHY DO YOU BLOCK OUR PATH? WE MUST CROSS THE STONE BRIDGE-- MANY LIVES DEPEND ON IT!
SSSSSSSS SSSSSSSS
YOU WILL NOT PASS. . .
WE ARE HERE TO KILL AND DESTROY THE HUMAN ARMY. . .
THERE HAS BEEN PEACE BETWEEN OUR PEOPLES FOR FIFTEEN GENERATIONS.
RETURN TO YOUR HOMES BEFORE ANY BLOOD IS SHED.

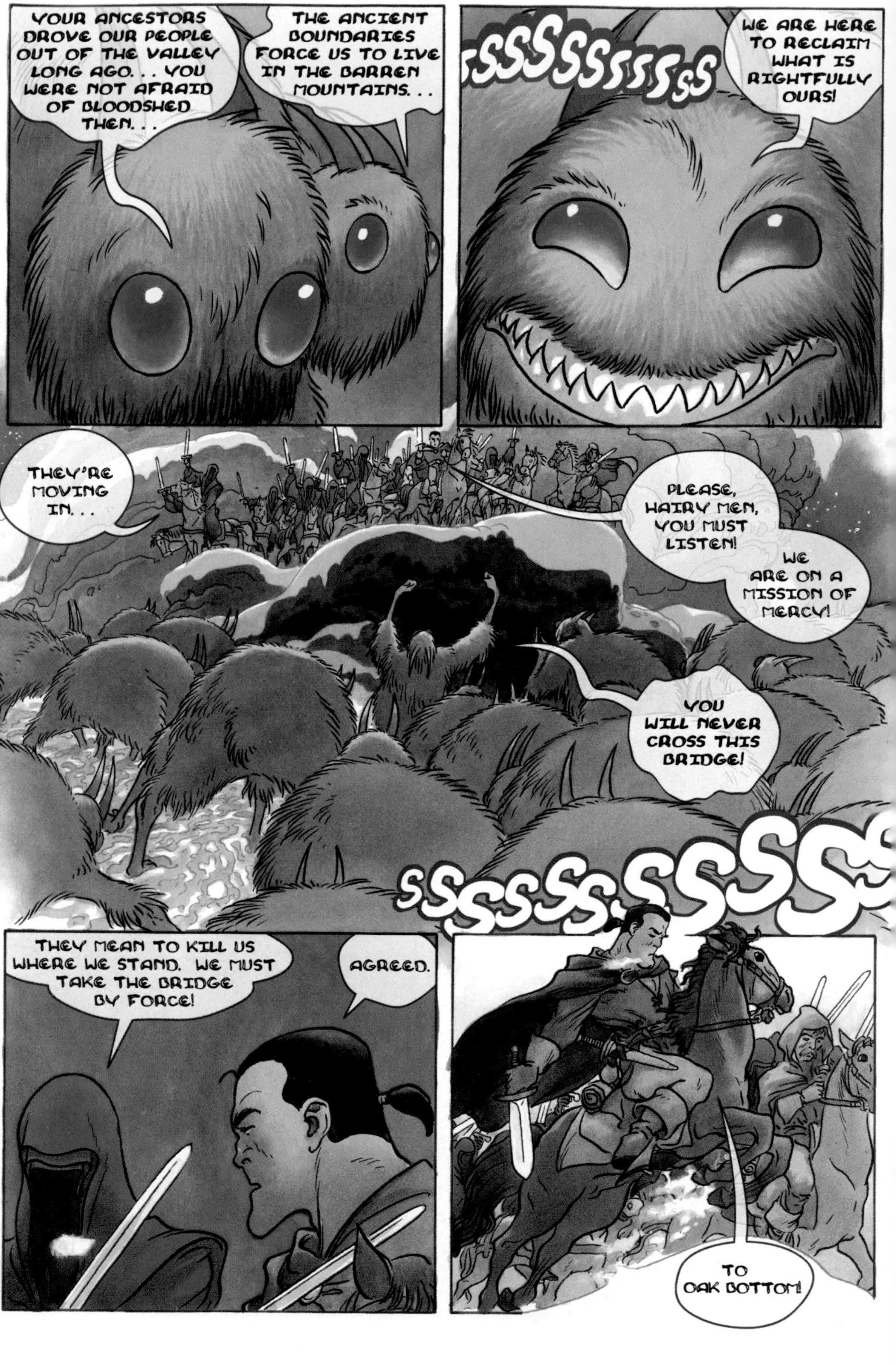

YOUR ANCESTORS DROVE OUR PEOPLE OUT OF THE VALLEY LONG AGO. . . YOU WERE NOT AFRAID OF BLOODSHED THEN. . .
THE ANCIENT BOUNDARIES FORCE US TO LIVE IN THE BARREN MOUNTAINS. . .
SSSSSSSSSSSSS
WE ARE HERE TO RECLAIM WHAT IS RIGHTFULLY OURS!
THEY'RE MOVING IN. . .
PLEASE, HAIRY MEN, YOU MUST LISTEN!
WE ARE ON A MISSION OF MERCY!
YOU WILL NEVER CROSS THIS BRIDGE!
SSSSSSSSSSSS
THEY MEAN TO KILL US WHERE WE STAND. WE MUST TAKE THE BRIDGE BY FORCE!
AGREED.
TO OAK BOTTOM!

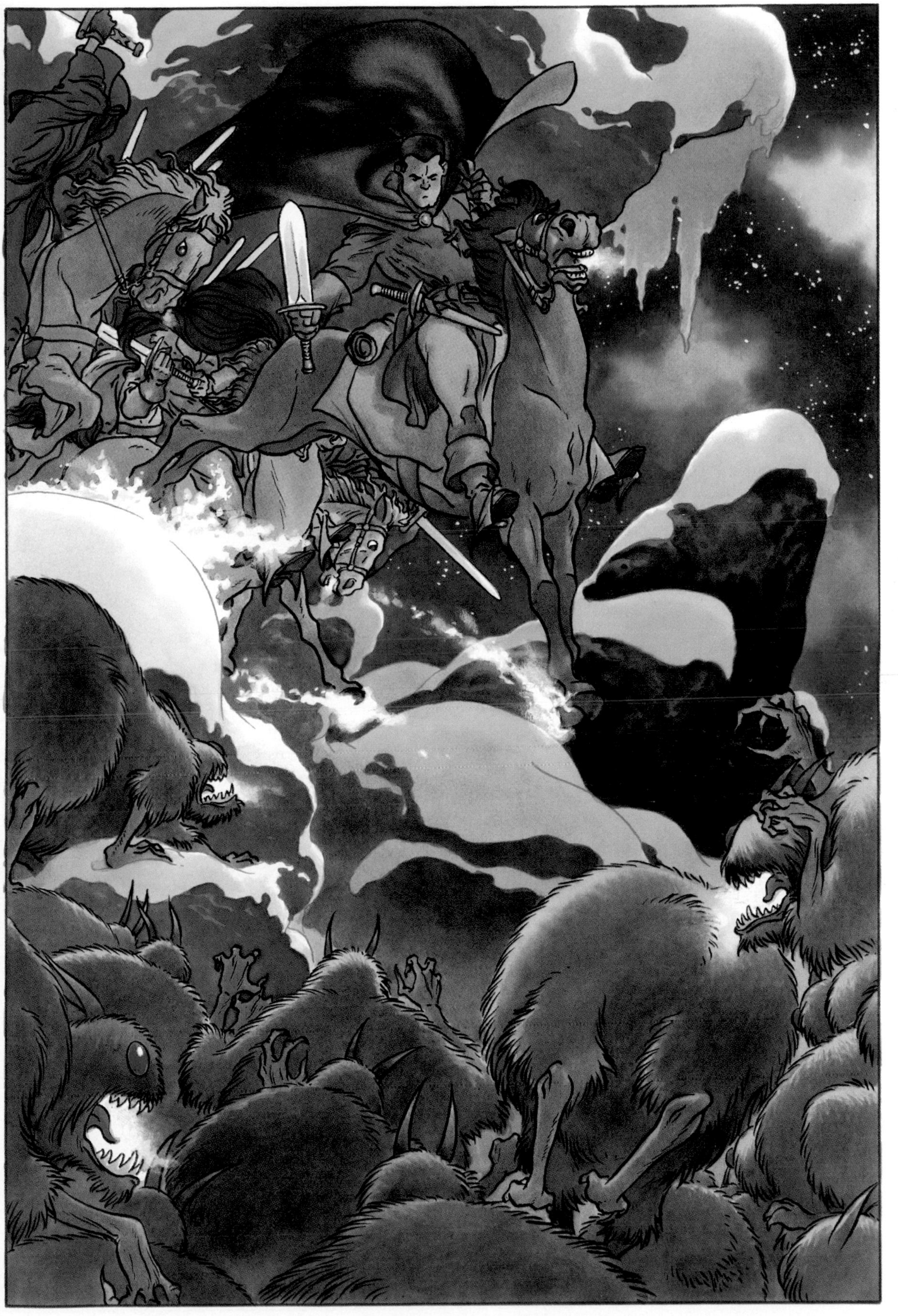

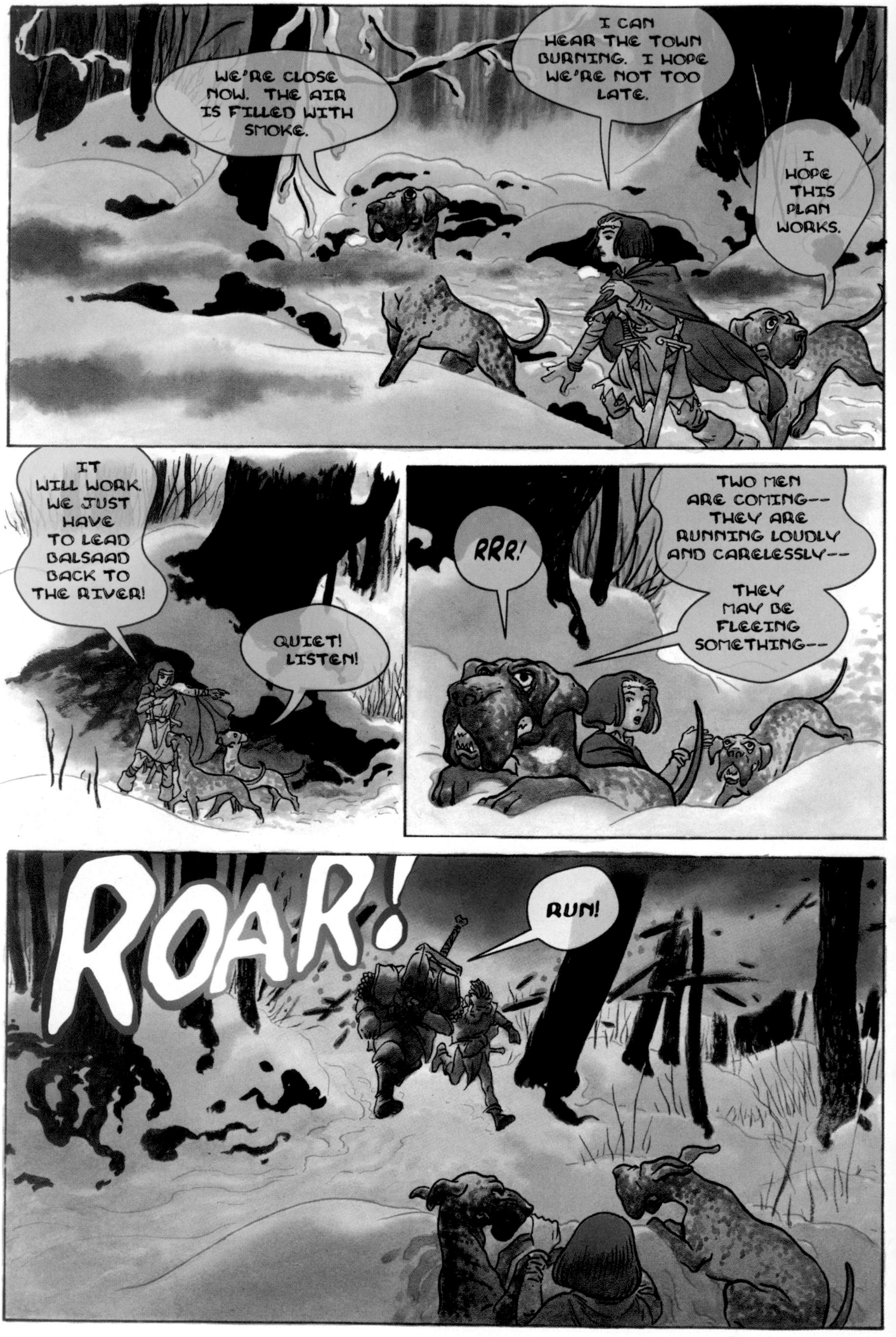
WE'RE CLOSE NOW. THE AIR IS FILLED WITH SMOKE.
I CAN HEAR THE TOWN BURNING. I HOPE WE'RE NOT TOO LATE.
I HOPE THIS PLAN WORKS.
IT WILL WORK. WE JUST HAVE TO LEAD BALSAAD BACK TO THE RIVER!
QUIET! LISTEN!
RRR!
TWO MEN ARE COMING-- THEY ARE RUNNING LOUDLY AND CARELESSLY--
THEY MAY BE FLEEING SOMETHING--
ROAR!
RUN!

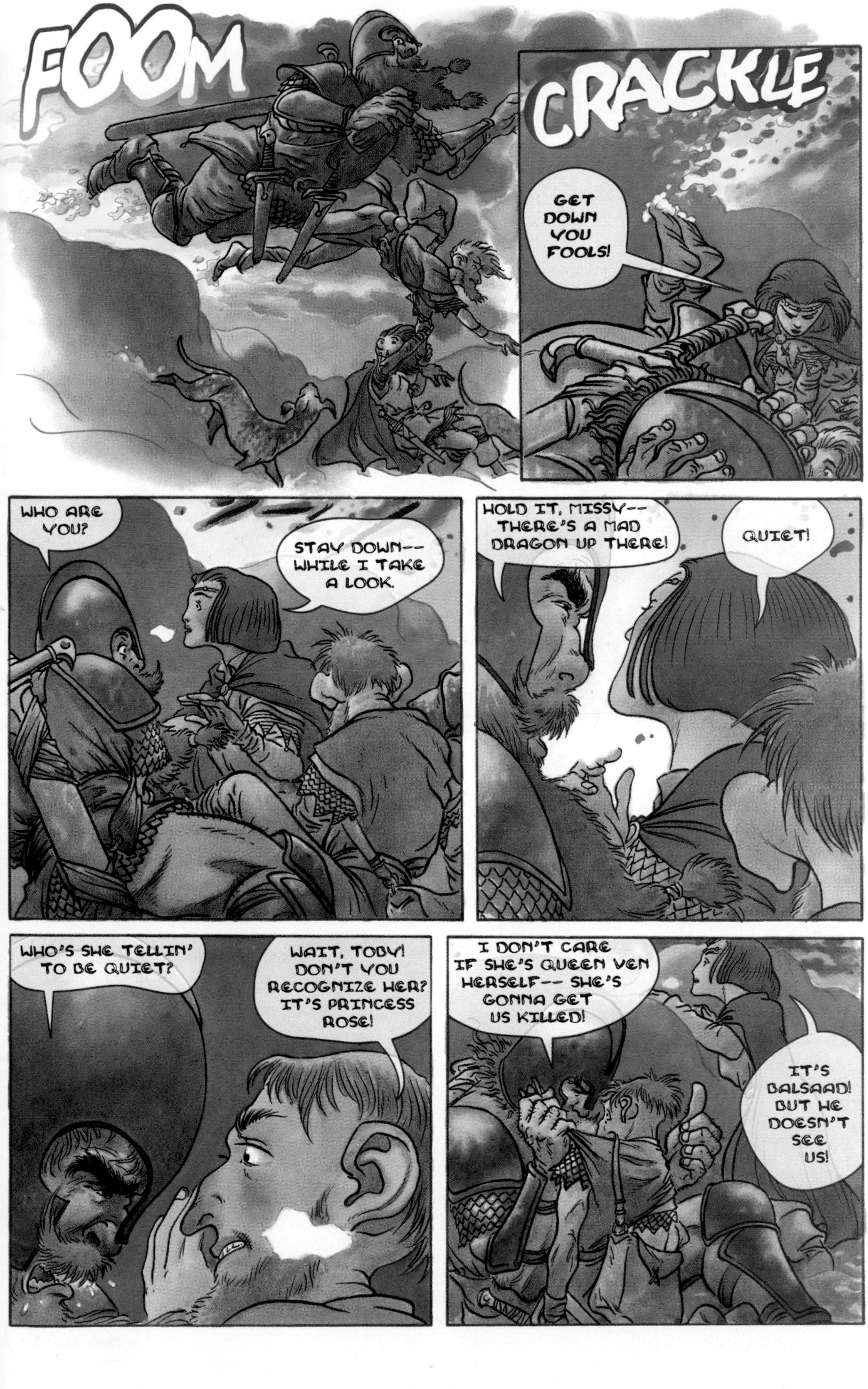
FOOM
CRACKLE
GET DOWN YOU FOOLS!
WHO ARE YOU?
STAY DOWN-- WHILE I TAKE A LOOK.
HOLD IT, MISSY-- THERE'S A MAD DRAGON UP THERE!
QUIET!
WHO'S SHE TELLIN' TO BE QUIET?
WAIT, TOBY! DON'T YOU RECOGNIZE HER? IT'S PRINCESS ROSE!
I DON'T CARE IF SHE'S QUEEN VEN HERSELF-- SHE'S GONNA GET US KILLED!
IT'S BALSAAD! BUT HE DOESN'T SEE US!

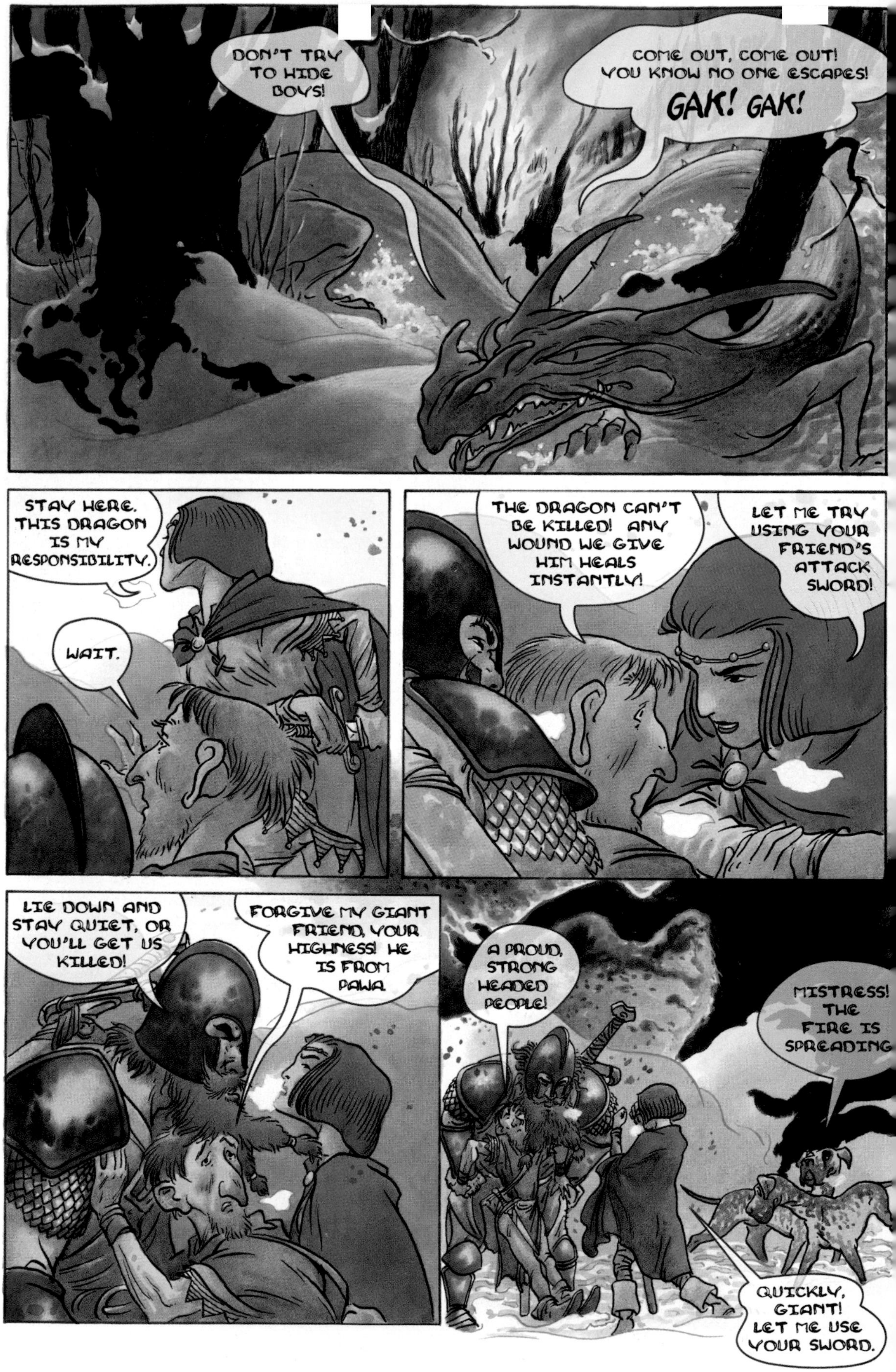
DON'T TRY TO HIDE BOYS!
COME OUT, COME OUT! YOU KNOW NO ONE ESCAPES!
GAK! GAK!
STAY HERE. THIS DRAGON IS MY RESPONSIBILITY.
WAIT.
THE DRAGON CAN'T BE KILLED! ANY WOUND WE GIVE HIM HEALS INSTANTLY!
LET ME TRY USING YOUR FRIEND'S ATTACK SWORD!
LIE DOWN AND STAY QUIET, OR YOU'LL GET US KILLED!
FORGIVE MY GIANT FRIEND, YOUR HIGHNESS! HE IS FROM PAWA
A PROUD, STRONG HEADED PEOPLE!
MISTRESS! THE FIRE IS SPREADING
QUICKLY, GIANT! LET ME USE YOUR SWORD.

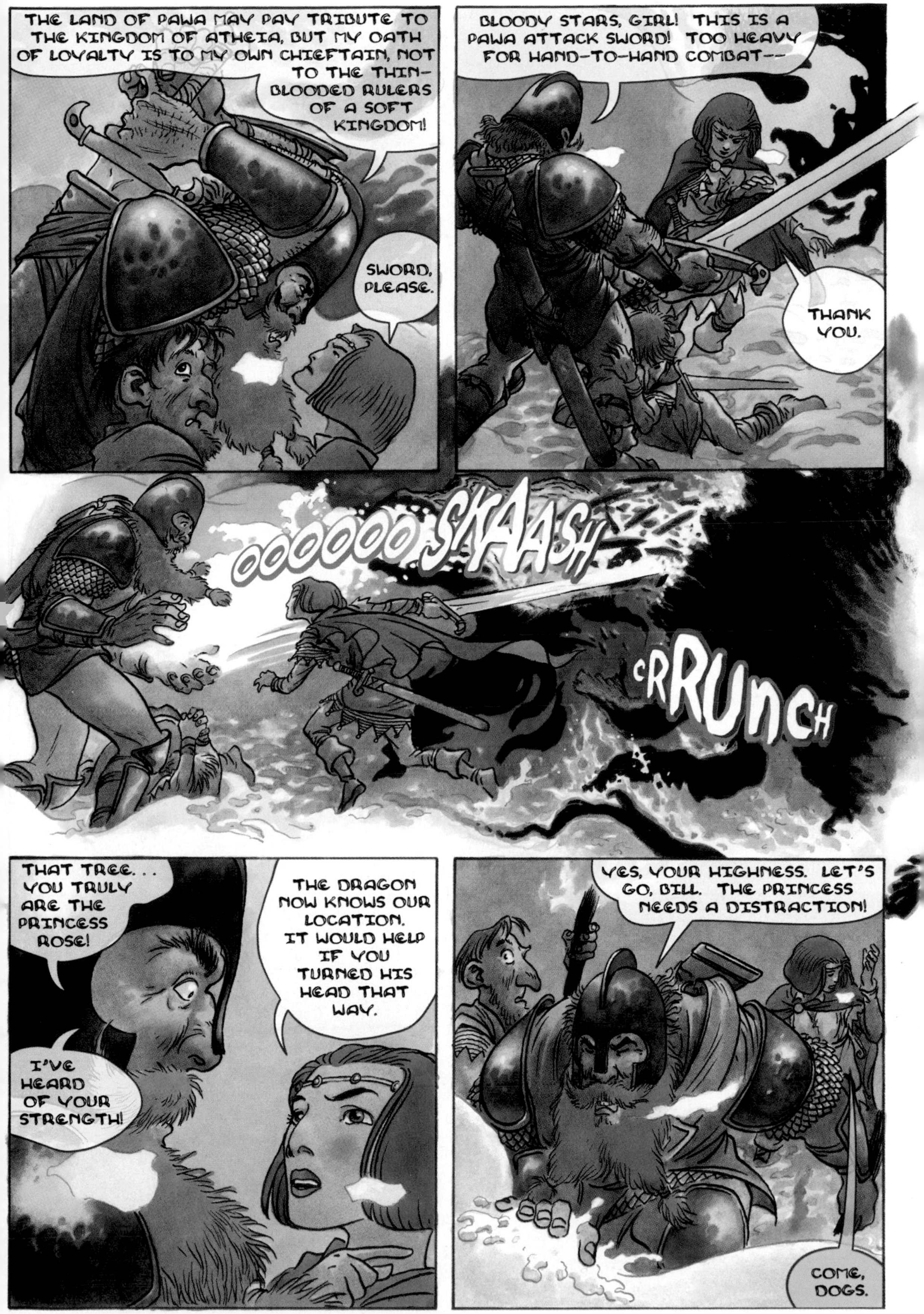
THE LAND OF PAWA MAY PAY TRIBUTE TO THE KINGDOM OF ATHEIA, BUT MY OATH OF LOYALTY IS TO MY OWN CHIEFTAIN, NOT TO THE THIN-BLOODED RULERS OF A SOFT KINGDOM!
SWORD, PLEASE.
BLOODY STARS, GIRL! THIS IS A PAWA ATTACK SWORD! TOO HEAVY FOR HAND-TO-HAND COMBAT--
THANK YOU.
OOOOOOO SKAASH
CRRUNCH
THAT TREE. . . YOU TRULY ARE THE PRINCESS ROSE!
I'VE HEARD OF YOUR STRENGTH!
THE DRAGON NOW KNOWS OUR LOCATION. IT WOULD HELP IF YOU TURNED HIS HEAD THAT WAY.
YES, YOUR HIGHNESS. LET'S GO, BILL. THE PRINCESS NEEDS A DISTRACTION!
COME, DOGS.

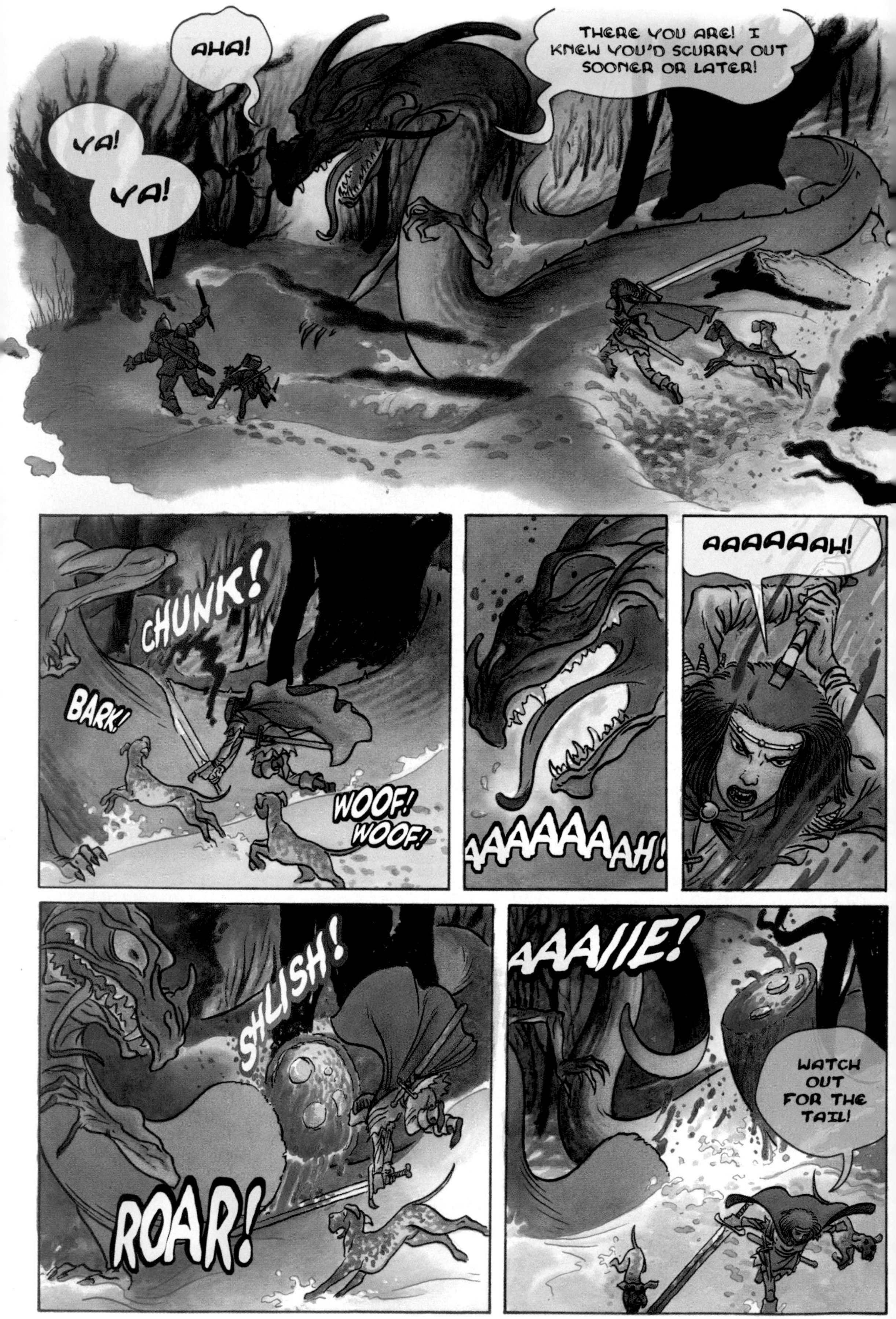

YA!
YA!
AHA!
THERE YOU ARE! I KNEW YOU'D SCURRY OUT SOONER OR LATER!
CHUNK!
BARK!
WOOF! WOOF!
AAAAAAAAH!
AAAAAAH!
SHLISH!
ROAR!
AAAIIE!
WATCH OUT FOR THE TAIL!

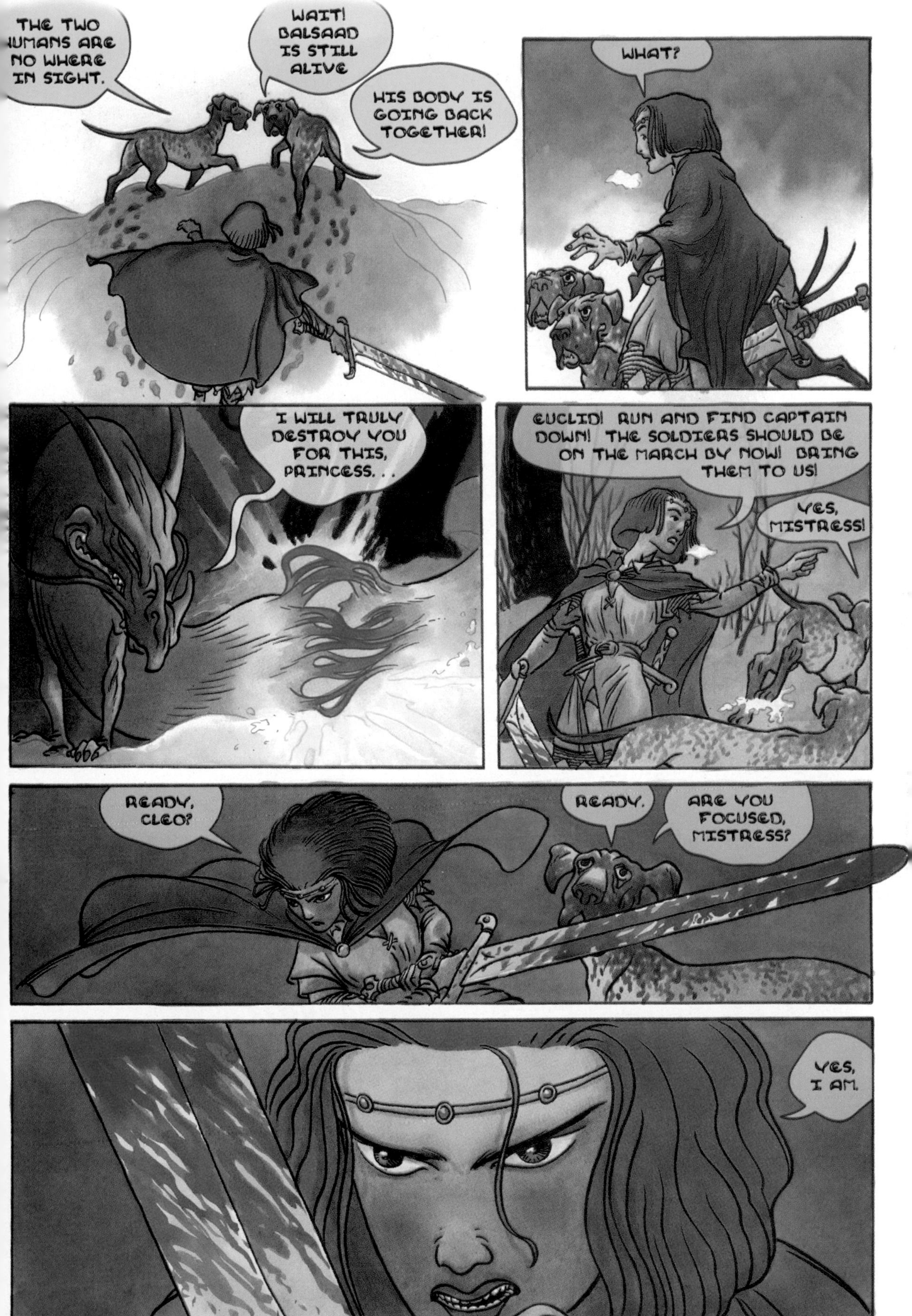
THE TWO HUMANS ARE NO WHERE IN SIGHT.
WAIT! BALSAAD IS STILL ALIVE
HIS BODY IS GOING BACK TOGETHER!
WHAT?
I WILL TRULY DESTROY YOU FOR THIS, PRINCESS. . .
EUCLID! RUN AND FIND CAPTAIN DOWN! THE SOLDIERS SHOULD BE ON THE MARCH BY NOW! BRING THEM TO US!
YES, MISTRESS!
READY, CLEO?
READY.
ARE YOU FOCUSED, MISTRESS?
YES, I AM.

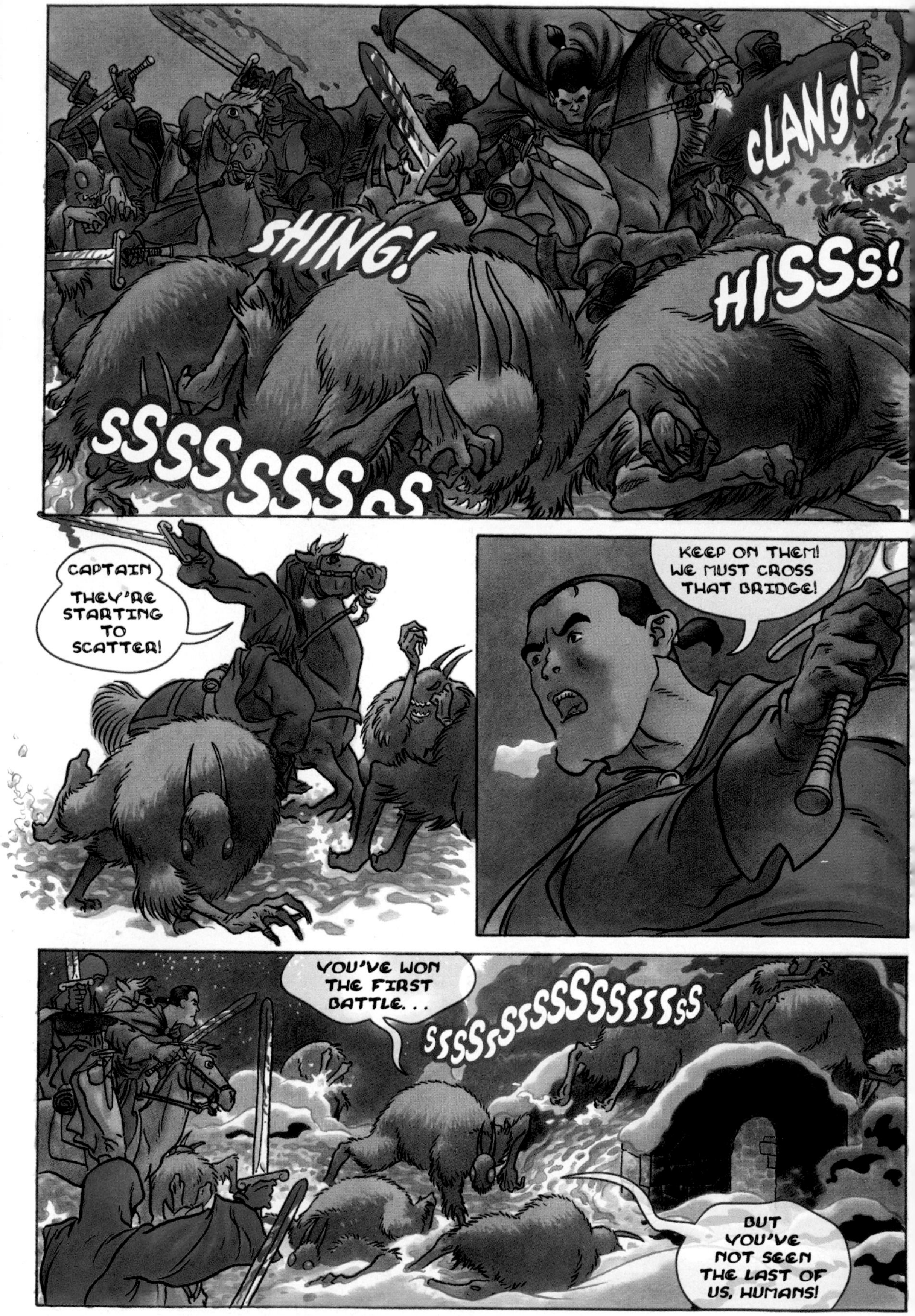
SHING!
CLANG!
HISSs!
SSSSSSSSS
CAPTAIN
THEY'RE STARTING TO SCATTER!
KEEP ON THEM! WE MUST CROSS THAT BRIDGE!
YOU'VE WON THE FIRST BATTLE. . .
SSSSSSSSSSSSSSSSS
BUT YOU'VE NOT SEEN THE LAST OF US, HUMANS!

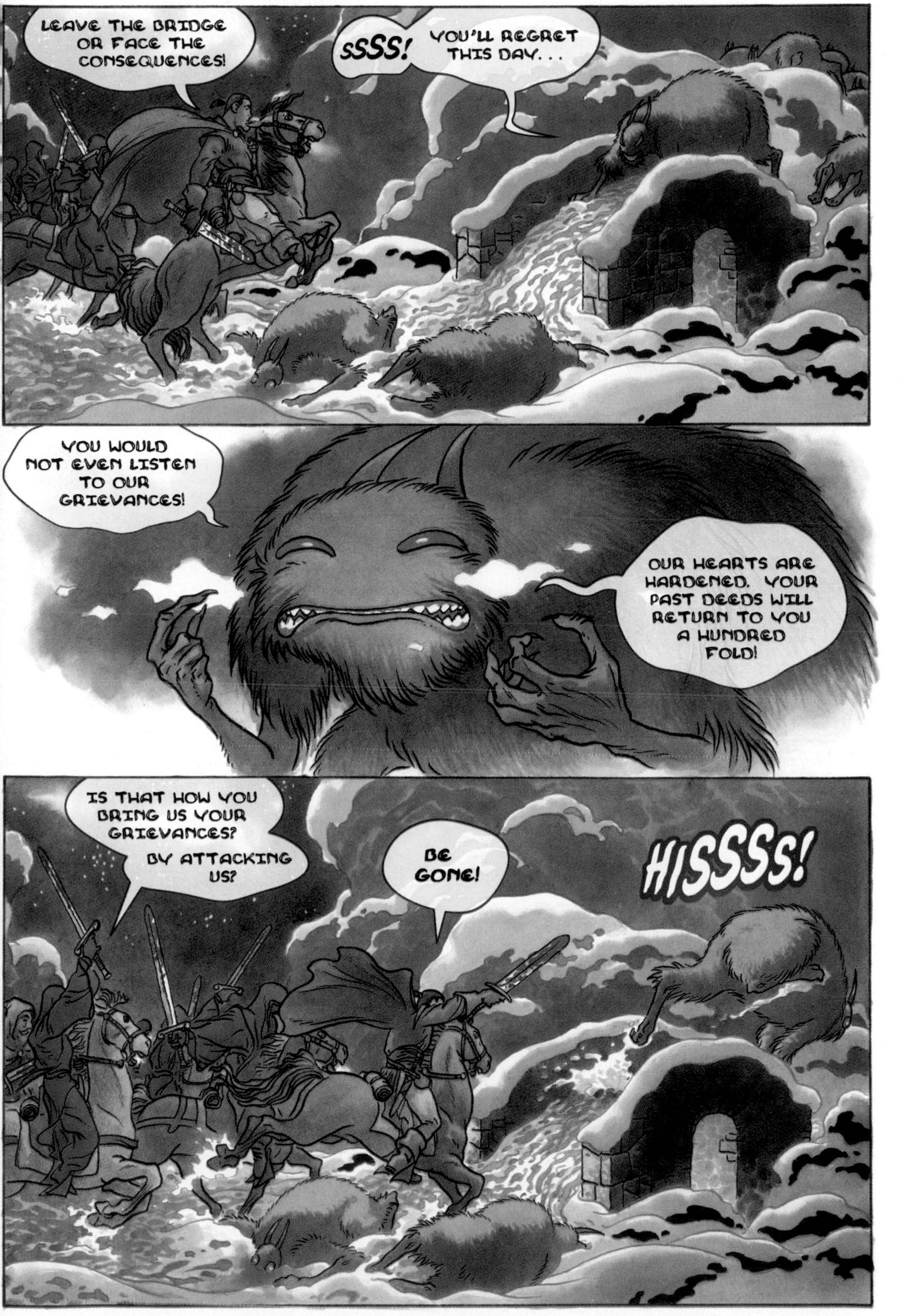
LEAVE THE BRIDGE OR FACE THE CONSEQUENCES!
sSSS!
YOU'LL REGRET THIS DAY...
YOU WOULD NOT EVEN LISTEN TO OUR GRIEVANCES!
OUR HEARTS ARE HARDENED. YOUR PAST DEEDS WILL RETURN TO YOU A HUNDRED FOLD!
IS THAT HOW YOU BRING US YOUR GRIEVANCES?
BY ATTACKING US?
BE GONE!
HISSSs!

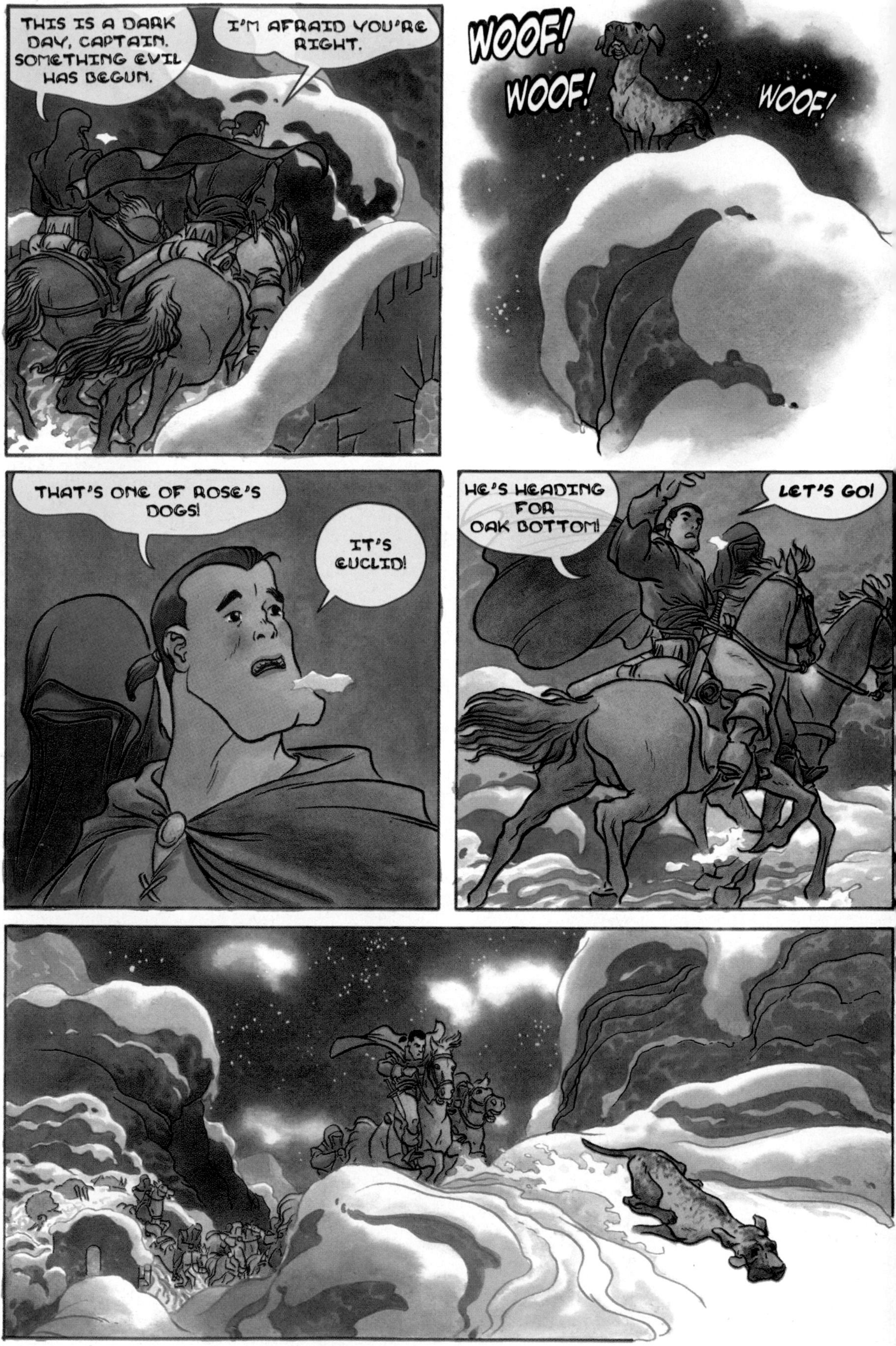
THIS IS A DARK DAY, CAPTAIN. SOMETHING EVIL HAS BEGUN.
I'M AFRAID YOU'RE RIGHT.
WOOF!
WOOF!
WOOF!
THAT'S ONE OF ROSE'S DOGS!
IT'S EUCLID!
HE'S HEADING FOR OAK BOTTOM!
LET'S GO!

THE
PROMISE

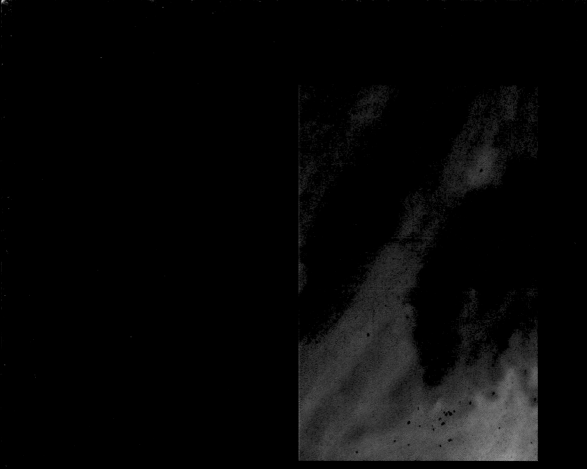

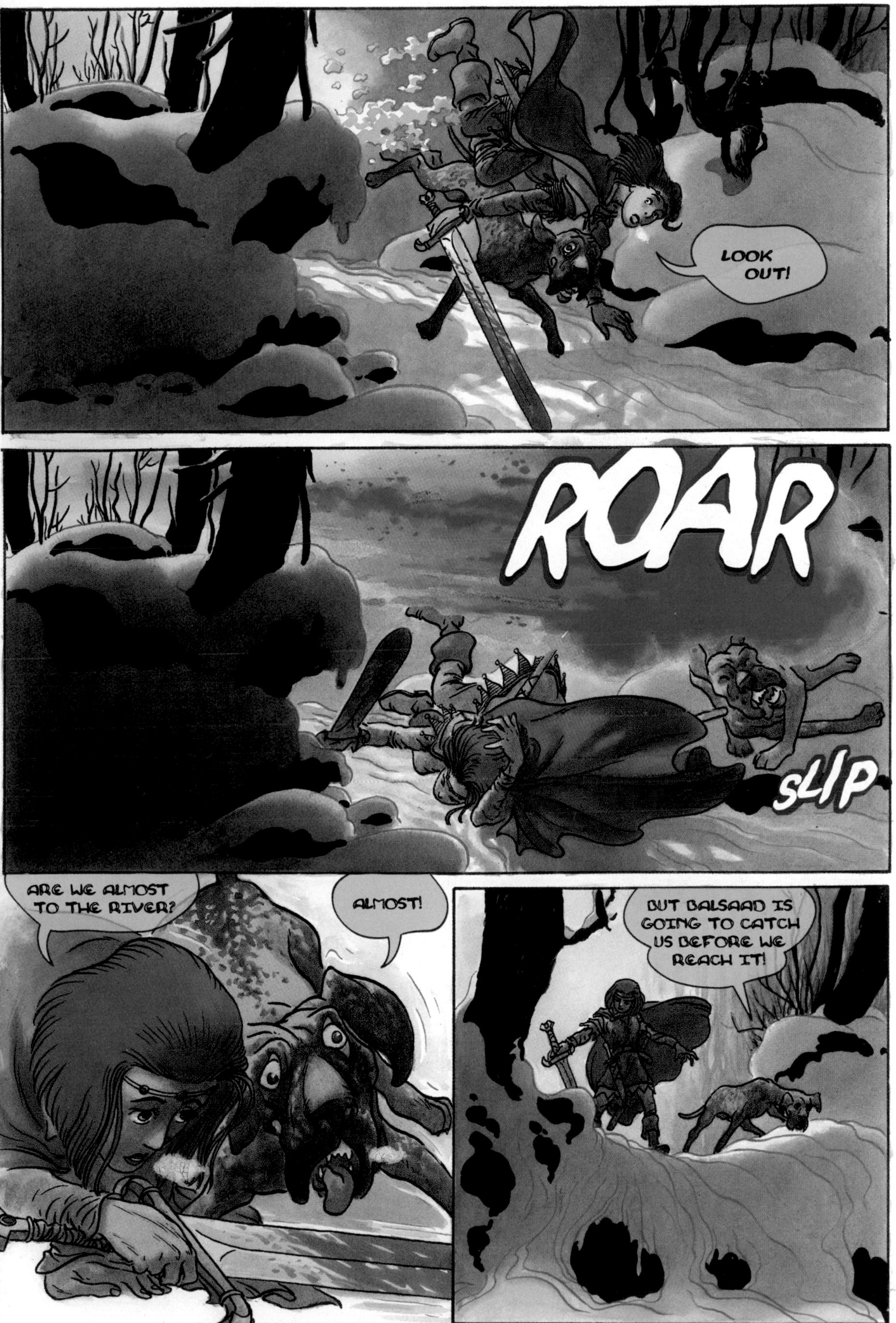
LOOK OUT!
ROAR
SLIP
ARE WE ALMOST TO THE RIVER?
ALMOST!
BUT BALSAAD IS GOING TO CATCH US BEFORE WE REACH IT!

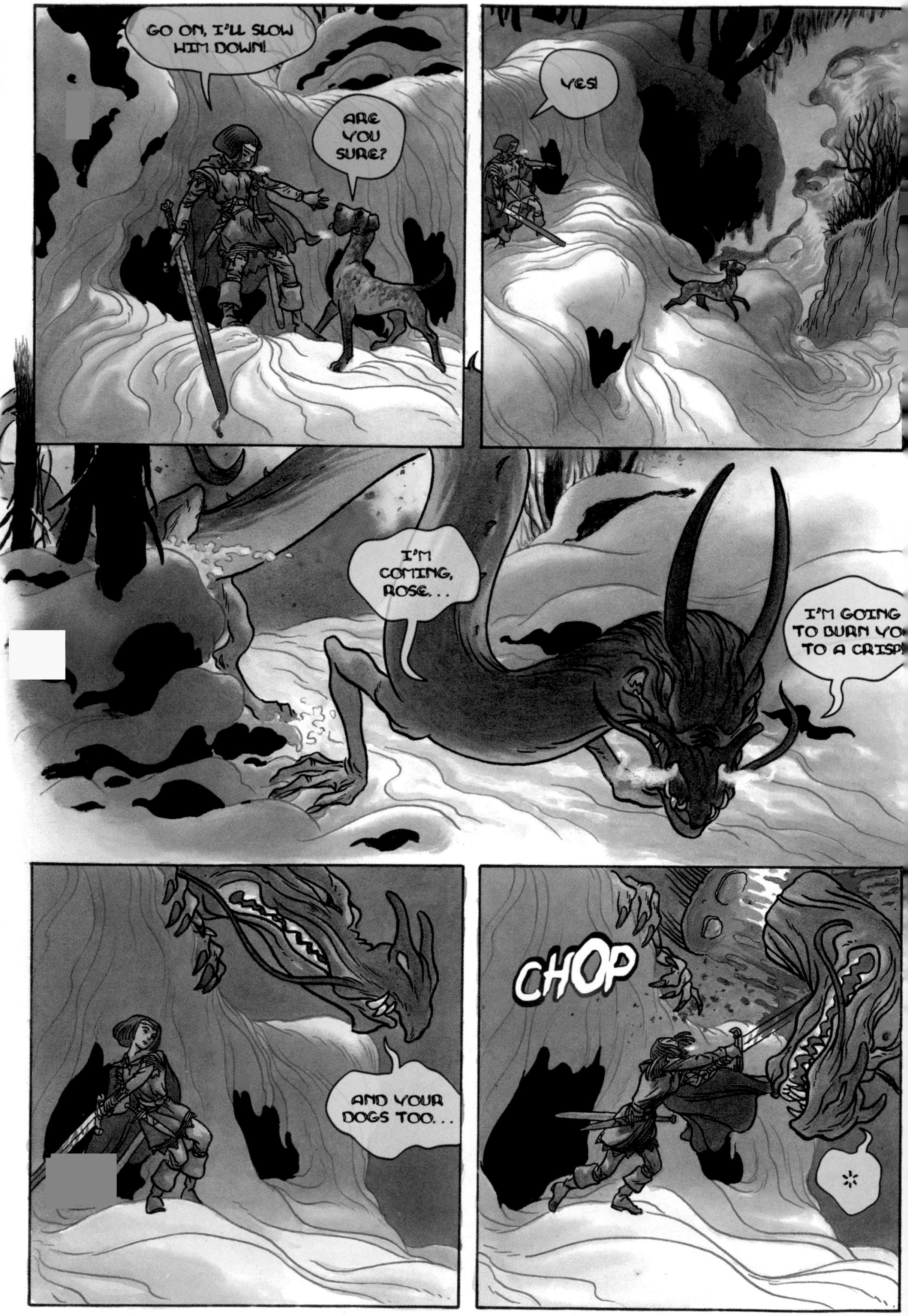
GO ON, I'LL SLOW HIM DOWN!
ARE YOU SURE?
YES!
I'M COMING, ROSE...
I'M GOING TO BURN YO TO A CRISP
AND YOUR DOGS TOO...
CHOP

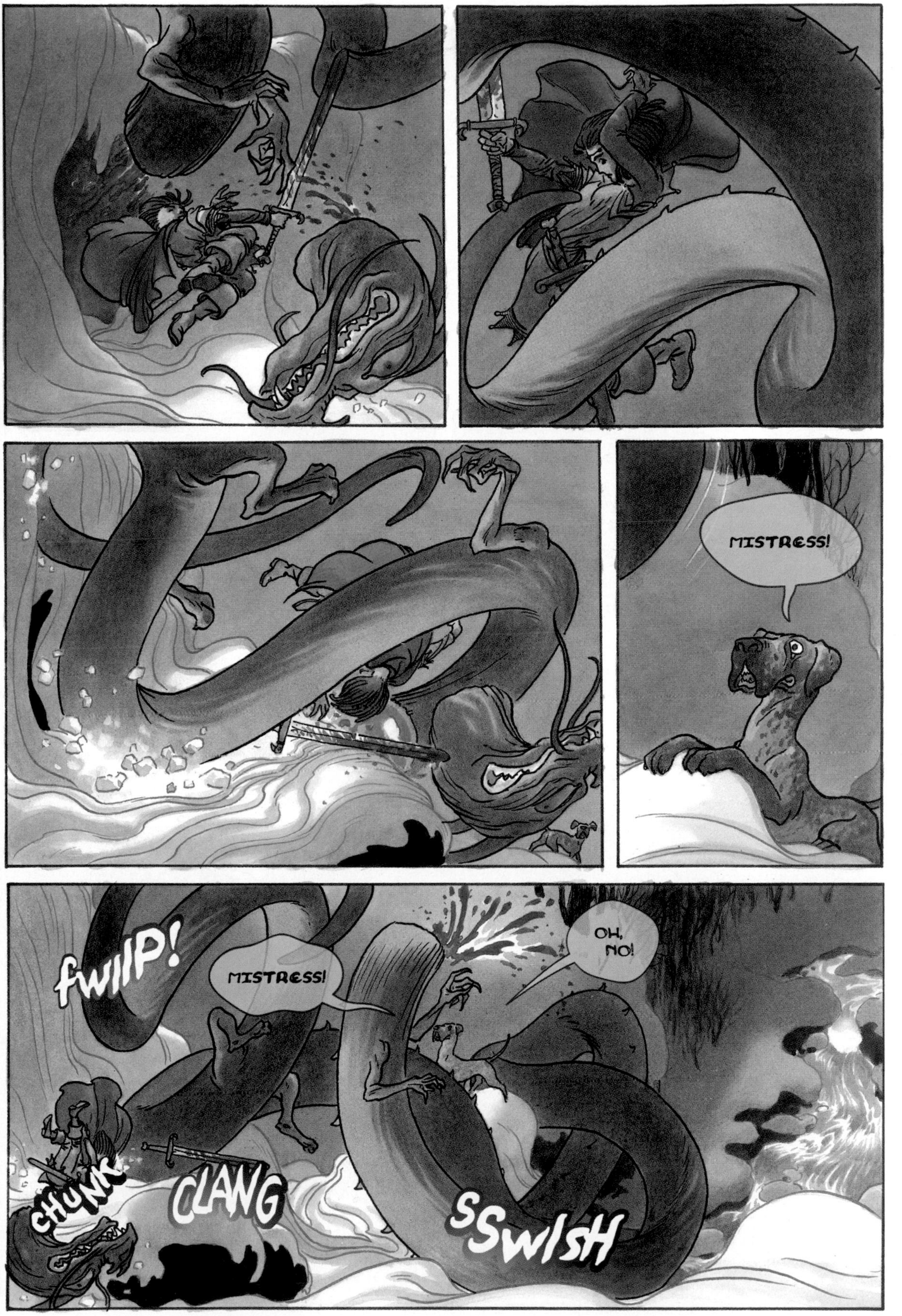
MISTRESS!
fwiiP!
MISTRESS!
OH, NO!
CHUNK
CLANG
SSWISH

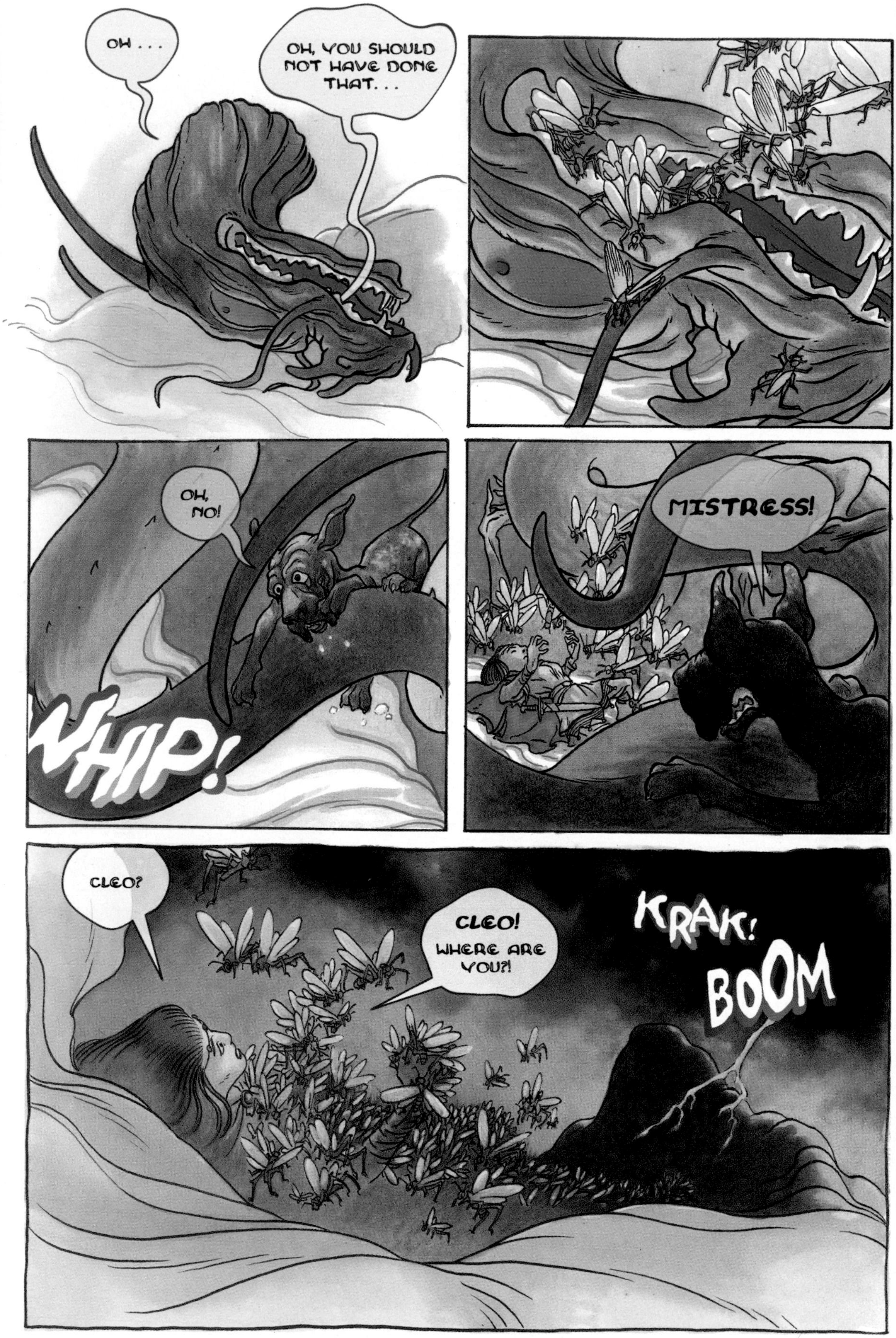
OH . . .
OH, YOU SHOULD NOT HAVE DONE THAT. . .
OH, NO!
WHIP!
MISTRESS!
CLEO?
CLEO! WHERE ARE YOU?!
KRAK!
BOOM

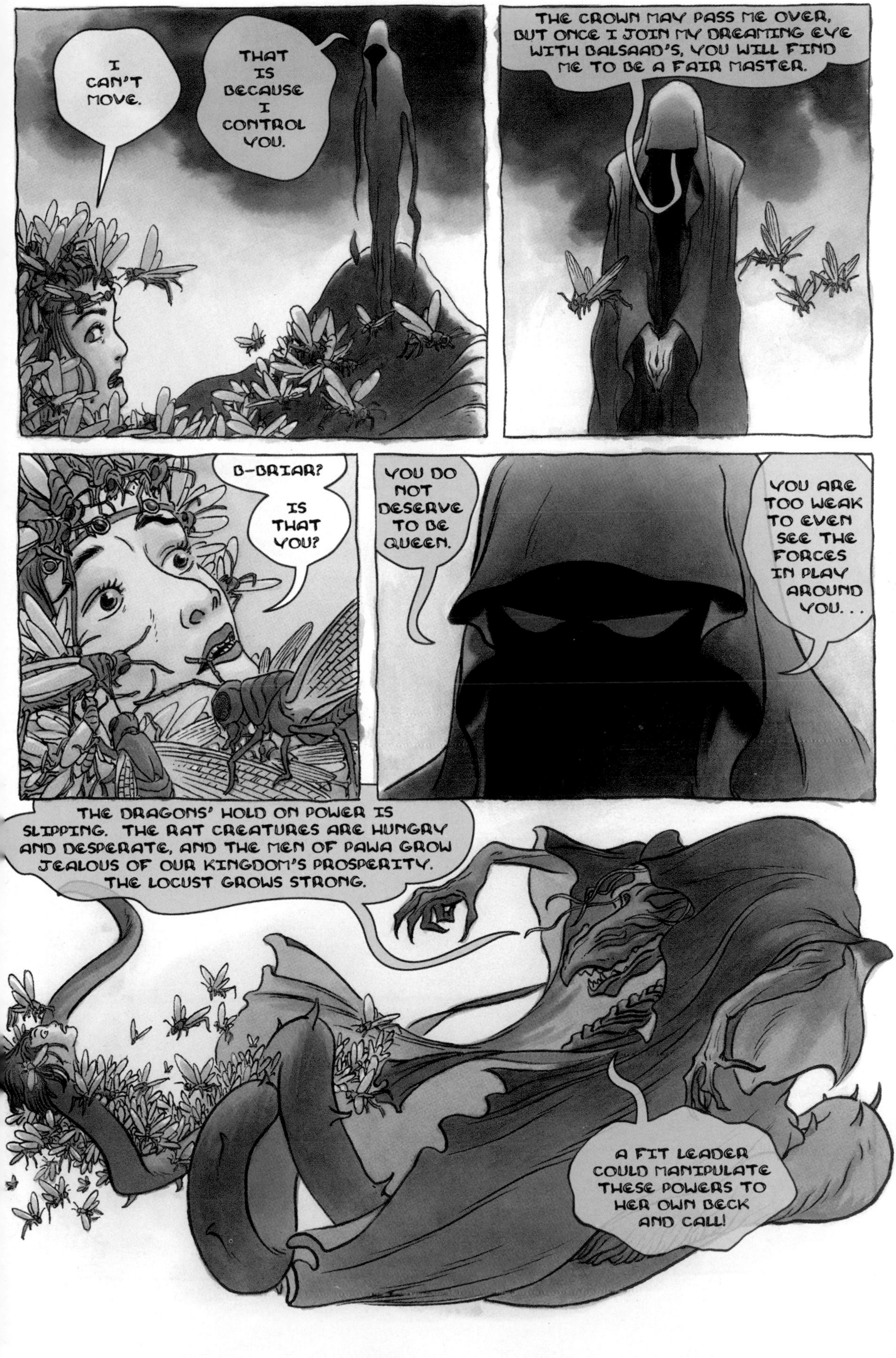
I CAN'T MOVE.
THAT IS BECAUSE I CONTROL YOU.
THE CROWN MAY PASS ME OVER, BUT ONCE I JOIN MY DREAMING EYE WITH BALSAAD'S, YOU WILL FIND ME TO BE A FAIR MASTER.
B-BRIAR?
IS THAT YOU?
YOU DO NOT DESERVE TO BE QUEEN.
YOU ARE TOO WEAK TO EVEN SEE THE FORCES IN PLAY AROUND YOU...
THE DRAGONS' HOLD ON POWER IS SLIPPING. THE RAT CREATURES ARE HUNGRY AND DESPERATE, AND THE MEN OF PAWA GROW JEALOUS OF OUR KINGDOM'S PROSPERITY. THE LOCUST GROWS STRONG.
A FIT LEADER COULD MANIPULATE THESE POWERS TO HER OWN BECK AND CALL!

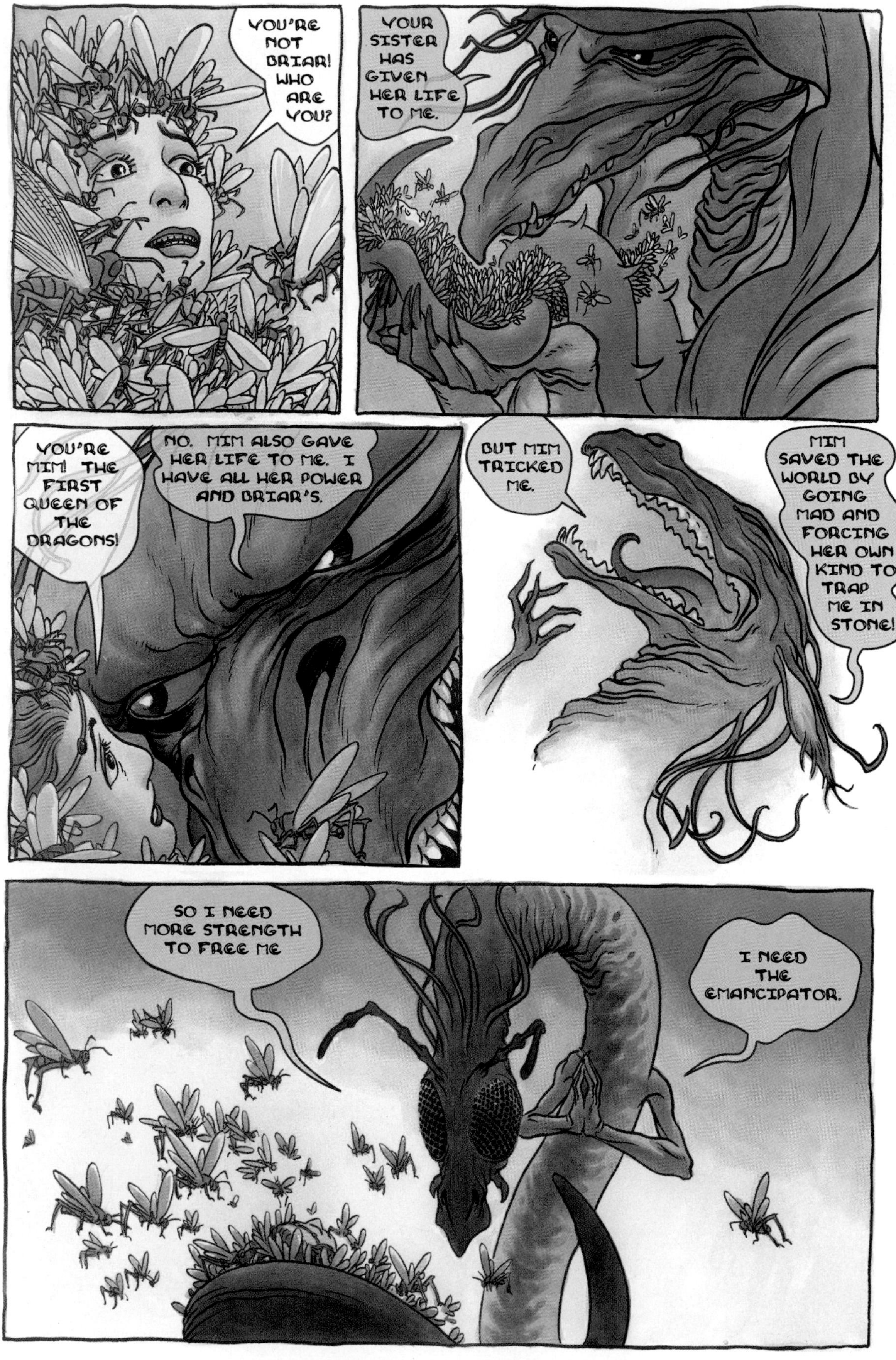
YOU'RE NOT BRIAR! WHO ARE YOU?
YOUR SISTER HAS GIVEN HER LIFE TO ME.
YOU'RE MIM! THE FIRST QUEEN OF THE DRAGONS!
NO. MIM ALSO GAVE HER LIFE TO ME. I HAVE ALL HER POWER AND BRIAR'S.
BUT MIM TRICKED ME.
MIM SAVED THE WORLD BY GOING MAD AND FORCING HER OWN KIND TO TRAP ME IN STONE!
SO I NEED MORE STRENGTH TO FREE ME
I NEED THE EMANCIPATOR.

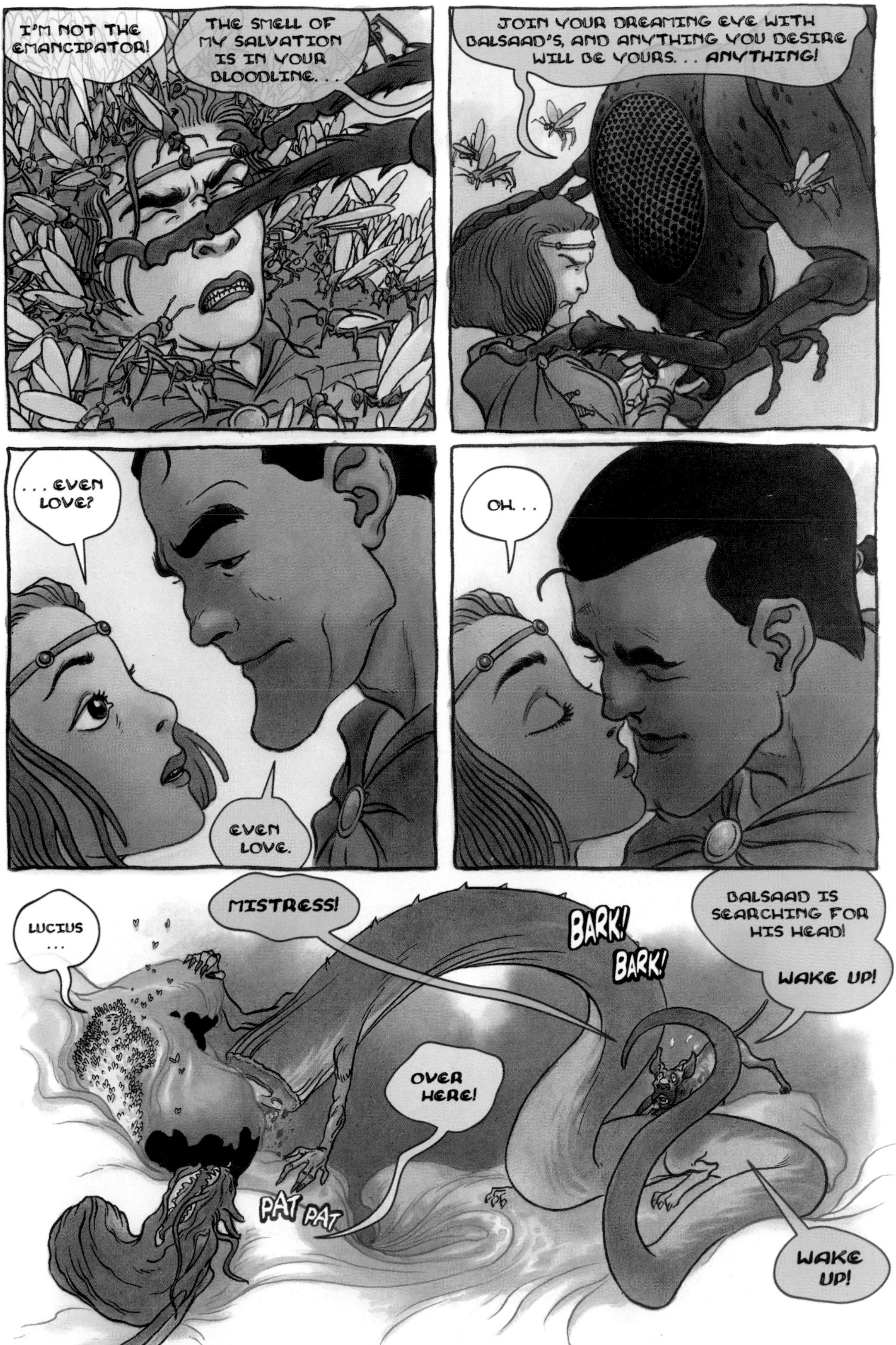
I'M NOT THE EMANCIPATOR!
THE SMELL OF MY SALVATION IS IN YOUR BLOODLINE...
JOIN YOUR DREAMING EYE WITH BALSAAD'S, AND ANYTHING YOU DESIRE WILL BE YOURS... ANYTHING!
...EVEN LOVE?
EVEN LOVE.
OH...
LUCIUS ...
MISTRESS!
BARK!
BARK!
BALSAAD IS SEARCHING FOR HIS HEAD!
WAKE UP!
OVER HERE!
PAT PAT
WAKE UP!

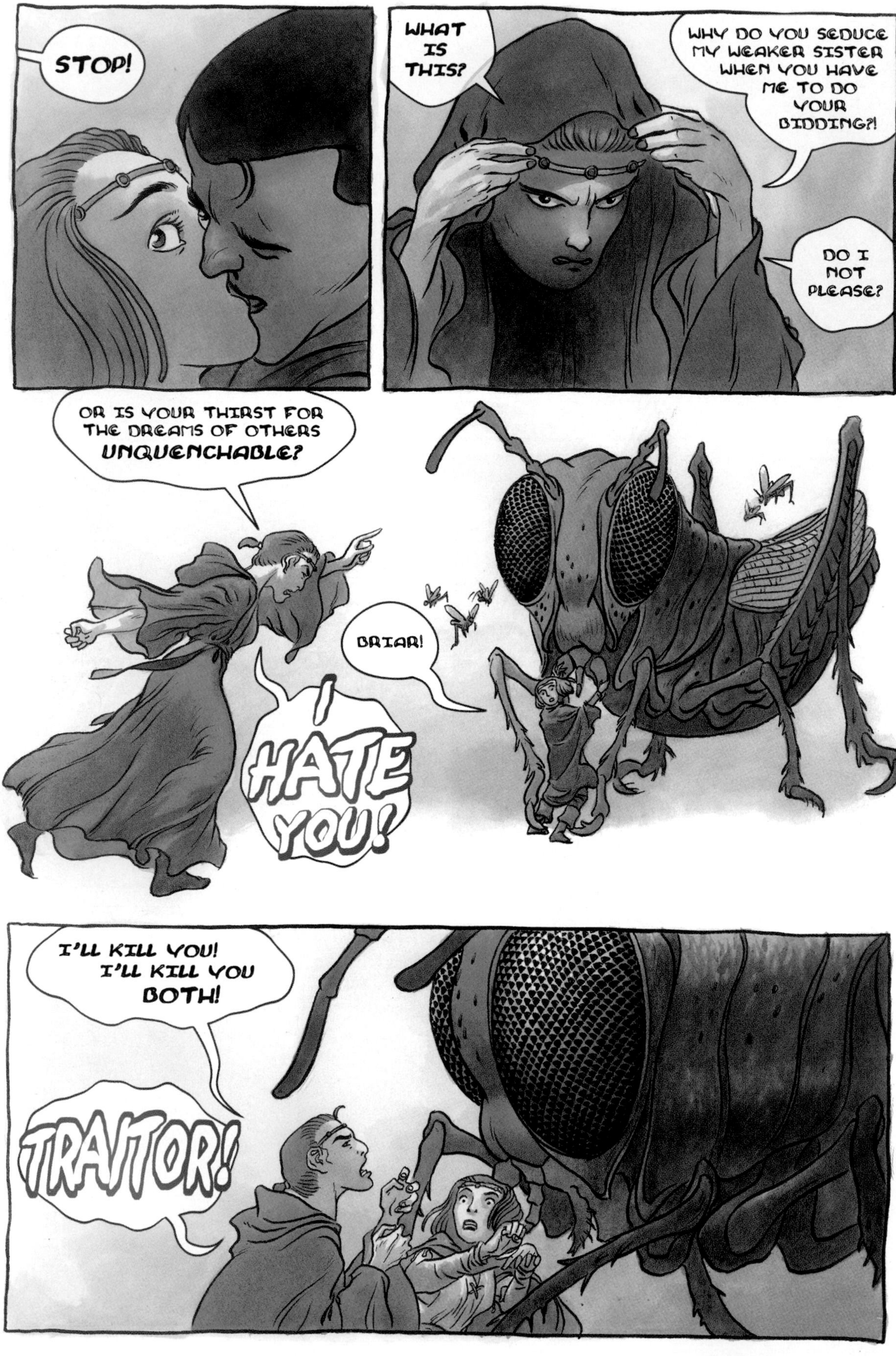
STOP!
WHAT IS THIS?
WHY DO YOU SEDUCE MY WEAKER SISTER WHEN YOU HAVE ME TO DO YOUR BIDDING?!
DO I NOT PLEASE?
OR IS YOUR THIRST FOR THE DREAMS OF OTHERS UNQUENCHABLE?
BRIAR!
I HATE YOU!
I'LL KILL YOU! I'LL KILL YOU BOTH!
TRAITOR!

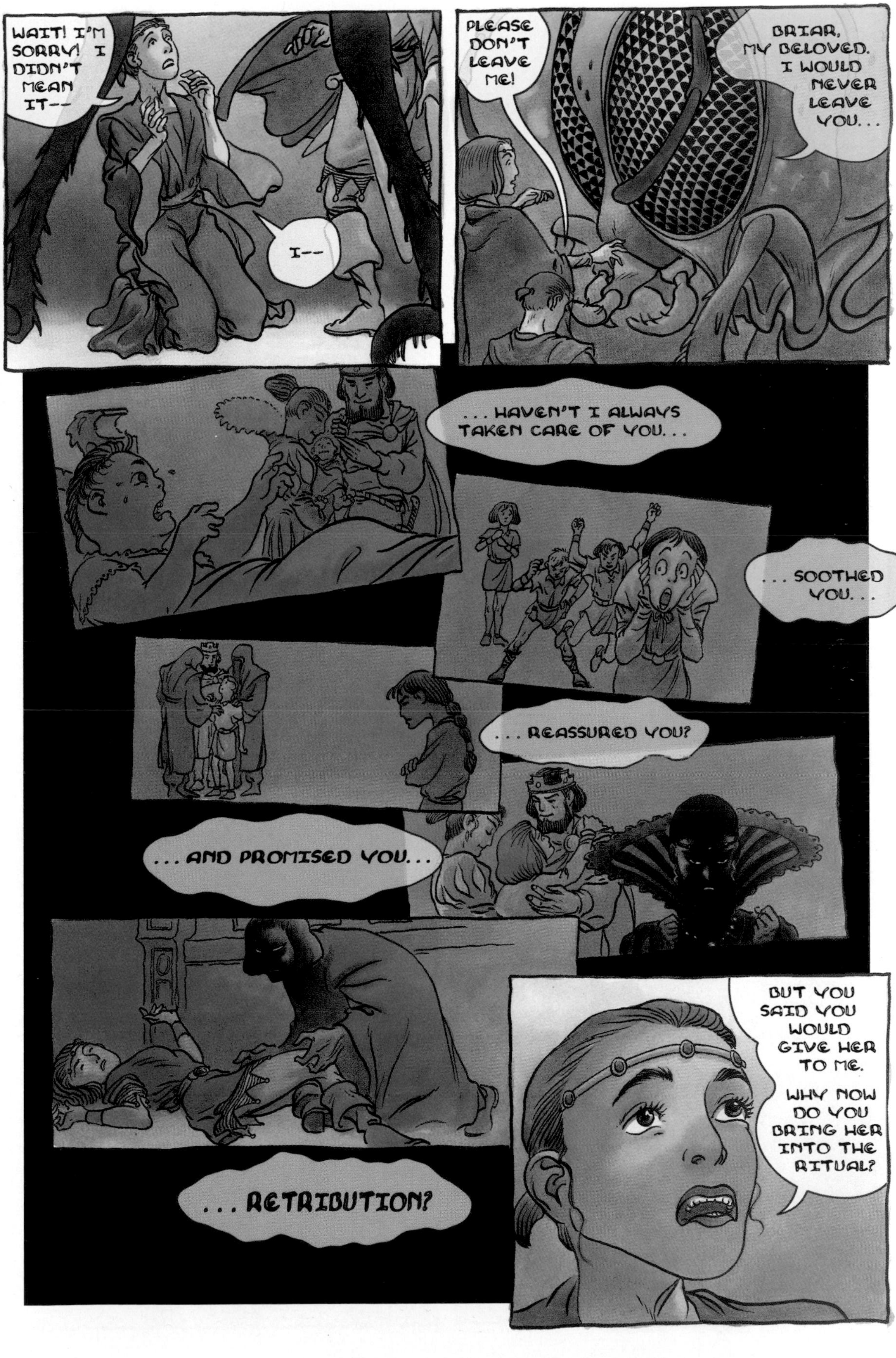
WAIT! I'M SORRY! I DIDN'T MEAN IT--
I--
PLEASE DON'T LEAVE ME!
BRIAR, MY BELOVED. I WOULD NEVER LEAVE YOU...
...HAVEN'T I ALWAYS TAKEN CARE OF YOU...
...SOOTHED YOU...
...REASSURED YOU?
...AND PROMISED YOU...
...RETRIBUTION?
BUT YOU SAID YOU WOULD GIVE HER TO ME.
WHY NOW DO YOU BRING HER INTO THE RITUAL?

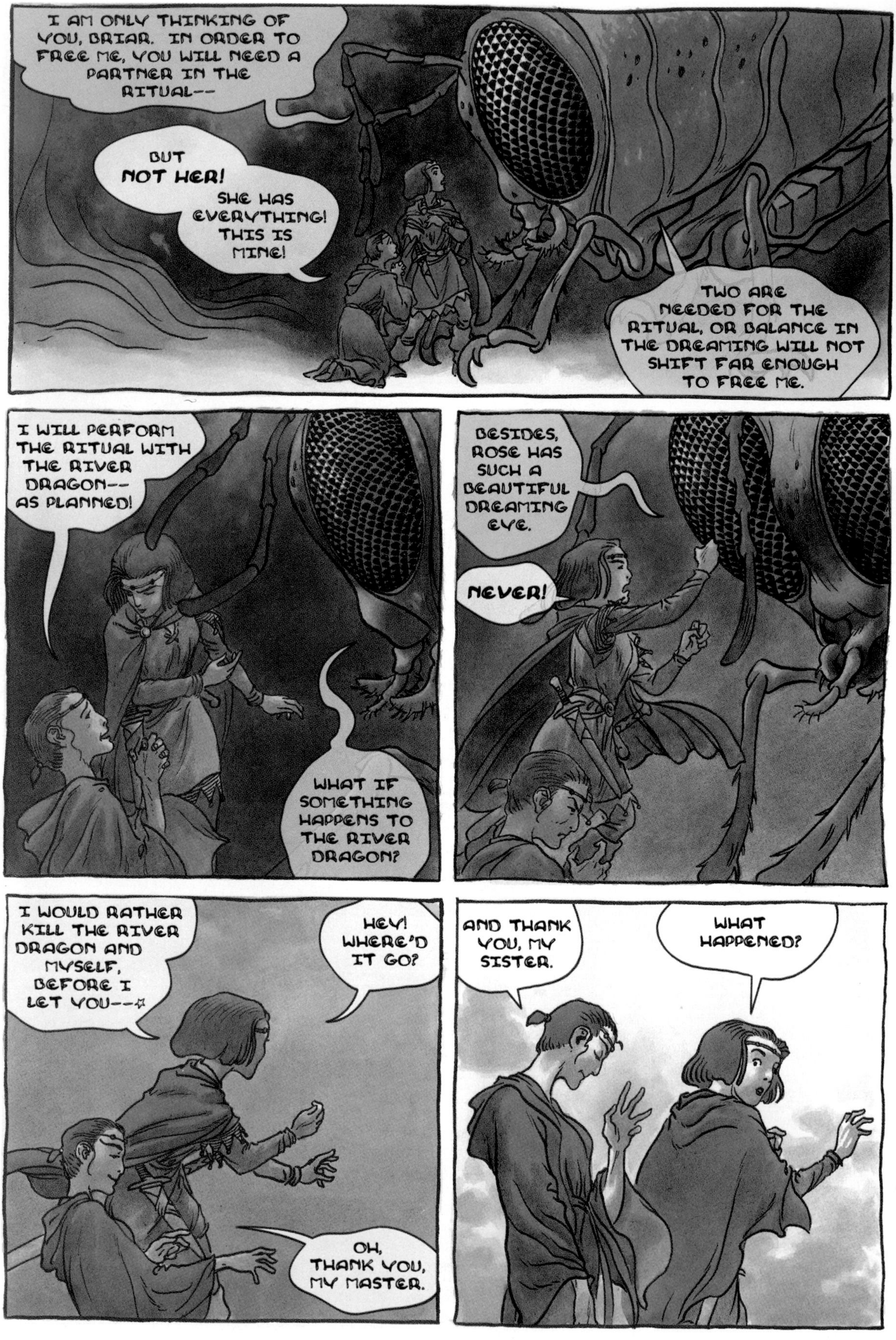
I AM ONLY THINKING OF YOU, BRIAR. IN ORDER TO FREE ME, YOU WILL NEED A PARTNER IN THE RITUAL--
BUT NOT HER!
SHE HAS EVERYTHING! THIS IS MINE!
TWO ARE NEEDED FOR THE RITUAL, OR BALANCE IN THE DREAMING WILL NOT SHIFT FAR ENOUGH TO FREE ME.
I WILL PERFORM THE RITUAL WITH THE RIVER DRAGON-- AS PLANNED!
WHAT IF SOMETHING HAPPENS TO THE RIVER DRAGON?
BESIDES, ROSE HAS SUCH A BEAUTIFUL DREAMING EYE.
NEVER!
I WOULD RATHER KILL THE RIVER DRAGON AND MYSELF, BEFORE I LET YOU--
HEY! WHERE'D IT GO?
OH, THANK YOU, MY MASTER.
AND THANK YOU, MY SISTER.
WHAT HAPPENED?

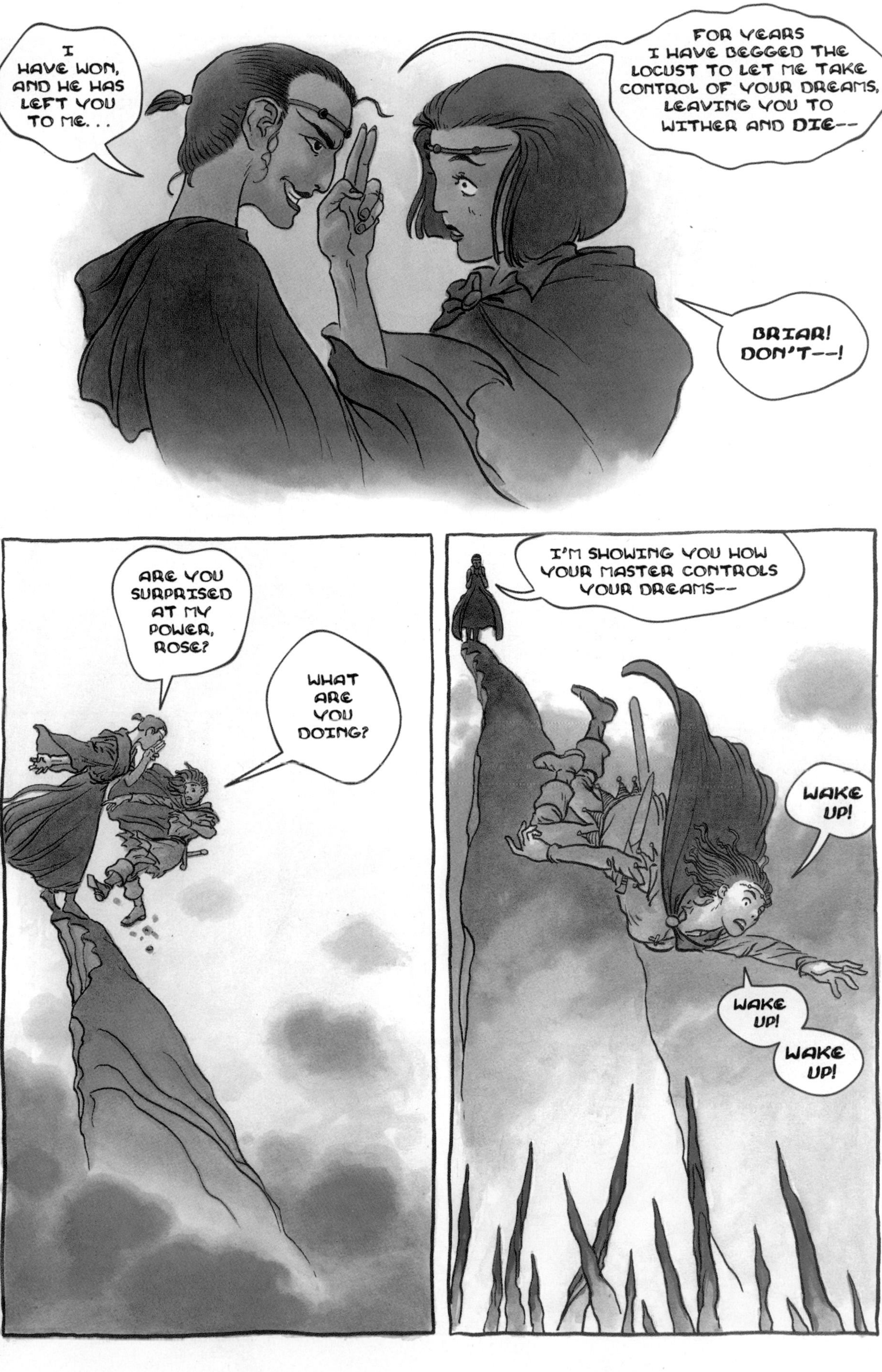
I HAVE WON, AND HE HAS LEFT YOU TO ME. . .
FOR YEARS I HAVE BEGGED THE LOCUST TO LET ME TAKE CONTROL OF YOUR DREAMS, LEAVING YOU TO WITHER AND DIE--
BRIAR! DON'T--!
ARE YOU SURPRISED AT MY POWER, ROSE?
WHAT ARE YOU DOING?
I'M SHOWING YOU HOW YOUR MASTER CONTROLS YOUR DREAMS--
WAKE UP!
WAKE UP!
WAKE UP!

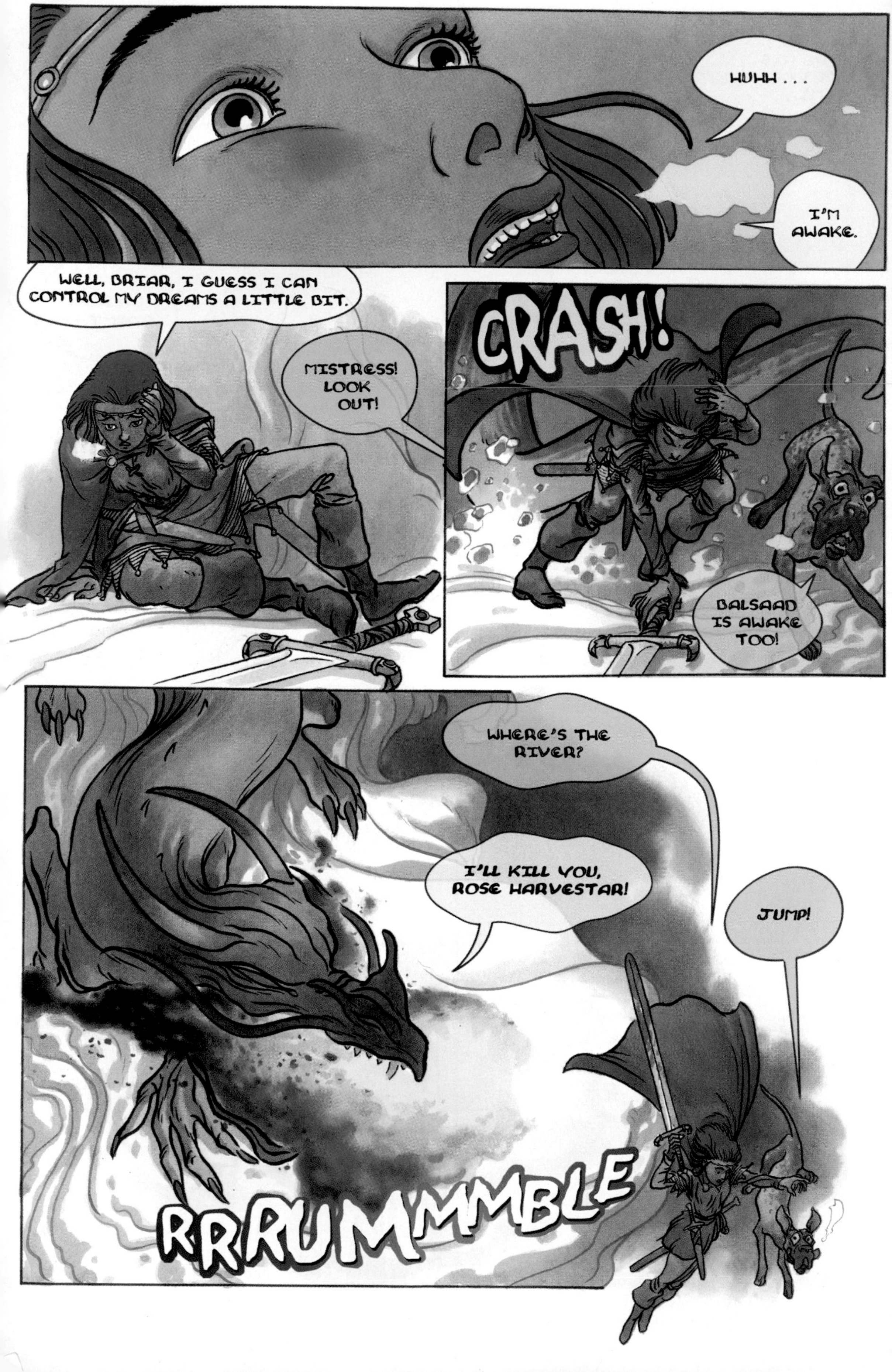
HUHH . . .
I'M AWAKE.
WELL, BRIAR, I GUESS I CAN CONTROL MY DREAMS A LITTLE BIT.
MISTRESS! LOOK OUT!
CRASH!
BALSAAD IS AWAKE TOO!
WHERE'S THE RIVER?
I'LL KILL YOU, ROSE HARVESTAR!
JUMP!
RRRUMMMBLE

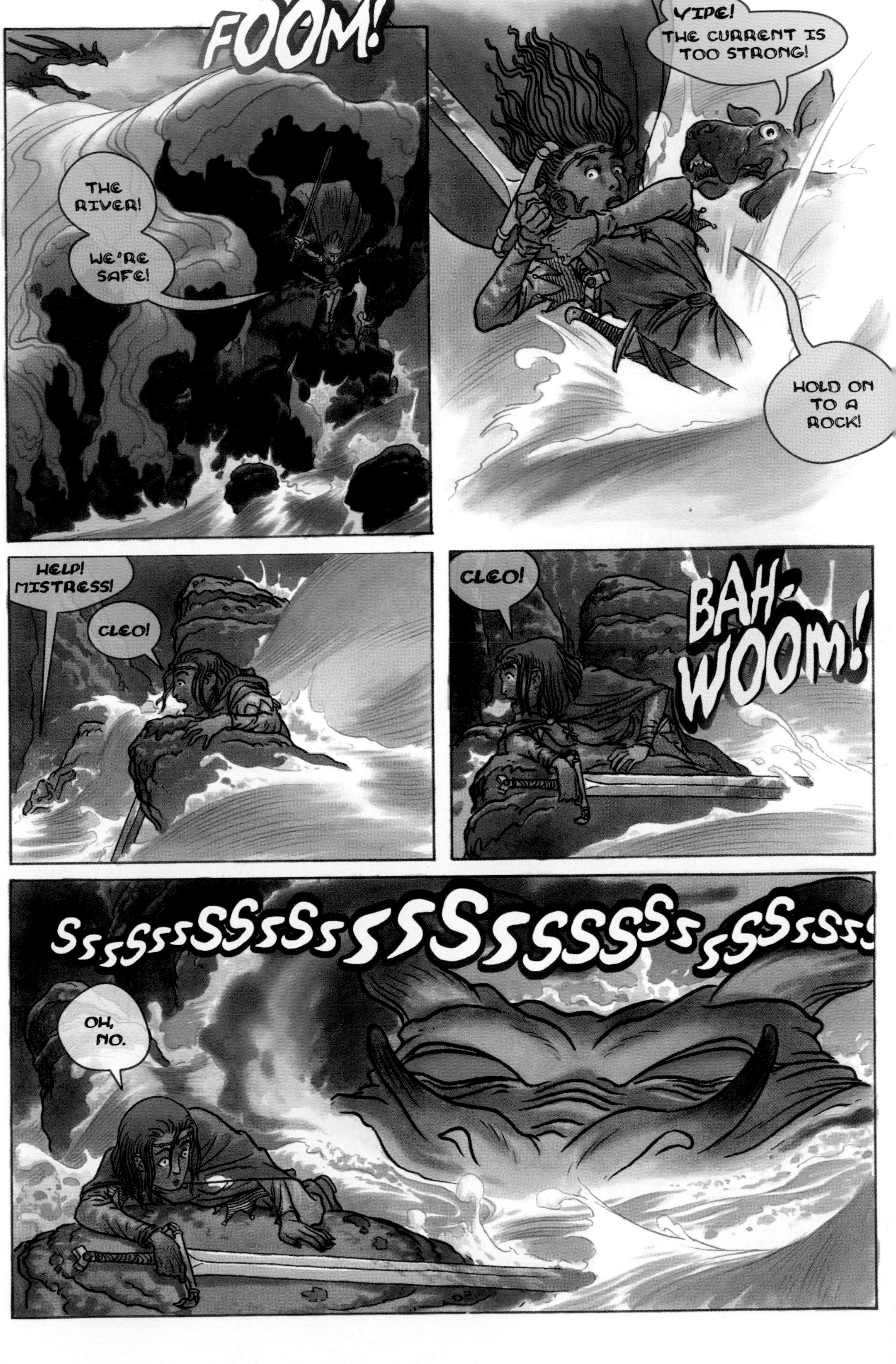
FOOM!
THE RIVER!
WE'RE SAFE!
YIPE! THE CURRENT IS TOO STRONG!
HOLD ON TO A ROCK!
HELP! MISTRESS!
CLEO!
CLEO!
BAH-WOOM!
SsSssSSsSssSSsssSSsSSsSs
OH, NO.

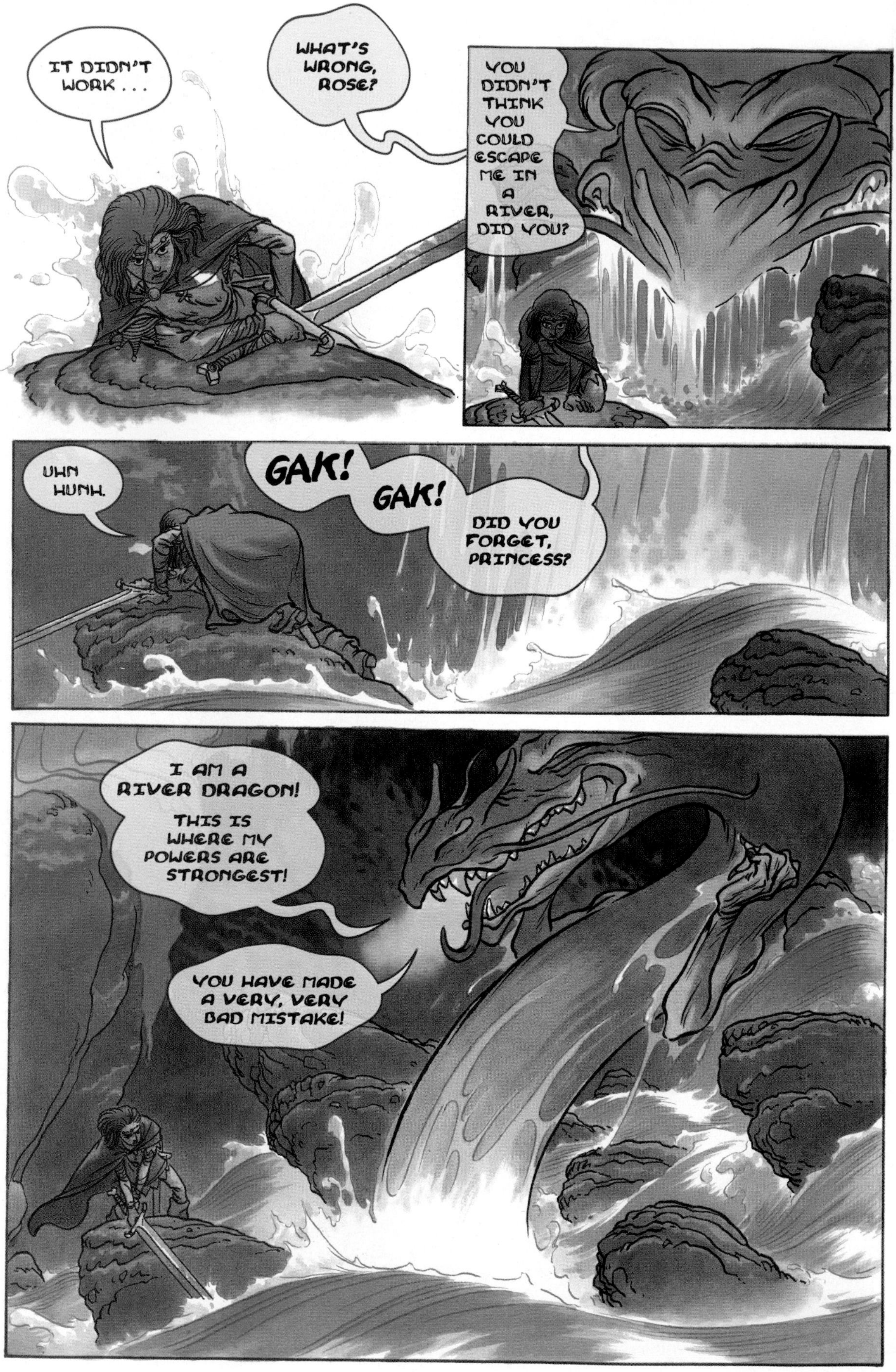
IT DIDN'T WORK . . .
WHAT'S WRONG, ROSE?
YOU DIDN'T THINK YOU COULD ESCAPE ME IN A RIVER, DID YOU?
UHN HUNH.
GAK!
GAK!
DID YOU FORGET, PRINCESS?
I AM A RIVER DRAGON!
THIS IS WHERE MY POWERS ARE STRONGEST!
YOU HAVE MADE A VERY, VERY BAD MISTAKE!

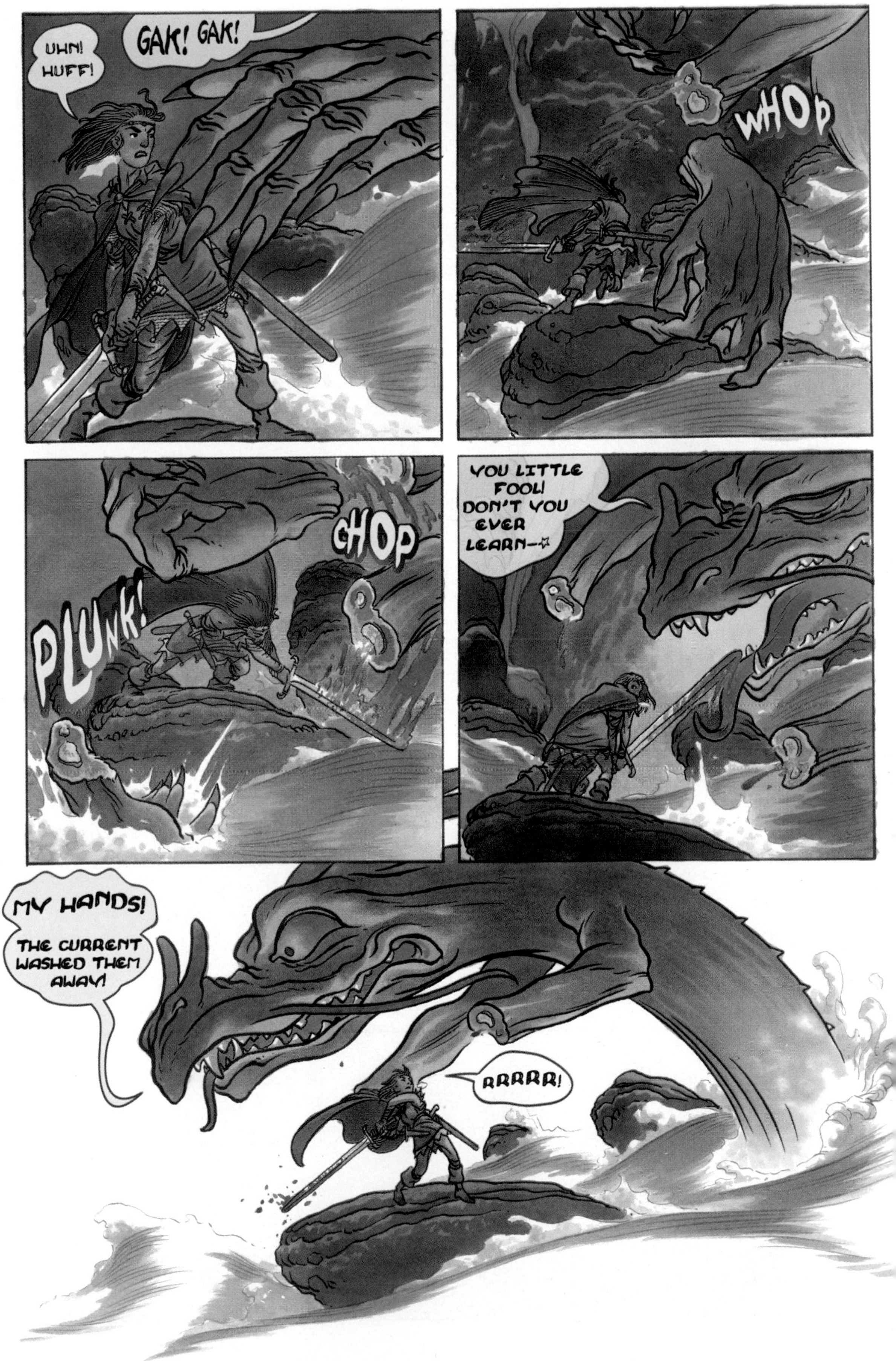
UHN! HUFF!
GAK! GAK!
WHOP
CHOP
PLUNK!
YOU LITTLE FOOL! DON'T YOU EVER LEARN--☆
MY HANDS!
THE CURRENT WASHED THEM AWAY!
RRRRR!

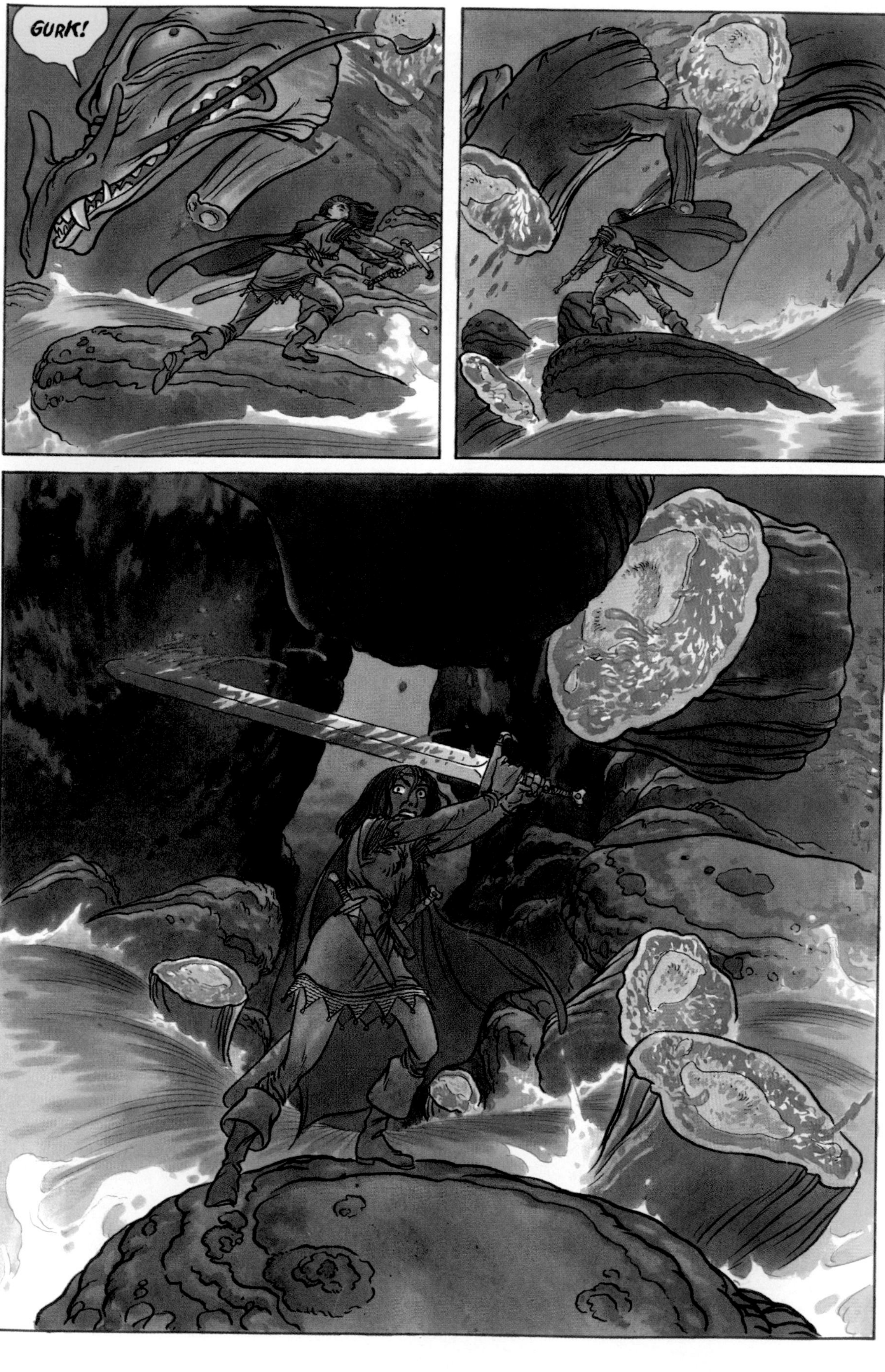
GURK!

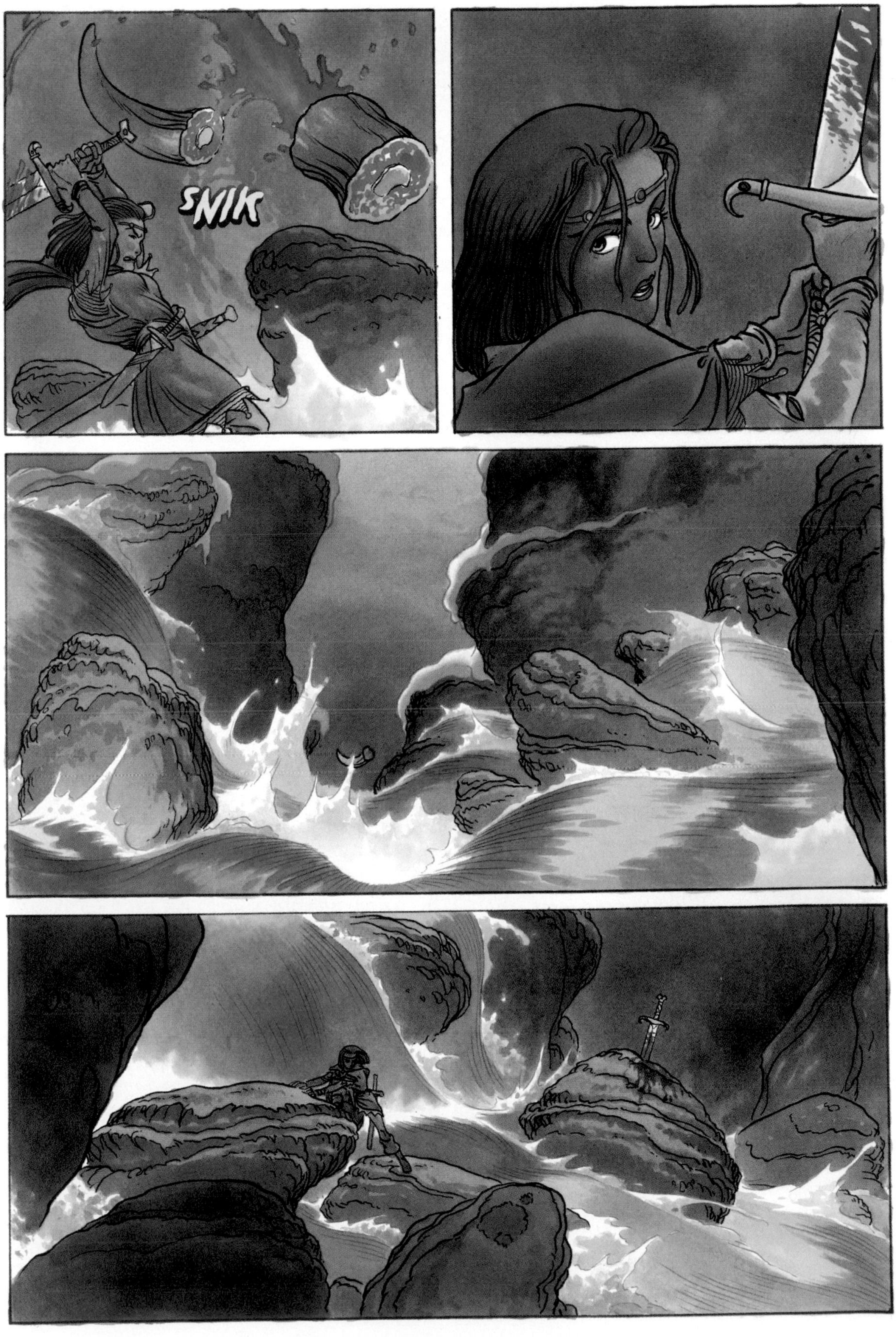
SNIK

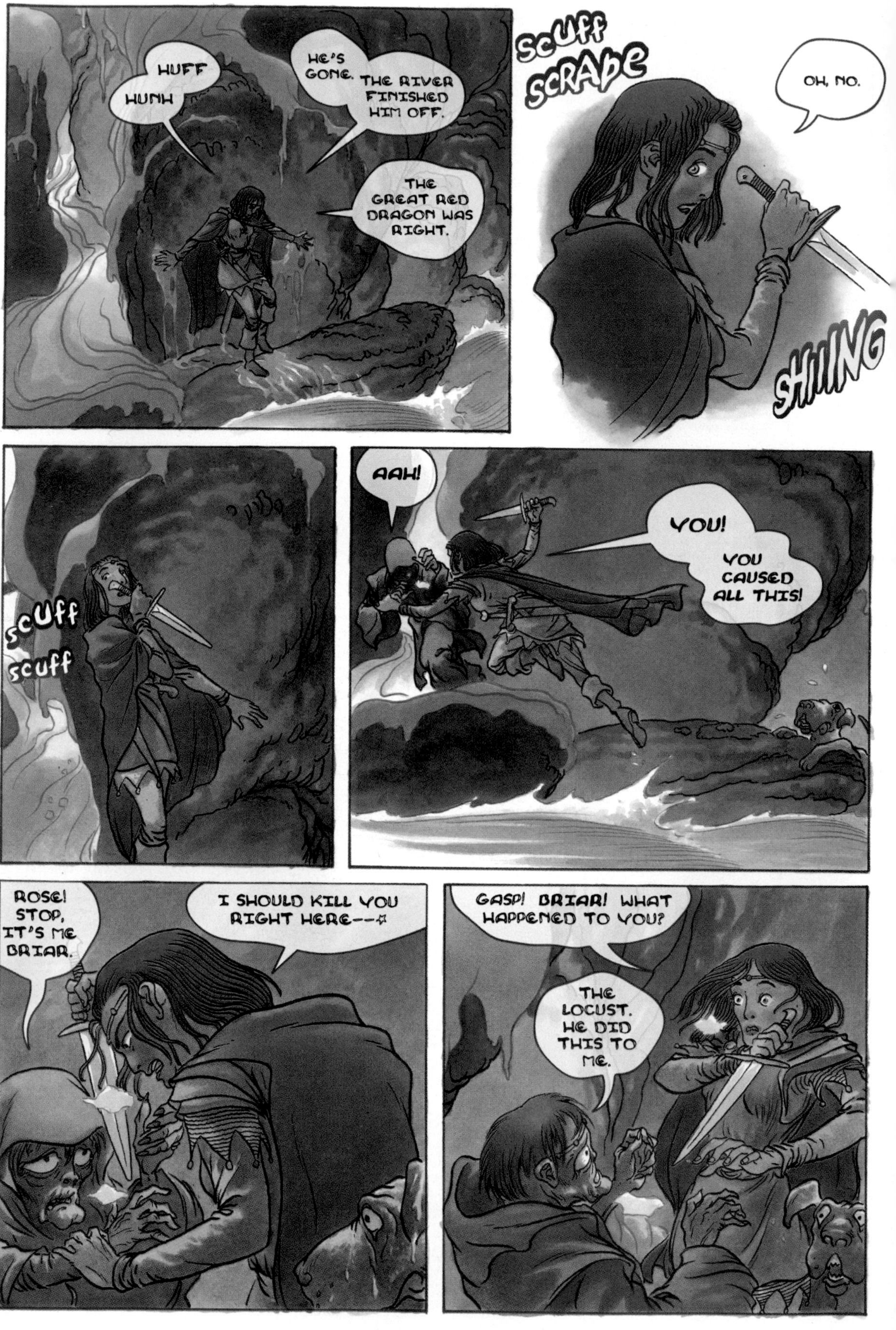
HUFF
HUNH
HE'S GONE.
THE RIVER FINISHED HIM OFF.
THE GREAT RED DRAGON WAS RIGHT.
scuff
SCRAPE
OH, NO.
SHIIING
scuff
scuff
AAH!
YOU!
YOU CAUSED ALL THIS!
ROSE! STOP, IT'S ME BRIAR.
I SHOULD KILL YOU RIGHT HERE--☆
GASP! BRIAR! WHAT HAPPENED TO YOU?
THE LOCUST. HE DID THIS TO ME.

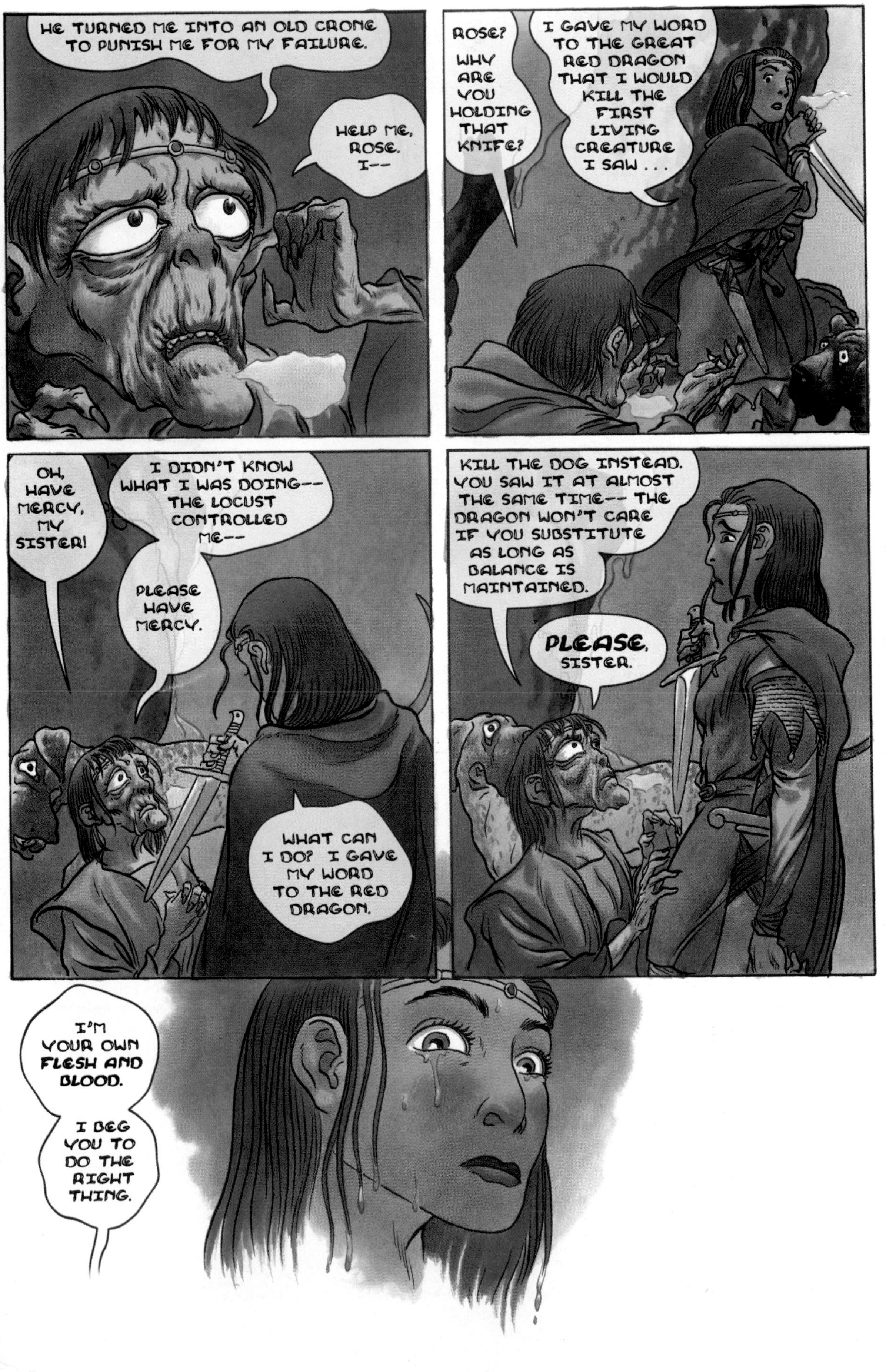
HE TURNED ME INTO AN OLD CRONE TO PUNISH ME FOR MY FAILURE.
HELP ME, ROSE. I--
ROSE? WHY ARE YOU HOLDING THAT KNIFE?
I GAVE MY WORD TO THE GREAT RED DRAGON THAT I WOULD KILL THE FIRST LIVING CREATURE I SAW . . .
OH, HAVE MERCY, MY SISTER!
I DIDN'T KNOW WHAT I WAS DOING-- THE LOCUST CONTROLLED ME--
PLEASE HAVE MERCY.
WHAT CAN I DO? I GAVE MY WORD TO THE RED DRAGON.
KILL THE DOG INSTEAD. YOU SAW IT AT ALMOST THE SAME TIME-- THE DRAGON WON'T CARE IF YOU SUBSTITUTE AS LONG AS BALANCE IS MAINTAINED.
PLEASE, SISTER.
I'M YOUR OWN **FLESH AND BLOOD.**
I BEG YOU TO DO THE RIGHT THING.

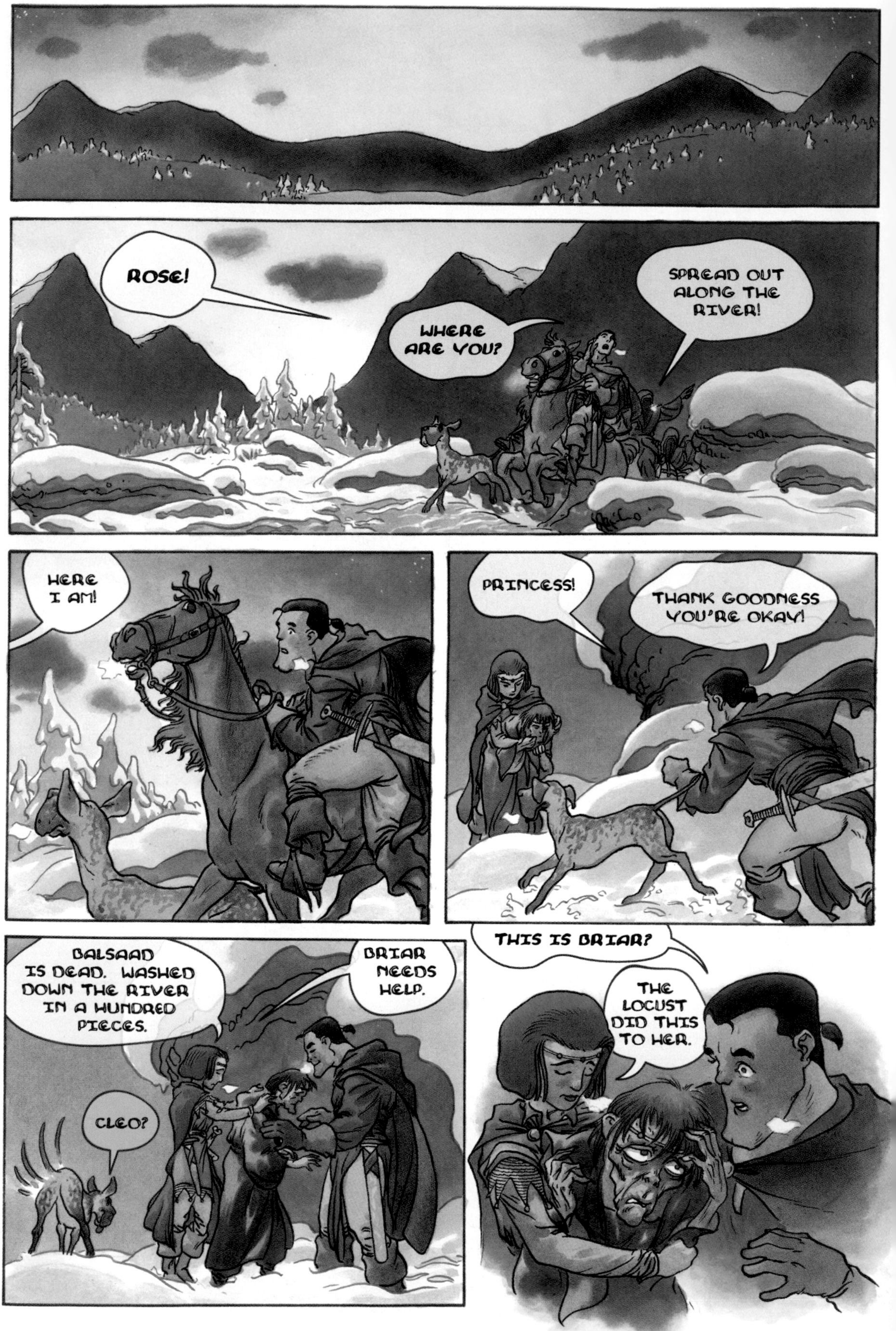
ROSE!
WHERE ARE YOU?
SPREAD OUT ALONG THE RIVER!
HERE I AM!
PRINCESS!
THANK GOODNESS YOU'RE OKAY!
BALSAAD IS DEAD. WASHED DOWN THE RIVER IN A HUNDRED PIECES.
BRIAR NEEDS HELP.
CLEO?
THIS IS BRIAR?
THE LOCUST DID THIS TO HER.

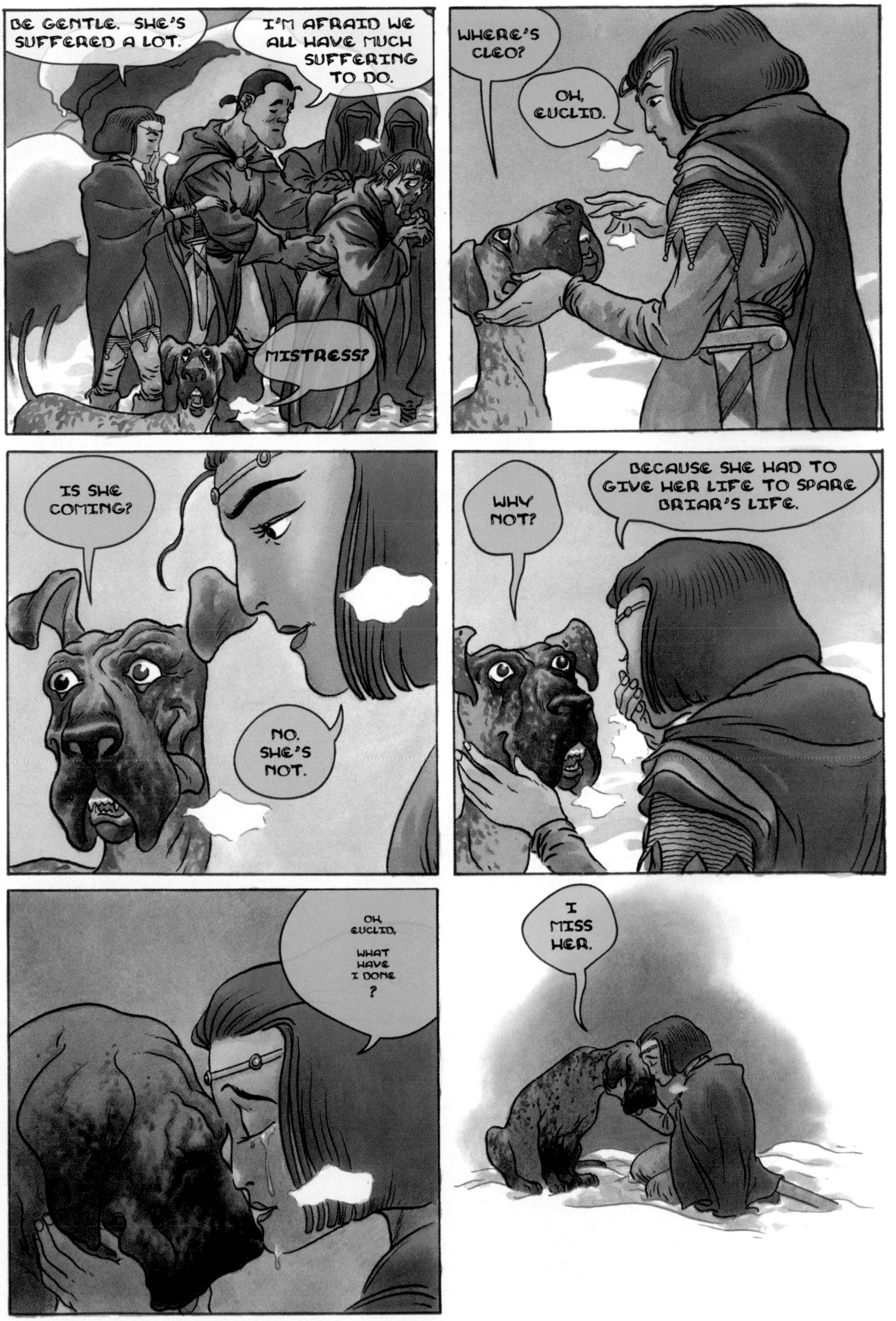
BE GENTLE. SHE'S SUFFERED A LOT.
I'M AFRAID WE ALL HAVE MUCH SUFFERING TO DO.
MISTRESS?
WHERE'S CLEO?
OH, EUCLID.
IS SHE COMING?
NO. SHE'S NOT.
WHY NOT?
BECAUSE SHE HAD TO GIVE HER LIFE TO SPARE BRIAR'S LIFE.
OH, EUCLID, WHAT HAVE I DONE ?
I MISS HER.

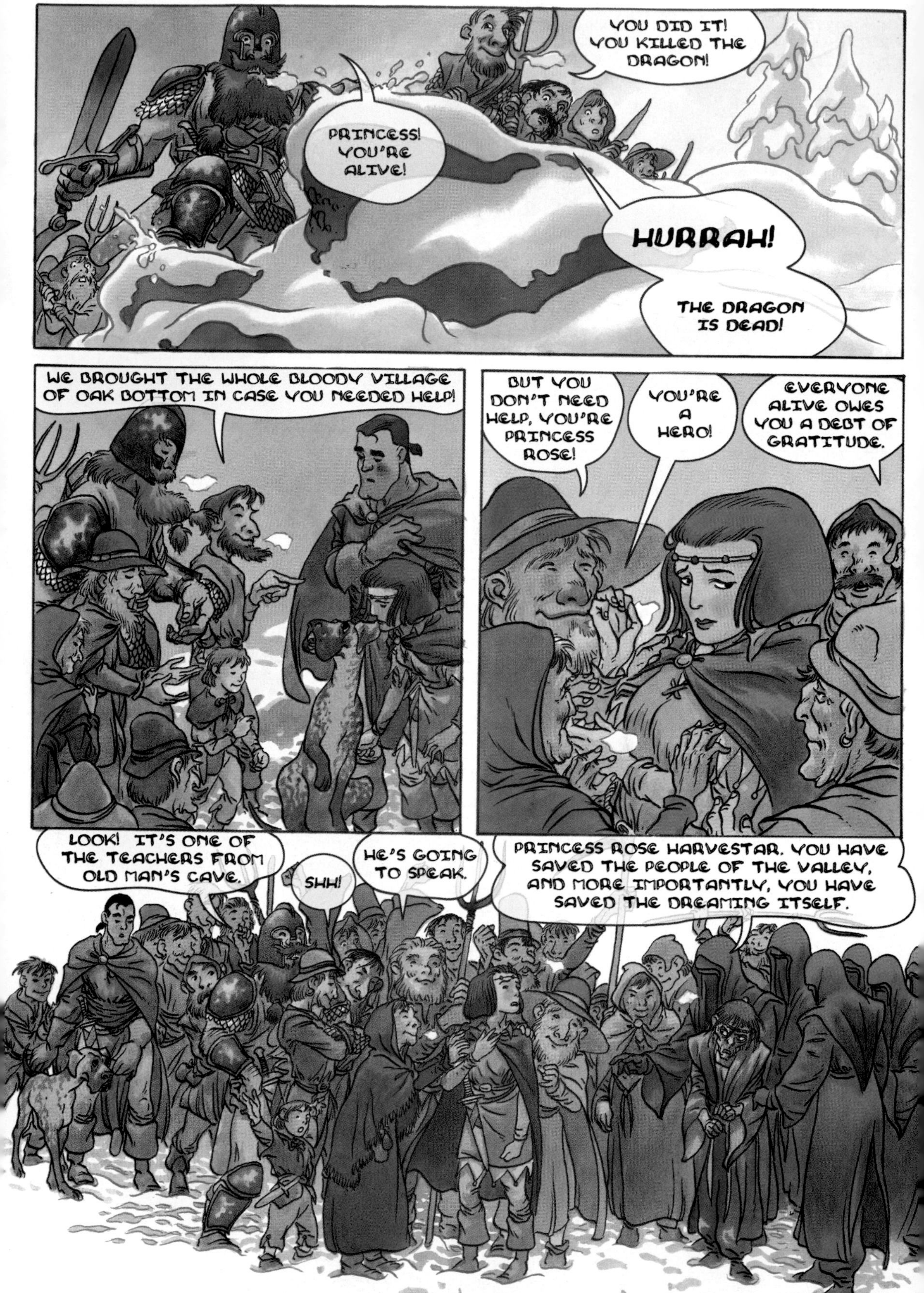
YOU DID IT! YOU KILLED THE DRAGON!
PRINCESS! YOU'RE ALIVE!
HURRAH!
THE DRAGON IS DEAD!
WE BROUGHT THE WHOLE BLOODY VILLAGE OF OAK BOTTOM IN CASE YOU NEEDED HELP!
BUT YOU DON'T NEED HELP, YOU'RE PRINCESS ROSE!
YOU'RE A HERO!
EVERYONE ALIVE OWES YOU A DEBT OF GRATITUDE.
LOOK! IT'S ONE OF THE TEACHERS FROM OLD MAN'S CAVE.
SHH!
HE'S GOING TO SPEAK.
PRINCESS ROSE HARVESTAR. YOU HAVE SAVED THE PEOPLE OF THE VALLEY, AND MORE IMPORTANTLY, YOU HAVE SAVED THE DREAMING ITSELF.

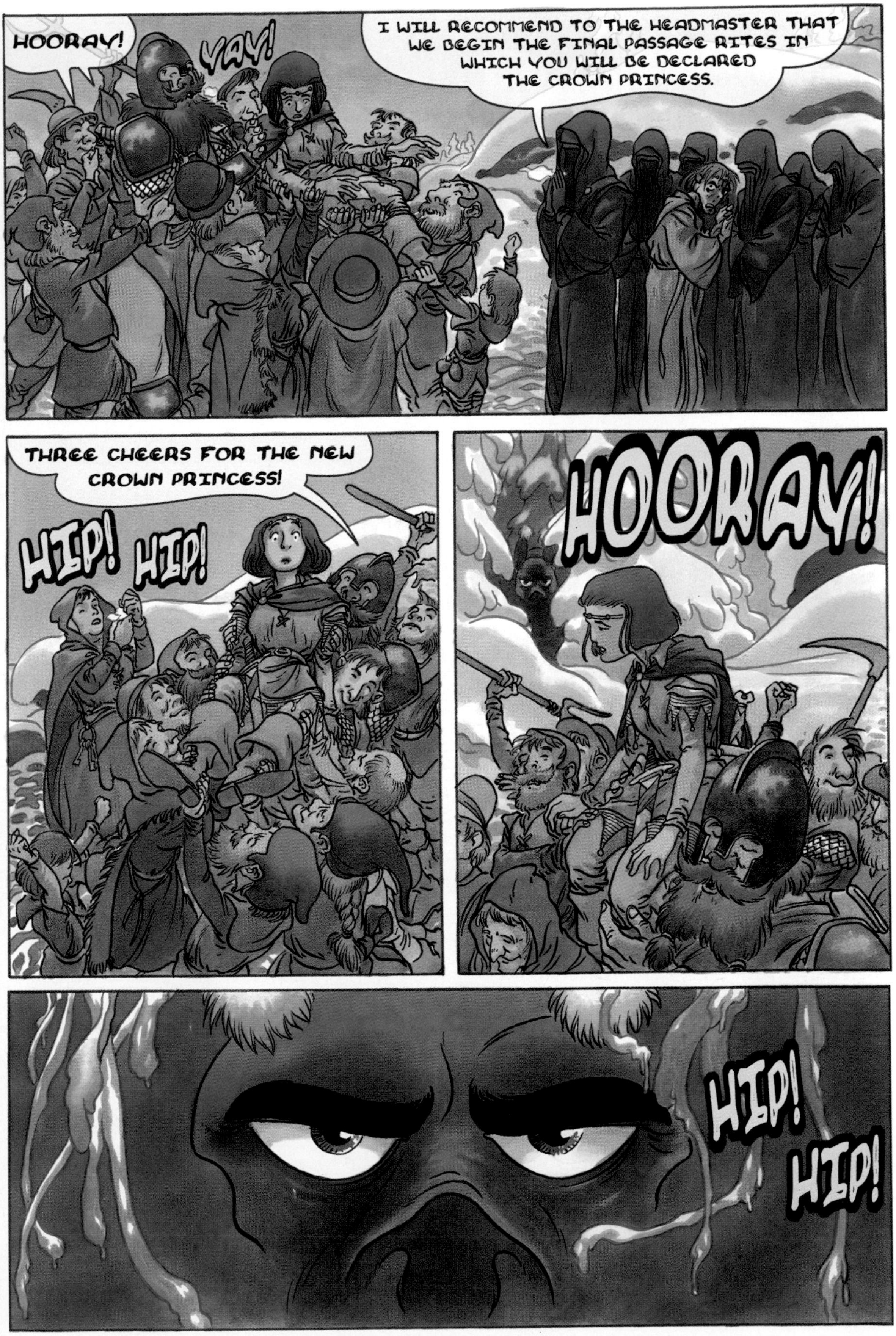
HOORAY!
YAY!
I WILL RECOMMEND TO THE HEADMASTER THAT WE BEGIN THE FINAL PASSAGE RITES IN WHICH YOU WILL BE DECLARED THE CROWN PRINCESS.
THREE CHEERS FOR THE NEW CROWN PRINCESS!
HIP! HIP!
HOORAY!
HIP! HIP!

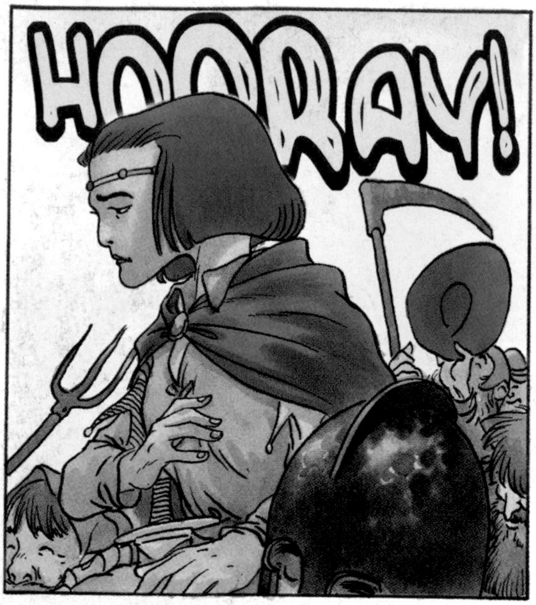
HOORAY!

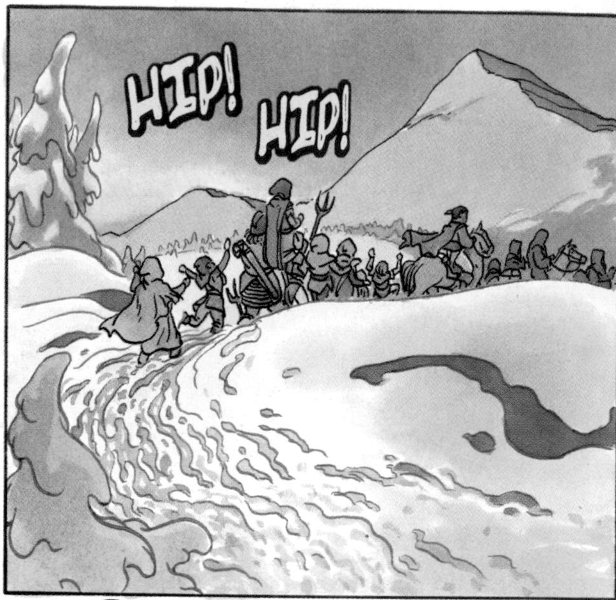
HIP!
HIP!

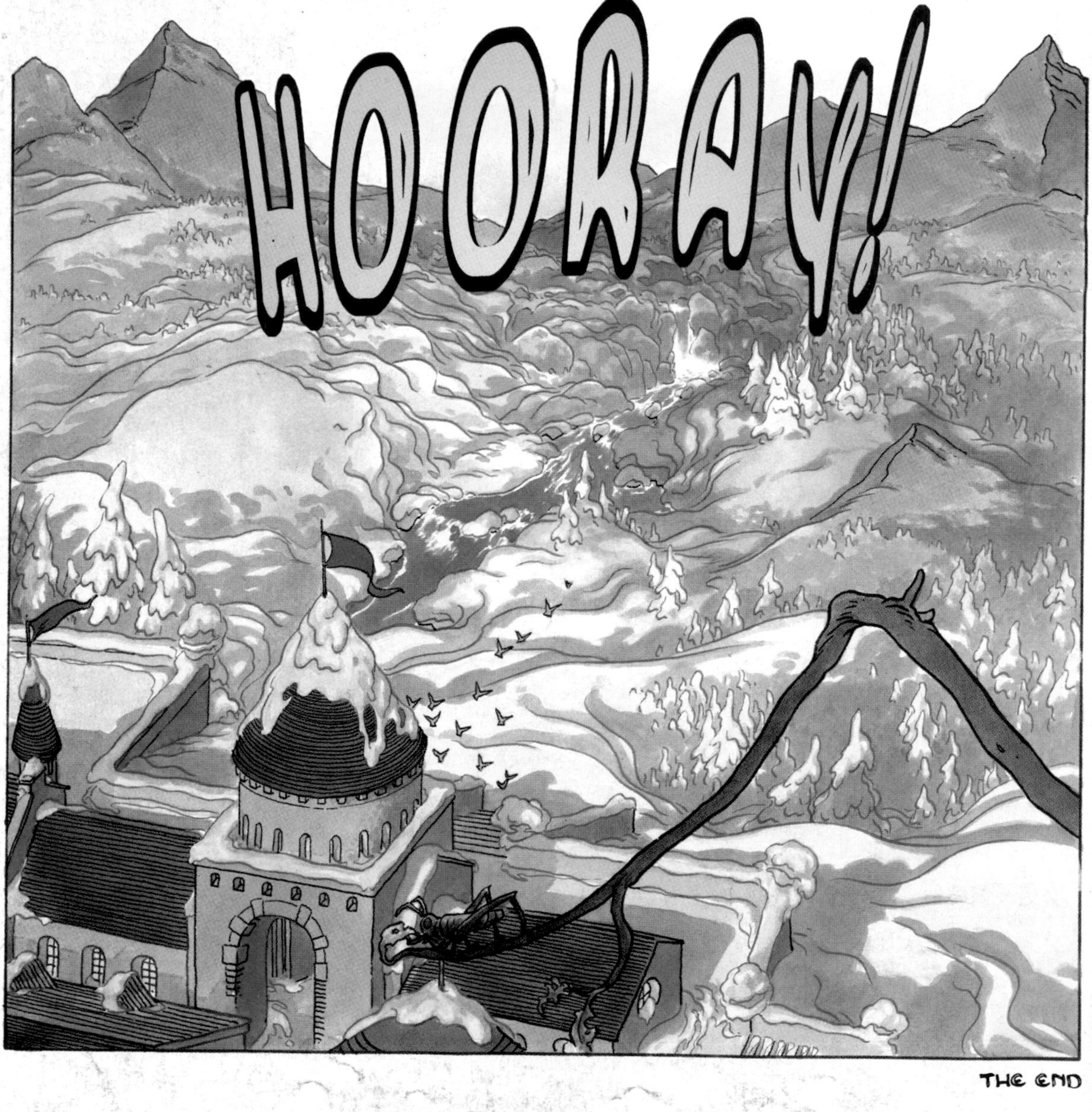
HOORAY!

THE END

BASED ON CHARACTERS FROM THE COMIC BOOK SERIES

ABOUT THE WRITER

Born and raised in the American mid-west, Jeff Smith learned about cartooning from comic strips, comic books, and watching animated shorts on TV. While most adults consider cartoons to be children's fare, Smith discovered early on that no topic of human experience — from the introspection of "Peanuts" or the politics of "Doonesbury" to the lyricism of "Pogo" — was beyond the wonderful world of comics. After four years of drawing comic strips for Ohio State's student newspaper starting in 1982, Smith co-founded the Character Builders animation studio in 1986. Then, in 1991, he launched the comic book "Bone".

"Bone" is currently printed in fifteen languages around the world, and was recently given the Eisner Award for Best Writer/Artist - Humor, as well as the Harvey Award for Best Cartoonist, Italy's Yellow Kid for Best Author, Spain's Premios Expocomic for Best Foreign Comic, France's Alph Art, and Finland's Lempi International for Best International Cartoonist.

ABOUT THE ILLUSTRATOR

Charles Dana Vess was born in 1951 in Lynchburg, Virginia and has been drawing ever since he could hold a crayon. He drew his first full-length comic when he was 10 and called it "Atomic Man." Minimalist in nature, it required no drawing of hands, feet or heads ("they just glowed"). Since then, he has painstakingly drawn thousands of hands, feet, and heads in great detail.

Charles graduated with a BFA from Virginia Commonwealth University, and worked in commercial animation for Candy Apple Productions in Richmond, Va. before moving to New York City in 1976. It was there that he became a freelance illustrator, working for many publications, including Heavy Metal, Klutz Press, and National Lampoon. His award-winning work has graced the pages of numerous comic book publishers, and has been featured in several gallery and museum exhibitions across the nation, including the first major exhibition of Science Fiction and Fantasy Art in 1980 at the New Britain Museum of American Art.

In 1991, Charles shared the prestigious World Fantasy Award for Best Short Story with Neil Gaiman for their collaboration on "Sandman #19" (DC Comics) -- the first and only time a comic book has held this honor. In the summer of 1997, Charles won The Will Eisner Comic Industry Award for best penciller/inker for his work on "The Book of Ballads and Sagas" (which he self-publishes through his own Green Man Press) as well as "Sandman #75". In 1999 he was awarded the World Fantasy Award for Best Artist for his work on "Stardust", a novel written by Neil Gaiman.

In the third issue of "The Book of Ballads and Sagas" published by Green Man Press, Jeff Smith adapted the humorous traditional ballad, "The Galtee Farmer". Now Charles and Jeff have turned their collaborative prowess to "Rose", the prequel to "Bone". This beautiful fully-painted series turns to earlier times in the lives of the characters of "Bone" and reveals many of the untold secrets of their turbulent past.

Following the "Rose" mini-series Charles' work will be featured in several illustrated book projects, including: "The Green Man: Tales from the Mythic Forest" (Viking Press), "A Circle of Cats" (a children's picture book from Penguin/Putnam), "Seven Wild Sisters" (Subterranean Press) and "A Storm of Swords" (MeishaMerlin Press). For information about these projects, or to see more of Charles Vess' work please visit his website: www.greenmanpress.com.

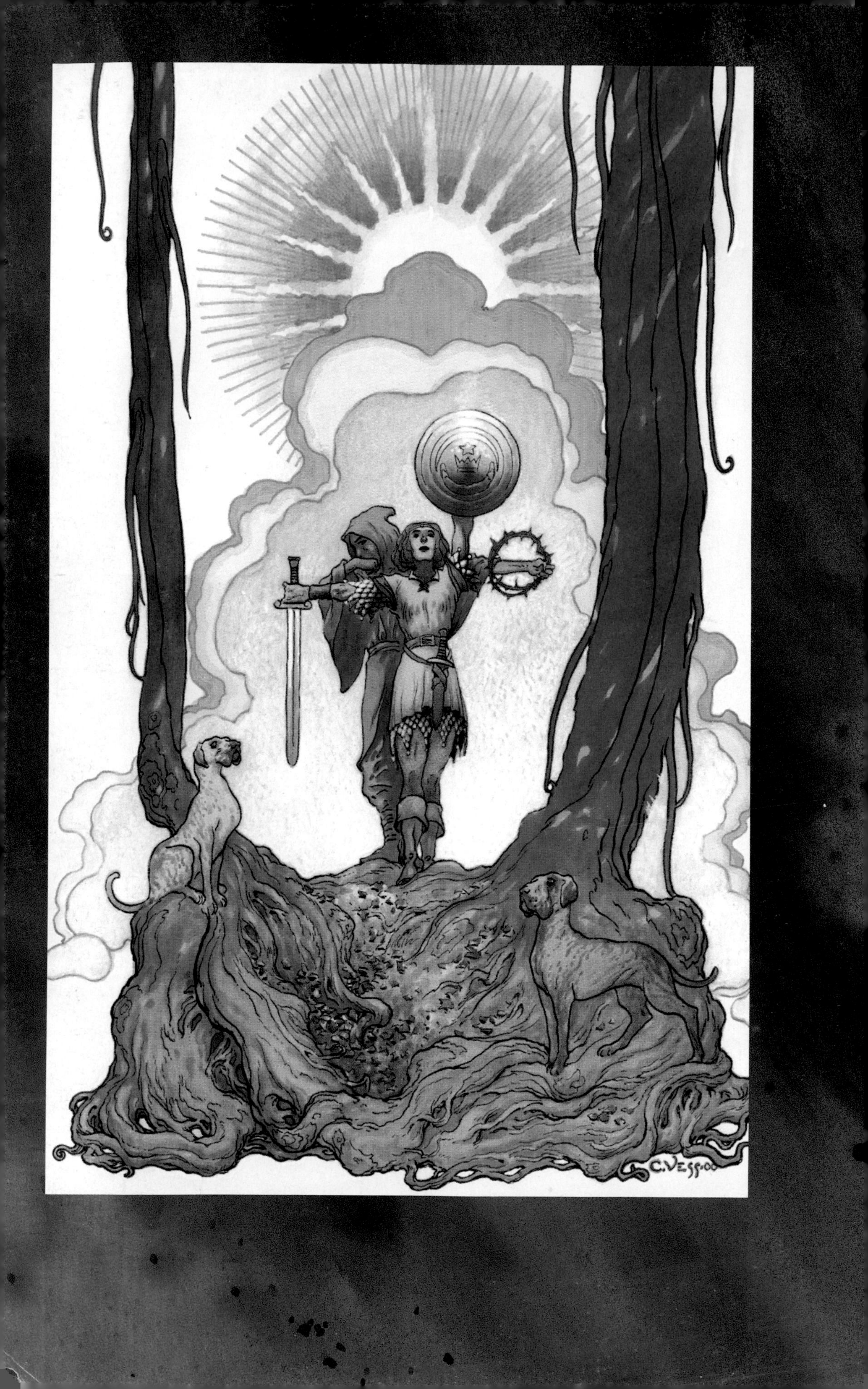
C.VESS.00

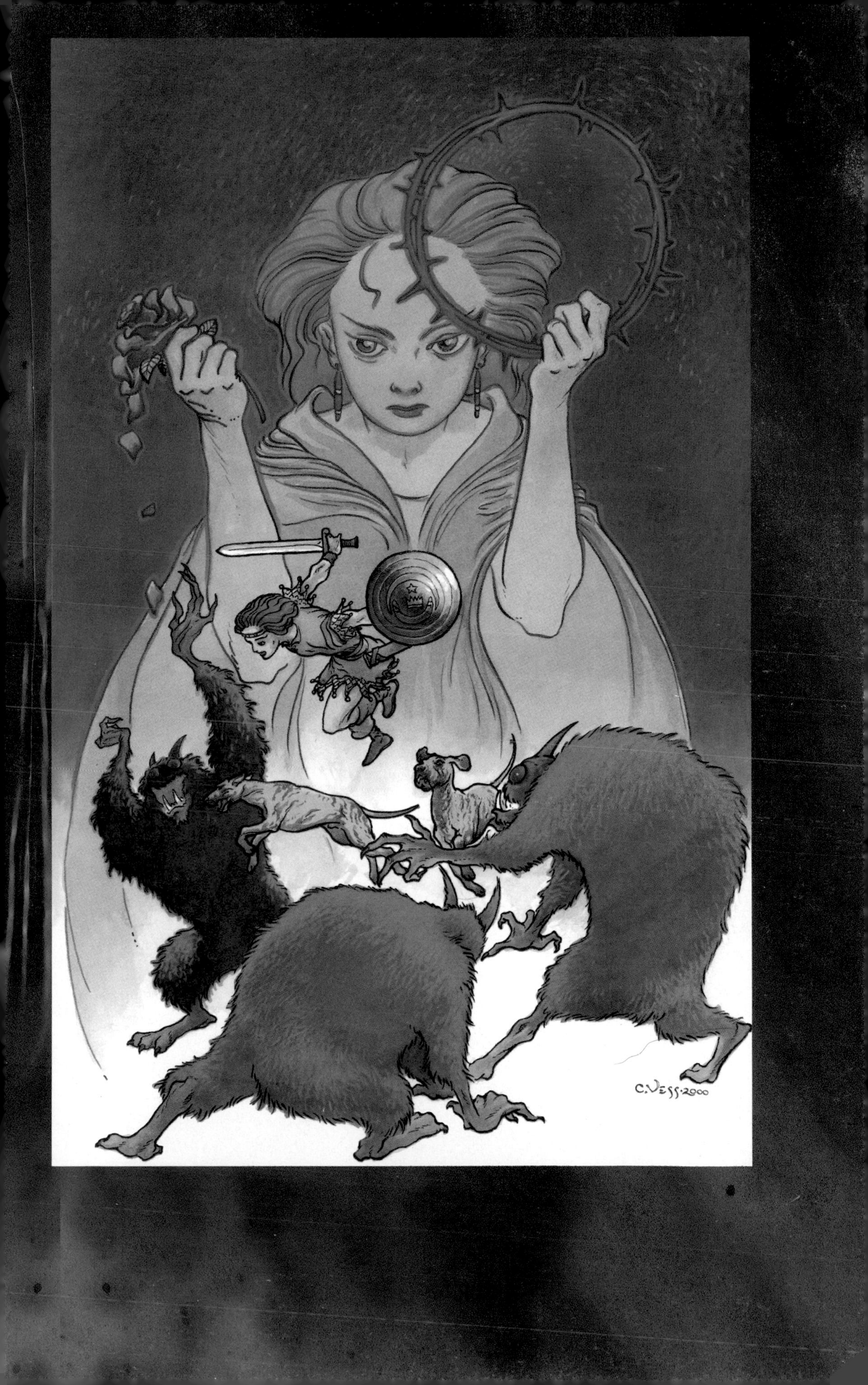
C.VESS·2000

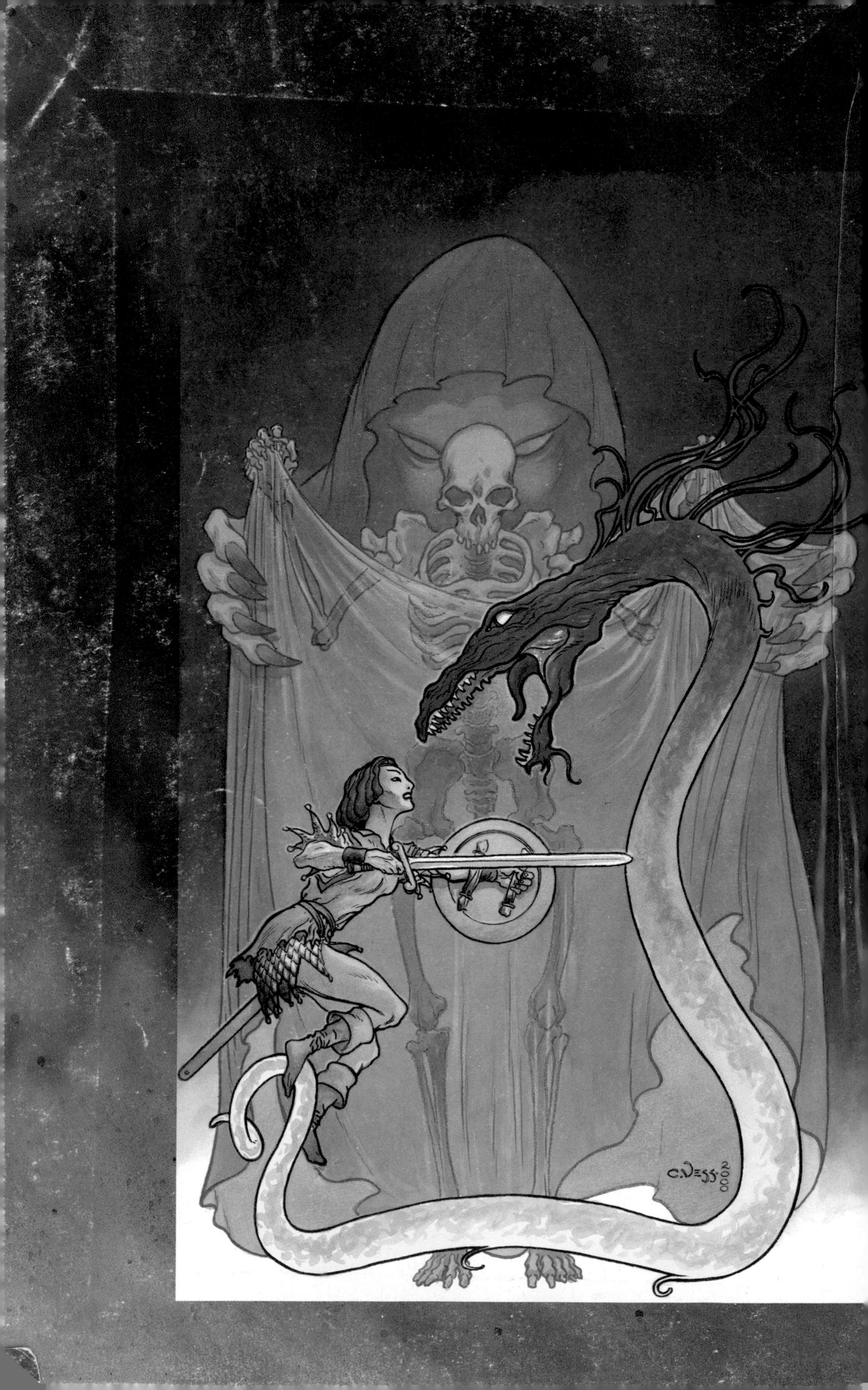
C.VESS·2000